Silent Partner

✦

Law Enforcement Adventures
FEAR NOTHING RISK EVERYTHING

Road Deputy
&
Steven King

iUniverse, Inc.
New York   Bloomington

Silent Partner

Law Enforcement Adventures
FEAR NOTHING RISK EVERYTHING

iUniverse books may be ordered through booksellers or by contacting:

iUniverse
1663 Liberty Drive
Bloomington, IN 47403
www.iuniverse.com
1-800-Authors (1-800-288-4677)

ISBN: 978-0-595-52330-6 (pbk)
ISBN: 978-1-4401-0511-1 (cloth)
ISBN: 978-0-595-62386-0 (ebk)

Printed in the United States of America

I am a Police Officer; my background includes six years of service in the Marine Corps and a few years as a Police Officer with a northern agency.

Training for the northern agency required I complete a five month criminal justice academy. I worked in the county jail in a correctional capacity. My current position required the successful completion of a five month academy as well. After which, I went through a fourteen week field training program. The first two weeks consisted of nothing but book work. We reviewed all of the agency's policies and the frequently used laws. This was also the time we were taught defensive driving and all about our "tools" of the trade. My "tools" include a 9mm Beretta handgun, an expandable baton, pepper spray, handcuffs, and a Remington shotgun. The next twelve weeks I rode alongside six field training officers, each for a period of two weeks.

Field Training Officers are supposed to let you do "your thing", and then evaluate you on your performance. Some jump in on every situation. It's like their egos force them to take control of the situation. Others sit back and watch without saying a word. They let you sink and drown and never offer a rope. The best are those that allow you to handle the situation and offer constructive criticism along the way. Needless to say, I longed for the day to be "cut loose".- Then, one day it happened. I was given a car, some equipment, and a badge and told to go out on my own. It was an unbelievable feeling.

The first day on my own I mostly just sat in my car. I wondered what, if anything, I should be doing. I think I failed to respond on several occasions when calls were dispatched in my area. It's difficult training your ear and brain to be conscious of the radio traffic 24/7 and to respond when your unit number is called.

I've been at it for a little while now. I guess you can still consider me a rookie.

Since entering this profession, people frequently ask exactly what it is that I do on a daily basis. This book chronicles my daily law enforcement activities and provides some insight into the "mind of an Officer".

Hopefully, you'll get to know me as a person as well since YOU are my Silent Partner.

Journal Key

D= Dispatched Call
S= Self Initiated Call
BU= Back Up for another Officer
W/M= White Male
B/M = Black Male
H/M= Hispanic Male
W/F= White Female
B/F= Black Female
H/F= Hispanic Female
YO= Year Old
FG= Friend Girl

All journal Entries are listed by date and are in military time, enjoy!

1900 (S) DISABLED MOTORIST

WHILE PATROLING MY AREA, I NOTICED A STATE TROOPER ON THE HIGHWAY. HE WAS OFF THE SIDE OF THE ROADWAY WITH A MAROON BLAZER. BELIEVING HE WAS ON A TRAFFIC STOP, I PULLED OFF TO ASSIST HIM. OTHER OFFICERS, AS WELL AS OTHER AGENCIES, FREQUENTLY ASSIST FELLOW OFFICERS FOR SAFETY PURPOSES. WE BELIEVE IN STACKING THE ODDS IN OUR FAVOR. A PERSON WITH BAD INTENTIONS IS LESS LIKELY TO "TRY SOMETHING" WHEN THEY'RE OUTMANNED. AS IT TURNS OUT, THE MOTORIST IN THE BLAZER HAD RUN OUT OF GAS. THE TROOPER WAS DRIVING A SMALLER VEHICLE AND HAD NO ROOM FOR ADDITIONAL PASSENGERS. AS I PULLED UP, HE WAS EXPLAINING HOW TO GET TO THE NEAREST GAS STATION. BEING THE KIND-HEARTED OFFICER THAT I AM, I OFFERED TO DRIVE THE MOTORIST THE THREE OR FOUR MILES TO THE GAS STATION. THE WHOLE WHILE I WAS ALL PLEASANT AND SMILES AND IN THE BACK OF MY MIND I'M THINKING IS THERE A PROBLEM WITH YOU GAS GAUGE, OR WHAT? I MEAN, I'M SURE WE'VE ALL PUSHED IT A TIME OR TWO, BUT MOST OF US KNOW JUST HOW FAR OUR NEEDLES CAN GO PAST THAT "E".

1935 (S) CITIZEN ASSIST

WHILE PARKED IN A TACO BELL PARKING LOT DOING PAPER WORK, I WAS APPROACHED BY SOME PEOPLE LOOKING FOR ANOTHER OFFICER. THE OFFICER HAD REQUESTED SOME INFORMATION FROM THEM, BUT GAVE THEM ONLY THE OFFICE NUMBER. BEING THAT WE'RE ON THE ROAD 99% OF THE TIME IT SEEMS TO ME HE REALLY DIDN'T WANT THEM TO FIND HIM. AT ANY RATE, I MANAGED TO LOCATE HIM OVER THE RADIO AND HE MADE CONTACT WITH THE PEOPLE.

1953 (S) CITIZEN ASSIST

I ALMOST MADE IT OUT OF THE TACO BELL PARKING LOT WHEN SOME TOURIST PULLED UP TO ME IN A BLUE VAN. THE FIRST THING THE LADY ASKED ME WAS WHETHER OR NOT I SPOKE SPANISH. BEING THAT I DONT, I TOLD HER,

"NO". I WILL HOWEVER, BE STUDYING PORTUGUESE SOON. I RECENTLY ENROLLED BACK IN COLLEGE AND THAT'S ONE OF MY CLASSES. CENTRAL FLORIDA IS LIKE THE NUMBER ONE DESTINATION FOR BRAZILIAN TOURISTS, AND THEY SPEAK PORTUGUESE. THE TOURIST WAS ABLE TO GET ACROSS TO ME THAT SHE WAS LOOKING FOR THE "LARGEST MCDONALDS". INSTEAD OF TRYING TO EXPLAIN TO HER HOW TO GET THERE, I TOLD HER TO FOLLOW ME. AFTER GETTING HER THERE, SHE SAID, "MUCHOS GRACIAS". I DON'T KNOW IF THAT'S HOW TO SPELL IT, BUT THAT'S WHAT IT SOUNDS LIKE.

2053
-I NEED TO FIND SOME ACTION 'CAUSE I'M GETTING KIND OF SLEEPY. I HAD TO GET UP EARLY TODAY, 3:30 PM. YEAH, I SAID EARLY. WHEN YOU WORK 6PM TO 6AM, THAT'S EARLY. I HAD TO PICK UP SOME EVIDENCE THAT THE STATE ATTORNEY WAS REQUESTING BEFORE WORK. IF SOMETHING EXCITING HAPPENS, I'LL WAKE RIGHT UP.

2109 (S) CITIZEN ASSIST
I HELPED A TOURIST FIND THE TURNPIKE.

2114
-I STOPPED IN BUMPER TO BUMPER TRAFFIC TO ALLOW A J-WALKER TO CROSS THE STREET. I GAVE HIM A "DIRTY LOOK" AS HE PASSED IN FRONT OF ME. THAT LOOK WAS FOR HIS OWN GOOD, HE COULD GET HURT OUT THERE.

2125 (S) TRAFFIC STOP
I STOPPED A MAZDA MINI VAN WITH AN EXPIRED TAG. THE DRIVER WAS AN OLD, PUERTO RICAN WOMAN. THIS I ASSUMED BECAUSE OF HER PUERTO RICAN DRIVERS LICENSE. SHE WAS DRIVING HER SON'S VEHICLE AND DIDN'T REALIZE THE TAG WAS EXPIRED. SHE WAS VERY POLITE. I GAVE HER A WRITTEN WARNING AND TOLD HER TO HAVE HER SON TAKE CARE OF THE PROBLEM.

2135 (D) STOLEN VEHICLE
I WAS DISPATCHED A STOLEN VEHICLE CALL. THE LOCATION WAS ON THE INTERSTATE, CLOSE TO WHERE I CONDUCTED

MY LAST TRAFFIC STOP. I TOLD THE DISPATCHER I WAS ON THE SCENE AND ASKED IF SHE COULD PROVIDE ME WITH FURTHER INFORMATION. ALL SHE COULD TELL ME WAS THAT A GREEN PONTIAC WAS STOLEN AND THAT IT WAS HEADING WEST ON THE INTERSTATE. THE VICTIM WAS SUPPOSEDLY IN A WHITE TAXI CAB IN PURSUIT OF THE PONTIAC. FINALLY, SHE SAID THE THEFT OCCURRED AT A CHEVRON GAS STATION, AND THAT I WAS TO MEET WITH THE VICTIM ONE EXIT FURTHER WEST AT ANOTHER CHEVRON. BETWEEN EXITING THE INTERSTATE AND TRYING TO GATHER MORE INFORMATION ON THE STOLEN CAR, I WAS APPROACHED BY SOME TOURISTS. THEY WERE LOOKING FOR DIRECTIONS TO A FRIEND'S HOUSE. IN A POLITE TONE OF VOICE AND WITH A SMILE ON MY FACE, I TOLD THEM I WAS DEALING WITH A STOLEN CAR SITUATION. I SAID THEY COULD FOLLOW ME TO THE GAS STATION, AND AFTER I WAS FINISHED WITH THE VICTIM, I COULD HELP THEM. THEY FOLLOWED. ONCE I MET WITH THIS SUPPOSED VICTIM, I FOUND THAT HE WAS MERELY AN EYE WITNESS WHO DIDN'T KNOW EXACTLY WHAT HE HAD WITNESSED. HE SAID HE WAS AT THE GAS STATION GASSING UP HIS CAB, WHEN ALL OF A SUDDEN THE GREEN PONTIAC TORE OFF THE PROPERTY RECKLESSLY INTO ONCOMING TRAFFIC. SHORTLY THEREAFTER, FOUR PEOPLE RAN OUT OF THE GAS MART YELLING, "HE JUST STOLE THAT CAR". THE CAB DRIVER THEN PROCEEDED TO CHASE THE PONTIAC. HE FOLLOWED THE PONTIAC ONTO THE INTERSTATE HEADING WEST. THAT'S WHEN HE CALLED 911. HE LOST SIGHT OF THE CAR ONE EXIT LATER. I ASKED IF IT WERE POSSIBLE THAT THIS WAS JUST A GAS DRIVE-OFF. THE CAB DRIVER SAID IT WAS POSSIBLE, BUT THE PEOPLE SAID HE STOLE THE CAR. IT BECAME CLEAR TO ME THAT ALTHOUGH THIS MAN HAD VERY GOOD INTENTIONS, HE REALLY DIDN'T KNOW WHAT WAS GOING ON. I NEED TO GO BACK TO THAT FIRST GAS STATION TO FIND THAT OUT.   AS FOR MY LOST TOURIST, I LOOKED UP THE STREET IN MY MAP BOOK AND IT WASN'T LISTED. THE CAB DRIVER EVEN ASKED HIS DISPATCHER TO LOCATE THE ADDRESS. THEY WERE UNABLE TO LOCATE IT AS WELL. WE ASKED THE GUY IF HE HAD A PHONE NUMBER AND COULD CALL FOR DIRECTIONS. HE SAID HE DID, BUT THEY WANTED TO SURPRISE THEM. (THE SURPRISE WAS GOING TO BE THEM NOT SEEING THEIR FRIENDS.) I WENT BACK TO THE FIRST GAS STATION AND SPOKE TO THE CLERK. SHE SAID THE PERSON IN THE PONTIAC HAD BEEN VERY IMPATIENT. HE WAS

RACING AROUND THE LOT, DOING DONUTS, AND TRYING TO PASS OTHER PATRONS. ANOTHER MOTORIST GOT MAD AT HIM, EXITED HIS VEHICLE AND WENT AFTER THE GUY IN THE PONTIAC. THAT'S WHEN HE SPED AWAY FROM THE GAS STATION. THUS BEGINS OUR TALE OF THE STOLEN VEHICLE.

2225 (S) TRAFFIC STOP

I CONDUCTED A TRAFFIC STOP OF A VAN. THE DRIVER WAS WEAVING BACK AND FORTH AS THOUGH HE WAS DRUNK OR SOMETHING. AFTER THE STOP, THE DRIVER, A W/M IN HIS LATE TWENTIES, GOT OUT OF THE VAN WEARING A GROCERY STORE UNIFORM. I SAID "WHAT'S THE DEAL, DUDE? YOU'RE ALL OVER THE ROAD. ARE YOU ASLEEP OR SOMETHING?" HE SAID HE HAD BEEN WORKING SINCE 8AM. I TOLD HIM TO TAKE IT EASY AND TO TRY AND GET HOME SAFELY.

2258 (S) TRAFFIC STOP

WHILE ON PATROL, I CONSTANTLY RUN TAGES ON MY MOBILE DATA TERMINAL (LAPTOP COMPUTER) TO CHECK THE VALIDITY OF TAGS, LICENSES AND "WHATNOT". SOMETHING AS MINOR AS AN EXPIRED TAG SOMETIMES LEADS TO MUCH MORE SERIOUS INFRACTIONS. I RAN A TAG ON A LITTLE RED MAZDA RX7. IT CAME BACK SHOWING THE OWNER'S LICENSE WAS SUSPENDED. I STOPPED THE CAR. THE DRIVER WAS A HISPANIC MALE IN HIS EARLY TWENTIES. HE WAS VERY POLITE THROUGHOUT THE STOP. SINCE HIS LICENSE WAS SUSPENDED, I HAD TO WRITE HIM A TICKET AND TAKE HIS LICENSE AWAY. SINCE IT WAS ONLY ONE SUSPENSION, I DIDN'T TAKE HIM TO JAIL.

2320 (S) TRAFFIC STOP

WHILE RANDOMLY RUNNING TAGS, I CAME ACROSS SOMEONE WHO HAD THREE SUSPENSIONS ON HIS LICENSE. I PULLED HIM OVER AND ASKED FOR HIS LICENSE. HE PULLED THE OLD "I'LL SLIP HIM MY MILITARY I.D. ALONG WITH MY LICENSE". I   PROMPTY GAVE HIM BACK HIS I.D. AS IF TO SAY, "DID I ASK YOU FOR THAT?" BESIDES, IT WASN'T A MARINE CORPS I.D. OOH RAH! (JUST KIDDING). AFTER VERIFYING HIS LICENSE WAS INVALID, I ARRESTED THE YOUNG MAN, WHO HAPPENED TO BE A YOUNG, WHITE, POSSIBLY HISPANIC, MALE. I REALLY FEEL BAD ARRESTING

PEOPLE, BUT, IT'S PART OF THE JOB. I TRY TO REMAIN AS
CONSISTENT AS POSSIBLE. IF THEY NEED TO GO (MEANING
TO JAIL, BASED ON THEIR VIOLATIONS), THEY TAKE THE
RIDE. I TRY TO MAKE IT AS PLEASANT AS POSSIBLE FOR MY
ARRESTEES. I EXPLAIN THE CHARGE AND WHAT THEY NEED
TO DO TO BE RELEASED. I DO WHAT I CAN FOR THEM WITHIN
THE REALM OF THE LAW. WE USUALLY PART COMPANY WITH
THEM IN A PLEASANT MOOD AND WISHING ME WELL. THEY
SOMETIMES THANK ME. (IMAGINE THAT) MANY TIMES, MY
DEMEANOR, OR THEIR DESPERATION CAUSES PEOPLE TO
OPEN UP TO ME. THEY TELL ME PERSONAL THINGS ABOUT
THEIR LIVES. IT'S KIND OF LIKE "TAXI CAB CONFESSIONS",
EXCEPT IN A POLICE CRUISER. AFTER ARRESTING THIS
YOUNG MAN, HE SAT QUIETLY IN MY BACK SEAT. HE
OPENED UP AFTER I SHIFTED FROM MY STERN ROLE TO A
MORE HUMAN ROLE AND EXPLAINED HIS CHARGE. ON THE
WAY TO THE JAIL HE BEGAN TALKING ABOUT HIS FAMILY.
HE SAID HE DIDN'T WANT TO CALL HIS PARENTS BECAUSE
THEY WOULD BE TERRIBLY UPSET WITH HIM. HE SAID HE
COULDN'T CALL HIS FRIENDS BECAUSE HE DIDN'T KNOW
THEIR NUMBER. HE SAID HE COULDN'T CALL HIS SISTER
BECAUSE THEY HAD BEEN FIGHTING RECENTLY. HE SAID
THEY WERE FIGHTING BECAUSE OF HER BOYFRIEND. HE
BEAT THE BOYFRIEND UP AT A RECENT WEDDING FOR
ACTING STUPID AND GETTING UP IN HIS FACE. HE GAVE
THE BOYFRIEND A "STRIKE" FOR BREAKING A SCREEN
OUT OF A WINDOW AT THEIR MOTHER'S HOUSE DURING
AN ARGUMENT WITH HIS SISTER. THAT WAS STRIKE 3. HE
HAD GIVEN HIM 2 STRIKES FOR AN EARLIER "OFFENSE". I
ASKED WHAT THAT WAS. HE HESITATED, BUT TOLD ME. HE
SAID HIS SISTER, WHO IS NOW 19, WAS A VIRGIN WHEN SHE
MET THE BOYFRIEND. AFTER THEY SLEPT TOGETHER FOR
THE FIRST TIME, THE BOYFRIEND GAVE HER A SEXUALLY
TRANSMITTED DISEASE. I AGREED THAT WARRANTS AT
LEAST "2 STRIKES".

2332
 -I ALMOST FORGOT, WHILE I HAD THE LAST GUY IN THE
BACK SEAT ON THE SIDE OF THE ROAD, I WAS APPROACHED
BY A TOURIST. HE PULLED OFF THE SIDE OF THE INTERSTATE
WHERE I WAS, FLASHING LIGHTS AND ALL, AND ASKED HOW

TO GET SOMEWHERE. IN MY ALWAYS PLEASANT TONE, I TOLD HIM.

0100
- AFTER LEAVING THE JAIL, I WENT TO A FAVORITE ESTABLISHMENT TO DINE. I SAT WITH ABOUT FOUR OTHER OFFICERS AND JOKED AROUND A BIT AS I ATE.

0145
-I WENT UP TO A LOCAL NIGHTCLUB. THEY WERE ABOUT TO LET OUT AND THE CROWD SOMETIMES GETS ROWDY. I ENCOUNTERED THE USUAL DRUNKS THAT WANTED TO PLAY "BEFRIEND THE LAW ENFORCEMENT OFFICER". THEY TRIED TO CONVERSE WITH ME AND I TRIED TO IGNORE THEM. I HAD TO HELP MANAGEMENT AND SECURITY BREAK UP A DISTURBANCE AND THROW SOME PEOPLE OFF PROPERTY.

0258
-I DROVE SOME DRUNKEN NEW ZEALAND TOURISTS BACK TO THEIR HOTEL. THEY WERE WALKING AND ASKED ME FOR A RIDE. I TOLD THEM THE SHERIFF'S OFFICE WAS NOT A TRANSPORT SERVICE. THEY WERE PLEASANT AND PERSISTANT IN THEIR DRUNKEN STATE, SO I GAVE IN. THEY SAID THEY SAW MY AGENCY ON "COPS" BEFORE.

0327
- AFTER DROPPING OFF THE NEW ZEALANDERS, I WENT BEHIND THEIR HOTEL TO DO SOME PAPERWORK. WHAT HAS TO BE MY FAVORITE SONG OF ALL TIME CAME ON THE RADIO. I HAD TO STOP WHAT I WAS DOING, CRANK THE RADIO, AND BOB MY HEAD FOR A FEW MINUTES. (DON'T TELL THE SHERIFF I CRANK THE RADIO IN MY CRUISER I MEAN, HIS CRUISER, I MEAN, THE TAX PAYING COUNTY CITIZEN'S CRUISER THAT I HAPPEN TO TAKE HOME EVERYDAY.)

0422
-I TURNED IN MY PAPERWORK FOR THE SHIFT. I HAVE ABOUT AN HOUR TO GO BEFORE GETTING OFF. I'M GOING TO SEE IF I CAN FIND A BAD GUY "RIGHT QUICK".

0427

- IT IS PRETTY RAINY OUT SO ON SECOND THOUGHT I'M GOING TO HIDE SOMEWHERE UNTIL THE END OF THE SHIFT.

0454 -

FRIENDGIRL (3) CALLED ME TO SEE WHAT I WAS UP TO. SHE'S A 23Y/O PUERTO RICAN FEMALE. SHE LOVES TO COOK FOR ME, AND IS VERY SWEET. I KEEP TELLING HER SHE'S TOO SWEET FOR ME. I TELL HER I'M A BAD GUY AND SHE SHOULD LEAVE ME ALONE (THE DISCLAIMER). I ALSO TELL HER I CAN'T GIVE HER THE TIME SHE DESERVES BECAUSE OF MY BUSY SCHEDULE. SHE TELLS ME SHE'S HAPPY WITH WHATEVER TIME I CAN GIVE HER. IT'S THE SAME WITH ALL THE WOMEN IN MY LIFE. THEY MEET ME AND THINK I'M A GOOD GUY, ONE THEY'D ENJOY BEING WITH. I LET THEM KNOW UP FRONT THAT I DON'T HAVE WHAT IT TAKES TO BE IN A RELATIONSHIP, TIME AND COMMITMENT, THEY NEVER LISTEN. I GUESS THEY THINK IF THEY HANG AROUND, I'LL COME AROUND, BUT MY PLATE'S TOO FULL. FRIENDGIRL (1) HAS BEEN IN THE PICTURE FOR MANY YEARS. SHE'S AN OLDER FEMALE FROM TRINIDAD. WE EVEN LIVED TOGETHER BRIEFLY. SHE EVEN FOLLOWED ME TO FLORIDA. SHE RECENTLY MOVED BACK OUT OF STATE THOUGH. I THINK SHE MAY BE GIVING UP ON ME. FRIENDGIRL (2) IS A 26Y/O BRAZILIAN GIRL. EXTREMELY SWEET, BUT INSISTS THAT I DO HAVE TIME FOR HER WHEN I REALLY DON'T. SHE RECENTLY SENT ME AN E-MAIL. IT BASICALLY SAID THAT I DIDN'T TRY HARD ENOUGH TO FIND TIME FOR HER, SO HAVE A GOOD LIFE. (I WONDER HOW LONG THAT WILL LAST) FRIENDGIRL (4) IS A 21Y/O BRAZILIAN AS WELL. SHE SPEAKS VERY LITTLE ENGLISH. SHE CAN SAY F--K YOU. SHE TRIED TO TEACH ME TO SAY IT IN PORTUGUESE, BUT I TOLD HER I DIDN'T WANT TO LEARN. I DON'T "CUSS".

0525 (D) ALARM AT A TOURIST RESORT

RESORT SECURITY WANTED TO MEET WITH AN OFFICER BECAUSE AN ALARM WAS GOING OFF. (I'M THINKING PERHAPS THIS SECURITY GUARD NEEDS TO GET A DOG) UPON MEETING WITH THE GUARD, I LEARNED SHE WAS NEW. THE S.O.P. (STANDARD OPERATING PROCEDURES) MANUAL WAS SITTING OUT ON HER DESK. IT INFORMED HER TO CALL 911 WHENEVER AN ALARM WENT OFF. SHE HAD ALREADY CHECKED THE

BUILDING AND DETERMINED ALL WAS WELL. I INFORMED HER OF THE R.L.O.P. (REAL LIFE OPERATING PROCEDURES). CALL US IF AFTER CHECKING THE BUILDING, YOU FIND ALL IS NOT WELL.

0554
  - I'M HEADED TO THE HOUSE. "SEE YA"

08/12

1745 (S) TRAFFIC STOP

I CONDUCTED A TRAFFIC STOP ON THE WAY TO WORK. AFTER RUNNING THE TAG, I FOUND THE CAR'S OWNER HELD A VALID I.D. ONLY, NO D.L. AFTER STOPPING THE CAR, I FOUND THAT THE OWNER'S DAUGHTER, A YOUNG WF WAS THE DRIVER. SHE EXPLAINED THAT HER FATHER, WHO WAS LEGALLY BLIND, HAD PASSED AWAY 2 MONTHS AGO. HE HAD PURCHASED THE CAR FOR HER.

1830

- AFTER BRIEFING, WHERE WE RECEIVE AN UPDATE ON THE LATEST ACTIVITY IN OUR AREA, I HEADED OUT FOR DINNER. ON THE WAY THERE I WAS DISPATCHED AN EMERGENCY, IN-PROGRESS CALL...

1830 (D) MAN DOWN

SECURITY AT A LOCAL RESORT ADVISED THAT A W/M WAS PASSED OUT IN FRONT OF THE BUILDING. TWO UNITS, WHO WERE BACKING ME, ARRIVED THERE FIRST. I WAS ON THE OTHER END OF MY ZONE, FIGHTING BUMPER-TO-BUMPER TRAFFIC. THEY ADVISED IT WAS IN FACT A SLIP AND FALL. IT WAS A MEDICAL CONCERN ONLY (NOT CRIMINAL), AND CLEARED THE CALL.

1842

-I DECIDED TO MAKE ANOTHER ATTEMPT AT GETTING DINNER. ON THE WAY THERE I GOT ANOTHER CALL...

1842

- A B/F WAS CAUSING A DISTURBANCE IN A PONDEROSA RESTAURANT. AGAIN, ANOTHER UNIT (OFFICER) ARRIVED ON THE SCENE BEFORE I DID. THEY CANCELLED ME, ADVISING THAT THE LADY HAD LEFT.

1900

- FINALLY, I MADE IT TO A "CHOW HALL". I HAD SOME PASTA AND PIZZA. NO DONUTS! NEVER DONUTS! AT LEAST IN UNIFORM.

2019 (S) CITIZEN ASSIST
I HELPED A TOURIST FIND THE LOCAL MALL.

2037 (D) DISTURBANCE
I RESPONDED TO A DISTURBANCE AT A GAS STATION. IT WAS A VERBAL ALTERCATION BETWEEN AN EMPLOYER AND A FORMER EMPLOYEE. THE EMPLOYER HAD A TRANSPORTATION COMPANY AND THE FORMER EMPLOYEE WAS A DRIVER. AFTER THE EMPLOYEE WAS DISMISSED, HE KEPT THE RADIO EQUIPMENT. HE HEARD ALL THE CALLS FOR SERVICE. IN SOME CASES HE WAS ABLE TO PICK UP THE FARES BEFORE THE PRESENT COMPANY DRIVERS COULD GET THERE. A FELLOW OFFICER CONVINCED THE MAN TO RETURN THE EQUIPMENT TO THE EMPLOYER. (YOU HAVE TO ADMIT THE GUY HAD A GOOD THING GOING FOR AWHILE. HE JUST CUT OUT THE MIDDLE MAN.) BEFORE I COULD LEAVE THE GAS STATION, I WAS BOMBARDED WITH LOST TOURISTS IN NEED OF DIRECTIONS.

2126 (D) SUSPICIOUS INCIDENT
A LOCAL RESIDENT, WHO WAS OUT OF TOWN, CALLED 911, DESIRING A CHECK OF HER HOME. SHE SAID SOMEONE CALLED HER CELL PHONE FROM HER RESIDENCE, AND NO ONE WAS SUPPOSED TO HAVE BEEN THERE. AS I ENTERED THE COMPLEX, I WAS FLAGGED DOWN BY A MIDDLE-AGED, B/M. HE SAID, "LOOK HERE MAN I NEED TO TALK TO YOU". I ASKED HIM WHAT THE PROBLEM WAS. HE SAID, "THERE'S A GIRL UP THERE IN MY APARTMENT AND SHE'S GOT TO GO". I TOLD HIM I WAS ON MY WAY TO ANOTHER CALL AND WOULD HELP HIM WHEN I WAS DONE. I LOCATED THE INITIAL CALLER'S RESIDENCE. I FOUND THE FRONT WINDOW UNLOCKED AND THE LIGHT AND A/C WERE ON. THE DISPATCHER GOT BACK IN TOUCH WITH THE CALLER. SHE SAID SHE LEFT THE LIGHT ON SO PEOPLE WOULD THINK SHE WAS HOME. SHE SAID SHE ALSO LEFT THE A/C ON, AND MAY VERY WELL HAVE FORGOTTON TO LOCK THE WINDOW. THE FRONT DOOR WAS LOCKED AND THE PLACE DIDN'T SEEM TO HAVE BEEN BURGLARIZED. I CLOSED UP AS BEST I COULD AND LEFT IT AT THAT. I DID ASK SOME PEOPLE IN THE AREA IF THEY HAD SEEN ANYONE AROUND THE APARTMENT. TWO OF THE PEOPLE I SPOKE TO WERE SOME COLLEGE EXCHANGE STUDENTS FROM ENGLAND (YOUNG, W/ F). THEY WERE JUNIORS. THEY HAD ONLY BEEN IN TOWN FOR

5 DAYS OF A 1 YEAR VISIT. THEIR TASK WAS TO WORK IN THE SERVICE INDUSTRY IN SOME CAPACITY DURING THAT TIME. THEY WERE EXTREMELY IMPRESSED WITH THE FACT THAT I HAD A GUN. (I GUESS IN ENGLAND, OFFICERS JUST CARRY A BATON, OR A LEATHER STRAP, OR SOMETHING) I GAVE THEM EACH MY BUSINESS CARD. THEY SAID, "GOOD, NOW WE CAN CALL YOU WHEN WE GET INTO TROUBLE". I CIRCLED BACK AROUND THE COMPLEX TO WHERE THE B/M WAS, BUT HE WAS GONE. OH WELL, I GUESS HE DECIDED HE COULD LIVE WITH HER ANOTHER DAY. EITHER THAT OR HE DIDN'T WANT ANY WITNESSES...

2212-I WENT TO 7 ELEVEN TO GET A DRINK AND RETURN SOME CALLS. FRIENDGIRLS (2) AND (3) HAD CALLED. FG (3), THE BRAZILIAN WHO SPEAKS LITTLE ENGLISH, ALSO KNOWS HOW TO SAY IN ENGLISH, "I LIKE YOU". SHE CALLS ME HER BOYFRIEND. I SPOKE BRIEFLY TO (2). THE TOURISTS REQUESTS FOR DIRECTIONS GOT TO BE TOO MUCH FOR ME, SO I ROLLED OUT.

2330 -I CALLED MYSELF TAKING A LITTLE SHORT CUT BEHIND SOME BUSINESSES ON A DIRT ROAD. ONCE I HIT THE DIRT ROAD, THERE WAS A BIG DROP OFF. THE ROAD AHEAD LOOKED ROUGH, BUT I WAS AT THE POINT OF NO RETURN. I ENDED UP GETTING MY VEHICLE STUCK IN THE MUD. (I SHOULD HAVE STAYED BACK THERE GIVING DIRECTIONS, HUH?) I MADE UP FOR IT THOUGH. WHILE I WAITED FOR A TOW TRUCK TO COME AND PULL ME OUT, I GAVE DIRECTIONS LEFT AND RIGHT.

0130 (D) ALARM
AFTER FINALLY GETTING MY CAR OUT OF THE MUD, I WAS DISPATCHED TO AN ALARM AT A GROCERY STORE. THE STORE WAS LOCKED UP TIGHT AND I HEADED TO EAT AGAIN.

0227 (S) TRAFFIC STOP
I STOPPED SOMEONE WITH A SUSPENDED LICENSE. I WROTE THEM A TICKET AND TOOK THEIR LICENSE.

0253 (S) TRAFFIC STOP
I RAN A TAG ON MY COMPUTER AND NOTHING CAME BACK. AFTER I STOPPED THE CAR, I FOUND A COUPLE, A B/M AND W/F, WHO WERE GOING HOME FOR THE EVENING. THEY PROVIDED

ME WITH A VALID REGISTRATION AND I ALLOWED THEM TO BE ON THEIR WAY.

0321(S) TRAFFIC STOP

I STOPPED AN OLDER, H/F, WHO WAS DRIVING A SMALL, RED VEHICLE, WITH A TAIL LIGHT OUT. HER DAUGHTER, WHO WAS IN HER EARLY TWENTIES, WAS IN THE PASSENGER SEAT. BASED ON THEIR ATTIRE AND THE AREA WE WERE IN, I KNEW THEY HAD JUST LEFT A NIGHTCLUB. SHE DIDN'T HAVE HER LICENSE ON HER, BUT SAID IT MUST BE IN THE TRUNK. I SAID SHE MUST HAVE ONE, OR ELSE HOW COULD SHE GET IN THE CLUB. I TOLD HER THAT WITHOUT I.D., NIGHTCLUB PERSONNEL WOULD HAVE NO WAY OF TELLING THAT SHE WAS 18 OR OVER. THAT MADE HER SMILE, AND IT MADE HER DAUGHTER LAUGH OUT LOUD. SHE WAS ABLE TO LOCATE THE LICENSE. I WARNED HER ABOUT THE LIGHT AND LET HER GO.

0331(S) TRAFFIC STOP

I WAS RIGHT BEHIND AN INDIVIDUAL WHO MADE A U-TURN, RUNNING A RED LIGHT. AFTER I LIT HIM UP, HE TOOK A WHILE BEFORE STOPPING. WHEN I CONFRONTED HIM (20'S H/M) I SAID, "YOU NOT ONLY RAN A LIGHT IN FRONT OF THE POLICE, BUT THEN YOU DON'T STOP". I TOLD HIM TO GET IT TOGETHER AND LET HIM GO. HE WAS VERY APOLOGETIC AND THANKFUL AS HE DROVE OFF.

0345 (S) TRAFFIC STOP

I CONDUCTED A TRAFFIC STOP. (NOTHING EXCITING)

0400 -I GOT A CALL FROM A FRIEND WHO WORKS A GRAVEYARD SHIFT AT A LOCAL HOTEL. I'LL CALL HER FRIENDGIRL (5). SHE'S A GREAT GIRL AND A REALLY GOOD FRIEND. SHE'S ONE OF THOSE PEOPLE WHO ARE SO GOOD A FRIEND THAT YOU WOULDN'T RISK "MESSING" THAT UP BY TAKING IT FURTHER.

0545 - ON THE WAY HOME I GOT ANOTHER CALL. A RESORT SECURITY OFFICER ADVISED A TRANSIENT WAS SLEEPING IN THE BATHROOM AND THAT IT WAS A CONTINUOUS PROBLEM. A COUPLE OF DAY SHIFT OFFICERS HEARD THE CALL ON THEIR WAYS TO WORK AND PICKED IT UP FOR ME.

0602 - ARMED ROBBERY

MY SHIFT ENDED AT 6AM. SHORTLY THEREAFTER, AS I SAT IN MY DRIVEWAY, I HEARD THE CALL GO OUT. 2 H/M HAD ROBBED A DRUG STORE AS MANAGEMENT WAS OPENING. AT GUNPOINT, THE 2 H/M USED DUCT TAPE TO BIND THE ARMS AND MOUTHS OF THEIR VICTIMS. THEY TOOK CASH FROM THE SAFE AND LEFT ONE OF THE VICTIMS WITH HEAD INJURIES. K-9 DOGS TRACKED THE SUSPECTS TO THE PARKING LOT BEFORE LOSING THEIR SCENT. THEY BELIEVE THE MEN FLED THE SCENE IN A VEHICLE. I turned my radio off and went inside.

08/13

1921 - ON THE WAY TO WORK I RETRIEVED A VOICE MESSAGE FROM FRIENDGIRL (3). SHE WISHED ME A GREAT DAY.

2000 - BRIEFING

2011 -I HEADED TO DINNER

2018 (S) TRAFFIC STOP
   WHILE ON THE WAY TO EAT, I NOTICED AN EXPIRED TAG ON A VEHICLE. THE DRIVER, A W/M IN HIS LATE THIRTIES, HAD THE CORRECT TAG IN THE TRUNK. HE HADN'T YET SWITCHED IT OUT. AFTER VERIFYING THE VALIDITY OF HIS LICENSE, I LET HIM GO.
   (I TRY TO GIVE A GENERAL DESCRIPTION OF THE PEOPLE I COME IN CONTACT WITH. THIS SHOWS YOU THAT I ENCOUNTER ALL TYPES. HOPEFULLY, I TREAT EVERYONE EQUALLY.)

2022 (D) DOMESTIC DISTURBANCE
   BLOODY SCENE. A H/F ATTACKED HER H/M HUSBAND AT HIS RESIDENCE. THE TWO HAVE BEEN SEPARATED FOR A WHILE, AND LIVE APART. THE WIFE WAS UPSET THAT THE HUSBAND WAS NOW LIVING WITH HIS NEW GIRLFRIEND. SHE WENT TO HIS HOUSE WITH THE COUPLE'S YOUNG DAUGHTER. SHE KNOCKED SEVERAL TIMES ON THE FRONT AND BACK DOORS. HE DIDN'T LET HER IN BECAUSE HE DIDN'T WANT TROUBLE. FINALLY, SHE BROKE OUT THE WINDOW WITH A CONCRETE BLOCK THAT WAS OUTSIDE. INITIALLY SHE TRIED GETTING THEIR DAUGHTER TO CLIMB THROUGH THE WINDOW AND UNLOCK THE DOOR. A FRIEND, WHO HAD ALSO COME WITH HER, WARNED HER AGAINST THAT. SHE SAID THE LITTLE GIRL MIGHT GET CUT. THE WIFE THEN DECIDED TO CLIMB THROUGH THE WINDOW HERSELF. ONCE IN, SHE RANSACKED THE KITCHEN. THE GIRLFRIEND LOCKED HERSELF IN A ROOM AND THE HUSBAND CAME DOWNSTAIRS. THE WIFE BEAT HIM WITH A GLASS FRAMED PICTURE THAT SHE HAD RIPPED FROM THE WALL. SHE STRUCK HIM ON HIS HEAD AND ARMS AS HE TRIED TO BLOCK THE BLOWS. HE WAS UNINJURED, BUT SHE GOT CUT PRETTY BADLY. PARAMEDICS WRAPPED HER UP PRETTY GOOD AND SHE WAS TAKEN TO JAIL. SHE WAS

CHARGED WITH DOMESTIC BATTERY AND BURGLARY TO AN OCCUPIED DWELLING.

2146 - AS I WAS CLEARING THE SCENE, I NOTICED FG3 HAD CALLED. I CALLED HER BACK, BUT NOW SHE WAS BUSY. SHE ASKED IF SHE COULD CALL ME BACK. I SAID "GOOD LUCK". (KEEP IN MIND, I HADNT EATEN YET AND HAD FOOD ON THE BRAIN.) SHE CALLED BACK JUST AS I REACHED THE "CHOW HALL". I HAD TO MAKE A DECISION (1) GO EAT, OR (2) ANSWER THE PHONE, DON'T EAT YET, AND RISK GETTING DISPATCHED A CALL. I DECIDED TO GO EAT. (WHAT WOULD YOU CHOOSE?)

2202 - FG3 AND 4 LEFT MESSAGES WHILE I WAS AWAY EATING.

2250 (S) TRAFFIC STOP
   I STOPPED A CAR WHOSE REGISTERED OWNER HAD A SUSPENDED LICENSE. I LEARNED THAT THIS B/M HAD A VALID LICENSE. IT WAS HIS MOTHER, THE OWNER OF THE CAR, WHO HAD A SUSPENDED LICENSE.

2310(S) TRAFFIC STOP
   I STOPPED A CAR WHOSE REGISTERED OWNER HAD 4 SUSPENSIONS ON HIS LICENSE. THE REGISTERED OWNER WAS IN THE PASSENGER SEAT AND HIS COUSIN WAS DRIVING (2 W/M'S). I THINK THEY MAY HAVE PULLED THE OLD "SWITH-A-ROO" AFTER I STOPPED THEM, BUT I DIDN'T SEE IT. I ASKED HIM WHY HE WAS DRIVING HIS COUSIN'S VEHICLE. HE SAID HIS COUSIN HAD BEEN DRINKING AND THEY WERE DOING THE RESPONSIBLE THING. I ADVISED HIM THAT HAD THE COUSIN WITH THE SUSPENSIONS BEEN DRIVING, HE'D BE GOING TO JAIL. I ALLOWED THEM TO GO ON THEIR WAY.

2320 (S) TRAFFIC STOP
   I STOPPED A CAR WITH AN UNASSIGNED TAG. THE DRIVER WAS ABLE TO PRODUCE VALID REGISTRATION AND I LET THEM GO.

2335 (S) TRAFFIC STOP

I STOPPED A CAR WITH A TAG ATTACHED THAT WASN'T ASSIGNED TO IT. THE DRIVER WAS A YOUNG W/F. SHE HAD THE CORRECT TAG, WHICH SHE RECENTLY RECEIVED IN THE MAIL, IN THE TRUNK. SHE SAID SHE DIDN'T APPRECIATE BEING PULLED OVER AND TREATED LIKE A CRIMINAL. I TOLD HER, "I'M SURE YOU'RE NOT A CRIMINAL. YOU ARE, HOWEVER, IN VIOLATION OF THE LAW AND ARE BEING TREATED ACCORDINGLY. THAT DIDN'T MAKE HER FEEL ANY BETTER. SHE SEEMED TO BE KIND OF SHAKEN UP.

2352 -I TOOK A QUICK BREAK FOR GAS AND A CAR WASH. I HAVE A SLIGHT HEADACHE. I DON'T KNOW IF IT'S FROM THE DESSERT I ATE OR FROM MY CELL PHONE.

2355 (D) PETIT THEFT

A TOURIST HAD A BACKPACK STOLEN WHILE DINING IN A HOTEL LOBBY. THIS WAS AN ASIAN WOMEN VISITING FROM CHINA. SHE WAS VISITING FLORIDA WITH HER HUSBAND AND THREE DAUGHTERS. THEY SPENT THE DAY AT AMUSEMENT PARKS AND DIDN'T REPORT THE THEFT, WHICH OCCURRED AT BREAKFAST TIME, UNTIL LATE. WHEN SHE REPORTED IT TO THE HOTEL STAFF, THEY TOLD HER TO CALL THE POLICE. THEY SAID THE POLICE WOULD QUESTION THE FACT THAT THEY TOOK SO LONG TO CALL. SHE ASKED ME IF THAT WAS GOING TO BE A PROBLEM. I TOLD HER NO. HAD IT BEEN A MORE SERIOUS OFFENSE, LIKE A SEXUAL BATTERY (RAPE), QUESTIONS MIGHT BE ASKED AS TO THE TIMELINESS OF THE REPORT. AS FOR A THEFT, NO. WE REALIZE PEOPLE WANT TO TAKE CARE OF THEIR BUSINESS AND CALL WHEN IT'S CONVENIENT FOR THEM. AFTER I TOLD HER THAT, SHE WAS PLEASED. SHE TOLD ME TO "CHALLENGE" THE HOTEL GUY ON MY WAY OUT. I TOLD HER I WOULD TO MAKE HER FEEL GOOD. ALL I SAID TO THE HOTEL GUY WAS, "HAVE A GOOD EVENING". THE LADY SIGNED HER STATEMENT IN CHINESE. I THOUGHT THAT WAS PRETTY COOL.

0100 - BACK ON THE PROWL

0106 (S) TRAFFIC STOP
AMOTHER WAS DRIVING HER SON'S CAR. THE SON'S LICENSE WAS SUSPENDED.

0124 (S) TRAFFIC STOP
I RAN THE TAG OF A CHEVROLET IMPALA. IT CAME BACK TO A BMW. IT WAS A B/F DRIVING. SHE WOULDN'T STOP WHEN I LIT HER UP. EVENTUALLY I GOT HER STOPPED AFTER SHE TURNED DOWN A SIDE STREET. ANOTHER OFFICER SHOWED UP TO BACK ME. WHEN I GOT THE LADY OUT OF THE CAR, SHE TOLD ME SHE KNEW HER LICENSE WAS SUSPENDED. SHE SAID HER BMW WAS IN THE SHOP, SO SHE PUT THE TAG ON HER BROTHER'S IMPALA. SHE SAID SHE DIDN'T STOP BECAUSE SHE HEARD WOMEN SHOULD ONLY STOP IN WELL LIT AREAS. I TOLD HER THAT EXCUSE WASN'T GOING TO FLY. SHE PULLED OFF A WELL LIT STREET DOWN A DARK ONE. SHE LATER TOLD ME SHE KEPT GOING BECAUSE SHE DIDN'T WANT TO GET LOCKED UP BACK THERE WHERE ALL THOSE "WHITE PEOPLE" WERE. SHE WANTED TO MAKE IT TO HER NEIGHBORHOOD. SHE WAS CRYING AND PRETTY HYSTERICAL AT FIRST. SHE CALMED DOWN AFTER BEING IN THE BACK SEAT FOR A WHILE. AFTER EXPLAINING HER CHARGES TO HER, SHE OPENED UP. SHE SAID THE BAD PEOPLE GET AWAY AND THE GOOD PEOPLE GET LOCKED UP. SHE SAID SHE WAS GOING TO REMEMBER ME FOR THE REST OF HER LIFE BECAUSE I LOCKED HER UP. I TOLD HER I'D GIVE HER MY CARD SO SHE COULD ATTACH A NAME WITH THE MEMORY. SHE LAUGHED. SHE SAID I WAS GOING TO LOCK HER UP WITH ALL THOSE CRAZY PEOPLE. I SAID THEY'RE GOOD PEOPLE REMEMBER. SHE THOUGHT THAT WAS FUNNY TOO. SHE SAID SHE HAD ONLY BEEN IN TOWN FOR TWO MONTHS AND I LOCKED HER UP BEFORE SHE COULD FIND A "MAN". SHE SAID SHE WAS MOVING BACK TO ATLANTA BECAUSE FLORIDA HAS BEEN NOTHING BUT TROUBLE. BEFORE IT WAS ALL OVER, SHE WAS ASKING ME IF I WAS MARRIED. I TOLD HER I WASN'T. SHE WANTED ME TO DRIVE HER AROUND ON ALL MY CALLS SO SHE WOULDN'T HAVE TO SPEND THE NIGHT IN JAIL. I TOLD HER I COULDN'T DO THAT. SHE SAID SHE HOPES THE OFFICER I TURN HER OVER TO IS AS NICE AS ME.

0356 -I HEADED TO THE STATION TO COMPLETE MY PAPERWORK.

0420 -I USED MY CELL PHONE AND GOT A STRANGE FEELING IN MY HEAD. IT WAS DEFINITELY THAT, AND NOT THE DESSERT, THAT GAVE ME THE HEADACHE. I MAY HAVE TO CANCEL MY PLAN. I DON'T WANT TO END UP LIKE THAT MAN WHO BELIEVES HE DEVELOPED BRAIN CANCER FROM USING A CELL PHONE.

0502 - ALL MY PAPER IS TURNED IN. IT'S TIME TO GO GET BREAKFAST AND COUNT DOWN TIL THE END OF MY WORKDAY.

08/16

1800-BRIEFING

1830 (D) ALARM
I WAS DISPATCHED TO AN ALARM AT A BUSINESS. I WAS UNABLE TO LOCATE THE ADDRESS AND CLEARED THE CALL.

1850 (BU) TRAFFIC STOP
I WENT TO BACK UP MY AREA PARTNER WHO WAS CONDUCTING A TRAFFIC STOP. THE REGISTERED OWNER OF THE VEHICLE WAS "WANTED". AS IT TURNED OUT, THE DRIVER (H/M) WAS NOT THE REGISTERED OWNER. THE WANTED INDIVIDUAL WAS HIS FRIEND AND HE WAS BORROWING THE CAR.

1907 (D) 911 HANG-UP
A CITIZEN (W/M) CALLED 911 AND DISCONNECTED THE LINE. THE DISPATCHER CALLED THE CALLER BACK, BUT WAS UNABLE TO GET THROUGH. WE GET A LOT OF THOSE, AND 99% OF TIME, THEY'RE ACCIDENTAL. THAT WAS THE CASE THIS TIME AS WELL.

1915-I WENT TO EAT

1930 -I WAS DISPATCHED TO ANOTHER 911 HANG-UP, BUT ANOTHER UNIT CLEARED THE CALL FOR ME.

2042 (D) CRIMINAL MISCHIEF
THE CABLE COMPANY WAS THE VICTIM (OLDER W/M) ON THIS CALL. A CONSTRUCTION COMPANY WAS DOING SOME ROADSIDE WORK WHERE CABLE WIRES WERE LAID. THE COMPANY INADVERTANTLY CUT SOME UNDERGROUND CABLES. THIS CAUSED ABOUT $75,000.00 WORTH OF DAMAGES AND LEFT HUNDREDS OF CUSTOMERS WITHOUT CABLE.

2135 (BU) SUSPICIOUS INCIDENT
THE CALLER WAS A YOUNG W/F WHO WAS HOME ALONE. SHE WAS POSITIVE THAT HER ROOMMATE WAS AT WORK, AND SHE HEARD SOME VOICES IN HER APARTMENT. SHE ALSO THOUGHT SHE SAW THE SHADOW OF A PERSON. AS IT TURNED OUT, NO

ONE BESIDES HER WAS IN THE APARTMENT. IT WAS LOCKED UP TIGHT. SHE WAS THRILLED AT THE FACT THAT 5 OFFICERS SHOWED UP TO HELP HER. AS WE LEFT, SHE STARTED ASKING WHETHER OR NOT WE KNEW CERTAIN OFFICERS. WE VIEWED THE CALL AS A CRY FOR ATTENTION. (WHATEVER)

2153-I WAS IN THE AREA OF THE CAR WASH SO I DECIDED TO CLEAN UP THE CRUISER.

2208 (D) DOMESTIC DISTURBANCE
ANOTHER HUSBAND/WIFE FIGHT (W/M W/F). THIS ONE WAS VERBAL ONLY. THE WIFE WANTED THE HUSBAND OUT. SHE FOUND OUT HE HAD A MISTRESS AND WANTED NOTHING ELSE TO DO WITH HIM. THEY BOTH ADMITTED THAT THINGS HADN'T BEEN GOOD FOR A LONG WHILE. SHE ALSO WANTED HALF OF WHAT WAS LEFT IN THE JOINT BANK ACCOUNT. THE HUSBAND AGREED TO LEAVE AND WAS LOADING THE CAR WITH HIS BELONGINGS WHEN MY AREA PARTNER AND I ARRIVED. HE GAVE HIS WIFE HER SHARE OF THE ACCOUNT BALANCE. SHE SEEMED TO THINK SHE WAS SHORT CUT. THE HUSBAND LEFT AND SAID HE WAS GOING TO A HOTEL FOR THE NIGHT. (I THINK HE PROBABLY WENT TO THE MISTRESS'. HE ALREADY MESSED UP, WHY SPEND 100 BUCKS ON A ROOM UNLESS OF COURSE, THE MISTRESS IS MARRIED TOO.)

2227 (BU) AGGRAVATED BATTERY
THIS WAS A CALL AT A JUVENILE DETENTION FACILITY. BOTH THE VICTIM (B/F) AND THE SUSPECT (W/F) WERE YOUNG TEENAGED GIRLS. RESCUE ALSO ARRIVED TO TREAT THE VICTIM FOR HER INJURIES. AS A JOKE, THE W/F POURED A CUP OF THE FOLLOWING MIXTURE IN THE FACE OF THE B/F: A CLEANING PRODUCT, TOOTHPASTE, SHAMPOO, LOTION, AND URINE. THE B/F DIDN'T THINK IT WAS TOO FUNNY. SHE PRESSED CHARGES AGAINST THE W/F AND HAD TO BE TAKEN TO THE HOSPITAL FOR EYE INJURIES.

2302 (D) SUSPICIOUS INCIDENT
THIS WAS A CALL IN A RETIREMENT COMMUNITY. AN ELDERLY W/F SAID A H/M WAS LOITERING IN THE NEIGHBORHOOD. HE AND ANOTHER PERSON WERE SITTING IN A VEHICLE THAT WAS PARKED IN FRONT OF HER HOUSE. THE H/M THEN

APPROACHED HER RESIDENCE AND KNOCKED ON THE FRONT PORCH SCREEN DOOR. THE W/F WENT TO THE DOOR, WITHOUT OPENING IT, AND ASKED HIM WHAT HE WANTED. HE SAID HE WAS OUT LOOKING FOR HIS CAT. THE WOMEN SAID, "AT 11:00 AT NIGHT? YOU BETTER LEAVE OR I'M GOING TO CALL THE POLICE!" THE H/M SAID, " I'LL BE OUT HERE A WHILE LOOKING FOR MY CAT". THE LADY THEN TOLD HIM SHE WAS CALLING THE POLICE NOW. BY THE TIME I ARRIVED, THE H/M WAS GONE. I TOLD THE LADY I'D DO A CHECK OF THE AREA AND PARK IN THE NEIGHBORHOOD FOR A WHILE.

2316 (D) SUSPICIOUS INCIDENT

MANAGEMENT OF POPEYE'S RESTAURANT CALLED ABOUT AN INCIDENT THAT OCCURRED IN THEIR DRIVE THRU. THE DRIVER OF ONE CAR DIDN'T THINK THE DRIVER OF ANOTHER CAR MOVED QUICKLY ENOUGH. DRIVER ONE GOT OUT HIS CAR TO CONFRONT DRIVER TWO. DRIVER ONE SAW THAT DRIVER TWO HAD A GUN IN THE CAR, AND BECAME FRIGHTENED. DRIVER TWO REASSURED DRIVER ONE THAT THE GUN WASN'T GOING TO BE USED ON HIM. HE SAID IT WAS FOR WHEN HE CAME BACK TO ROB POPEYE'S LATER. MANAGEMENT DECIDED TO CLOSE AN HOUR EARLY. ANOTHER OFFICER AND I WAITED ON PROPERTY UNTIL THAT TIME. (THE CHICKEN WAS SMELLING SO GOOD WE DECIDED TO HAVE SOME AND BISCUITS TOO, OF COURSE.)

0000 (D) GRAND THEFT

A TOURIST HAD SOME PROPERTY STOLEN FROM THEIR HOTEL ROOM. A HUSBAND AND WIFE (W/M W/F) WERE VISITING FLORIDA FROM PENNSYLVANIA WITH THEIR TWO DAUGHTERS. WHILE THEY WERE OUT AT AN AMUSEMENT PARK, SOMEONE STOLE THE WIFE'S WEDDING RINGS FROM HER SUITCASE. SHE WASNT CONCERNED WITH THE COST OF THE RINGS, IT WAS, OF COURSE, THEIR SENTIMENTAL VALUE. A KEY INTERROGATION DETERMINED THAT ONLY THE TOURISTS AND THE MAID ENTERED THE ROOM. IT'S PRETTY CLEAR, EITHER THE LADY LOST THE RINGS OR THE MAID STOLE THEM. THAT'S FOR THE DETECTIVE TO FIGURE OUT. I JUST GATHER AS MUCH INFO AS POSSIBLE TO MAKE IT EASY ON THEM.

0100 -I WENT TO A SHOPPING PLAZA TO COMPLETE

SOME PAPERWORK. I CALLED TO CHECK MY
MESSAGES ON THE HOME PHONE. I HAD THREE; TWO
WERE EX-GIRLFRIENDS, AND THE OTHER WAS MY
DAUGHTER'S MOM. THEY LIVE UP NORTH. SHE WAS
ASKING IF I WANTED THEM TO COME TO FLORIDA FOR
CHRISTMAS. I ALSO HAVE A SON FROM MY EX-WIFE.
THEY LIVE OUT OF STATE AS WELL. I SEE THEM EACH
ABOUT 2 OR 3 TIMES A YEAR.

0240 -I WENT UP TO EXXON TO GET A DRINK. I NOTICED
A COUPLE OF PEOPLE LOITERING IN VEHICLES IN THE
PARKING LOT. I ASKED ONE W/M WHAT HE WAS UP TO. HE
SAID HE WAS WAITING FOR SOMEONE. I APPROACHED
THE OTHER VEHICLE AND RAN THE TAG. THE OWNER'S
LICENSE WAS SUSPENDED. THE OWNER (H/M), WHO
WAS A STORE EMPLOYEE, WAS IN THE DRIVER SEAT
TAKING A BREAK, I GUESS. IF HE HAD A LICENSE I
WOULD HAVE TAKEN IT AWAY. IF HE HAD BEEN DRIVING
I WOULD HAVE WRITTEN HIM A TICKET. HE CLAIMED
HE COULDN'T FIND IT. HE ALSO CLAIMED HE DIDN'T
KNOW IT WAS SUSPENDED. I BELIEVE HIS LICENSE WAS
TAKEN AWAY ON ANOTHER OCCASION. AT ANY RATE,
I WARNED HIM. IF I SEE HIM DRIVING, AND HE HASN'T
SQUARED HIS LICENSE AWAY, HE TAKES THE RIDE.

0300 (S) TRAFFIC STOP
   I STOPPED A YOUNG W/F WITH AN EXPIRED NY TAG ALONG A
WINDING, DARK ROAD. AFTER STOPPING HER, SHE SAID SHE
HAS BEEN LIVING IN FLORIDA FOR ABOUT A YEAR. SHE SAID
SHE HASN'T HAD THE MONEY TO SWITCH OVER HER TAG YET.
I TOLD HER THAT IN THE EYES OF THE LAW, THAT WAS NO
EXCUSE. SHE AGREED. I GAVE HER A WRITTEN WARNING AND
TOLD HER NOT TO STOP ON SUCH A DARK ROAD AGAIN.

0322 (S) TRAFFIC STOP
   I WAS PATROLLING THE INTERSTATE AND RUNNING TAGS
AT RANDOM. (WE WERE ON A CLEAR CHANNEL WHICH MEANS
OTHER UNITS WERE ON AN EMERGENCY CALL AND ALL RADIO
TRAFFIC WAS RESTRICTED, WITH THE EXCEPTION OF THOSE
UNITS.) I WAS BEHIND TWO VEHICLE AND RAN THEM BOTH.
I LIKE TO STAY BEHIND A CAR UNTIL THE RESULTS COME

BACK. I RAN ONE CAR, A WHITE HONDA ACCORD, AND WAS AWAITING THE RESULTS. I THEN RAN THE OTHER VEHICLE. THAT VEHICLE WAS EXITING THE INTERSTATE. I WANTED TO STAY BEHIND IT, BUT DIDN'T WANT TO EXIT UNTIL THE HONDA INFO CAME BACK. AT THAT MOMENT, THE HONDA INFO CAME BACK. THE TAG ON IT WAS STOLEN. I LIT THE CAR UP BUT THE DRIVER WOULD NOT STOP. THAT USUALLY INDICATES THE CAR IS STOLEN. ANOTHER DRIVER, WHO WAS IN FRONT OF THE HONDA, STOPPED HIS VEHICLE IN RESPONSE TO MY EMERGENCY EQUIPMENT (LIGHTS AND SIREN). THAT JAMMED UP THE HONDA AND FINALLY HE STOPPED. THE DRIVER (H/M) IMMEDIATELY GOT OUT THE CAR AND WALKED BACK TOWARD MINE. I ORDERED HIM BACK TO THE HONDA WHERE I IMMEDIATELY HANDCUFFED HIM. HE BECAME HYSTERICAL AND WANTED TO KNOW WHY HE WAS BEING ARRESTED. I TOLD HIM I WAS DETAINING HIM UNTIL I FOUND OUT MORE ABOUT THE STOLEN TAG ON HIS CAR. HE REALLY LOST IT THEN. HE SAID HE DIDN'T STOP AT FIRST BECAUSE HE KNEW HIS LICENSE WAS SUSPENDED. HE SAID HE KNEW NOTHING ABOUT A STOLEN TAG THOUGH. I PLACED THE H/M IN MY BACK SEAT. MY PARTNER ARRIVED TO BACK ME UP. THERE WAS A T-SHIRT AROUND THE STEERING COLUMN AND THE IGNITION WAS PUNCHED. I CONFIRMED THAT THE CAR WAS IN FACT STOLEN. THE H/M SAID IT WAS HIS FRIEND'S CAR. HE SAID HE SPENT THE EVENING WITH HIM AND HIS GIRLFRIEND. HIS FRIEND TOLD HIM HE COULD TAKE THE CAR BECAUSE HE DIDN'T FEEL LIKE TAKING HIM HOME. I ASKED HIM WHY HE DIDN'T GET SUSPICIOUS WHEN HE SAW THE PUNCHED IGNITION. HE SAID HIS FRIEND TOLD HIM HE LOST HIS KEY. WHAT ABOUT THE SHIRT AROUND THE COLUMN? THAT WAS BECAUSE HIS FRIEND DIDN'T WANT TO ATTRACT ATTENTION. (YEAHHH!) HE SAID HIS FRIEND ASSURED HIM THE CAR WASN'T STOLEN. AT ANY RATE, HE WAS GOING TO JAIL. I EXPLAINED TO THE H/M THAT HIS FRIEND WASN'T THERE TO CONFIRM HIS STORY. ALL I HAD WAS HIM, THE SUSPENDED LICENSE, THE STOLEN TAG, AND THE STOLEN CAR. I SAID IF HE WAS REALLY A FRIEND, HE'D COME FORWARD AND COME CLEAN ABOUT THE CAR. I ASKED WHAT HIS FRIEND'S NAME WAS. HE ONLY KNEW THE FIRST NAME. (SOME FRIEND. HUH?)

08/17

1800-BRIEFING

1826-I WENT TO EAT, BUT WAS DISPATCHED A CALL...

1835 (D) DISABLED MOTORIST
A CALLER ADVISED THAT A WOMAN'S CAR HAD STALLED AT A BUSY INTERSECTION. I CHECKED THE AREA AND WAS UNABLE TO LOCATE HER.

1845 - I MADE IT TO A LOCAL RESTAURANT TO EAT. ONE OF THE MANAGER'S (W/F) THERE LIKES ME. SHE SAT AT MY TABLE AND TALKED TO ME THE WHOLE TIME I WAS EATING. (SWEET GIRL)

1945 (S) TRAFFIC STOP
I STOPPED A CAR WITH A TAG THAT WASN'T REGISTERED TO IT. THE DRIVER WAS A B/M, 6'-05", 375 LBS. HIS RECORD INDICATED THAT HE WAS A VIOLENT, CAREER CRIMINAL. I ARRESTED HIM AND CHARGED HIM WITH DRIVING WITH A SUSPENDED LICENSE AND ATTACHING A TAG THAT WASN'T ASSIGNED. HE SAID HE WAS PLANNING TO TAKE CARE OF ALL THAT ON PAY DAY. INSTEAD OF TOWING HIS CAR, I LET HIS GIRLFRIEND, WHO WAS WITH HIM, TAKE IT. HE LATER EXPLAINED THAT HIS RECORD WASN'T QUITE AS IT SEEMED. HE SAID HE GOT CAUGHT UP WITH SOME PEOPLE WHEN SOME BAD THINGS WENT DOWN. HE SAID HE'S BEEN CLEAN SINCE HE GOT OUT SEVERAL YEARS AGO. HE WAS NOW WORKING AS A PREP COOK IN A POPULAR, LOCAL RESTAURANT. (HE HAD A CALM DEMEANOR AND GAVE ME NO TROUBLE AT ALL DURING THE ARREST.)

2130 -I CHECKED MY MESSAGES AND I HAD TWO CALLS. ONE WAS FROM FG3 AND THE OTHER WAS A MALE FRIEND OF MINE. FOR WHATEVER REASON, HE'S ONE OF THE
FEW MALE FRIENDS I HAVE. HE WORKS SECURITY AT A LOCAL HOTEL. I ALSO RETURNED THE CALL OF ONE OF THOSE EX-GIRLFRIEND'S THAT CALLED ME EARLIER.

2150 (BU) TRAFFIC STOP
  I WENT TO ASSIST ANOTHER UNIT WHO WAS CONDUCTING A TRAFFIC STOP.

2315-I WENT TO GAS UP THE CRUISER AND ENDED UP ASSISTING SOME TOURISTS.

2330 - A TOURIST FLAGGED ME DOWN. HE HAD LOCKED HIS KEYS INSIDE HIS RENTAL CAR. WE DON'T CARRY SLIM JIMS. I BELIEVE WE'RE NOT PERMITTED TO ASSIST IN THESE MATTERS FOR LIABILITY REASONS. I ALWAYS TRY TO HELP THOUGH. I CARRY A COUPLE OF WIRE HANGERS IN MY TRUNK. THE W/M AND I (HE SOUNDED LIKE HE WAS FROM AUSTRALIA) BOTH TRIED UNSUCCESSFULLY. HE APPRECIATED MY TRYING AND SAID HE'D CALL THE RENTAL COMPANY.

0010 -I WORKED ON SOME PAPERWORK.

0054 (D) ARMED ROBBERY
  A B/M CAB DRIVER WAS ROBBED BY TWO BLACK MALES IN THEIR EARLY TWENTIES. THE CAB DRIVER'S SHIFT HAD ENDED AND HE WAS HEADING HOME. THE 2 B/MS FLAGGED HIM DOWN AND HE AGREED TO GIVE THEM A RIDE. WHEN THEY GOT DOWN THE ROAD, THE B/MS ATTACKED THE CAB DRIVER. THEY BEAT HIM OVER HIS HEAD WITH THEIR FISTS AND SOME METAL OBJECTS. THE DRIVER WAS UNSURE, BUT BELIEVES ONE OF THE B/MS WAS USING A GUN. THE DRIVER BEGGED FOR HIS LIFE AND TOLD THEM HE'D GIVE THEM ALL THAT HE HAD. HE REMOVED HIS DAY'S EARNINGS FROM HIS BREAST POCKET AND HANDED IT TO THEM. IT WAS A MERE $30.00. AFTER TAKING HIS CAR KEYS, THE B/MS FLED THE AREA ON FOOT. K-9 RESPONDED, BUT WERE UNABLE TO DEVELOP A STARTING POINT FOR THE DOG TO TRACK. OUR HELICOPTER WAS TIED UP ON ANOTHER CALL. RESCUE RESPONDED TO TREAT THE DRIVER FOR HIS INJURIES. I FOLLOWED THE AMBULANCE THAT TRANSPORTED HIM TO THE HOSPITAL. HE RECEIVED STITCHES FOR LACERATIONS ON HIS FACE AND HEAD. WHILE I WAS AT THE HOSPITAL, ANOTHER OFFICER ADVISED HE HAD A POTENTIAL SUSPECT DETAINED. IT WAS A BLACK MALE WHO FIT THE DESCRIPTION OF ONE OF THE

ATTACKERS. HE WAS SEEN RUNNING IN THE AREA WHERE THE ROBBERY OCCURRED. HE CLAIMED HE WAS OUT JOGGING. (YEAHHH!) I TOOK THE CAB DRIVER BACK TO THE SCENE TO LOOK AT THE GUY. THE DRIVER IDENTIFIED HIM AS ONE OF THE ATTACKERS. I ARRESTED THE B/M AND CHARGED HIM WITH ARMED ROBBERY, FOR WHICH THERE IS NO BOND. I'LL NEVER KNOW FOR SURE, BUT I THINK HE WAS GUILTY. IF HE IS FOUND GUILTY IT WILL BE A SHAME. A 22YO, B/M WHOSE LIFE IS RUINED OVER A BAD CHOICE, $30.00, AND SOME KEYS.

0900 - THANKS TO THE TWO IDIOTS WHO DECIDED TO VICTIMIZE A HARD WORKING CITIZEN MY WORK DAY WAS A 15 HOUR ONE. THE INITIAL CALL WENT OUT AT 12:54 AM. I FINISHED ALL THE PAPERWORK AROUND 9:00 AM. WHAT MAKES IT EVEN WORSE IS THAT I CAN'T GET PAID MONEY FOR MY OVERTIME. UNTIL THE NEW BUDGET COMES OUT, EARNING COMPENSATORY TIME IS OUR ONLY OPTION. THAT'S GOTTA SUCK, RIGHT?

08/21

1800-BRIEFING

1820 - (D) MISSING PERSON
   I WAS DISPATCHED TO A MISSING PERSON CALL AT THE CONVENTION CENTER. THE MISSING PERSON WAS A 41YO W/ F WHO WAS SEPARATED FROM HER PARTY. THE PARTY HAD CALLED IT IN. (NOW YOU TELL ME HOW IN THE "HAYO" IS A 41YO ANYTHING MISSING) AFTER ARRIVING, AND WALKING THE 10 MILES THROUGH THE CENTER, I MET WITH THE PARTY. THEY HAD ALREADY REUNITED WITH THEIR MISSING PERSON. I TOLD THEM TO COME UP WITH A PLAN TO MEET AT A PARTICULAR LOCATION NEXT TIME. WE ALL HAD A BIG LAUGH (MINE FAKE, OF COURSE) AND I CLEARED THE CALL.

1842 - (D) BURGLARY TO A VEHICLE
   THIS WAS A BURGLARY TO A VEHICLE THAT OCCURRED AT A MECHANIC'S GARAGE. THE VEHICLE WAS LEFT THERE FOR ABOUT A MONTH, AWAITING REPAIR PARTS. STOLEN FROM THE CAR WAS THE STEREO. ALL OF THE VICTIMS CD'S WERE LEFT THERE. THE VICTIM JOKED THAT THE THIEF MUST NOT HAVE LIKED HIS TASTE IN MUSIC.

1937-I WENT TO DINNER

2012-I WENT BACK ON PATROL.

2025 - (D) PETIT THEFT
   I RESPONDED TO A LOCAL HOTEL ON A THEFT CALL. TOURISTS FROM ENGLAND HAD THEIR PROPERTY (PURSE) STOLEN WHILE DINING AT A MALL. THE SUSPECTS GOT AWAY WITH ONLY CREDIT CARDS, WHICH WERE PROMPTLY CANCELLED.

2116- GASSED UP THE CRUISER.

2343 -I PULLED UP TO 7/11 TO GET A PINT OF "BEN & JERRY'S NEW YORK SUPER FUDGE CHUNK". A YOUNG, HISPANIC COUPLE WAS AT THE PUMP AND CALLED ME OVER. THEY TOLD ME THEY HAD NO MONEY AND

COASTED INTO THE GAS STATION ON FUMES (MY INTERPRETATION). THEY WANTED TO KNOW IF THERE WAS SOMETHING I COULD SAY TO THE CLERK TO ENABLE THEM TO GET ENOUGH GAS TO GET HOME. IN THE BACK SEAT WAS NOT ONE, BUT TWO BABIES IN CAR SEATS. AFTER I TOLD THEM I COULDN'T TALK TO THE CLERK FOR THEM, THEY ASKED IF I COULD GIVE THEM SOME MONEY. I LECTURED THEM ABOUT GOING OUT WITHOUT

SUFFICIENT GAS IN THE CAR AND PLACING THEIR CHILDREN IN JEOPARDY. I THEN PULLED MY LAST $5.00 FROM MY POCKET AND GAVE IT TO THEM. (I'M A COP SO I'M SURE I'M MORE BROKE THAN THEY ARE DON'T FORGET, I HAVE TWO KIDS MYSELF. THEY'RE ALWAYS CHEAPER WHEN YOU'RE WITH THEIR MOTHER.)

0005 -I WENT TO THE PUBLIX PARKING LOT TO DO MY PAPERWORK. AFTER I WAS DONE, I WENT TO ANOTHER 7/11 TO EXCHANGE MY ICE CREAM FOR ANOTHER ONE. MY NEW YORK SUPER FUDGE CHUNK HAD FREEZER BURN. THIS TIME I GOT TRIPPLE CARAMEL CHUNK. IN AN EFFORT TO NOT DEFRAUD THE KIND MERCHANTS, I THREW IT OUT AFTER EATING HALF OF IT. I HAD EATEN HALF OF THE OTHER BEFORE DECIDING THE FREEZER BURN WAS JUST UNACCEPTABLE.

0238 -I GOT ALL MY PAPERWORK TURNED IN.

0345 - (S) TRAFFIC STOP
I STOPPED A CAR WHOSE OWNER HAD A SUSPENDED LICENSE. THIS WAS A YOUNG B/M WHO HAD JUST GOTTEN OFF WORK AT A RESTAURANT. HE SAID THIS WAS ONE OF THREE JOBS HE HAD. HE RECENTLY WENT THROUGH A DIVORCE AND SIMPLY COULDN'T PAY HIS TRAFFIC TICKETS. I ARRESTED HIM FOR THIS OFFENSE. HE TOLD ME HE HAD BECOME A CHRISTIAN ONE YEAR AGO AND HAD JUST BEEN BAPTIZED IN JANUARY. FOR THIS REASON, HE DIDN'T FEEL COMFORTABLE ABOUT LYING ABOUT HIS LICENSE. I ALLOWED HIM TO DRIVE HIS CAR BACK TO THE RESTAURANT WHERE HE WORKED AND TO TELL HIS MANAGER HE MIGHT NOT BE IN FOR A WHILE.

THE REST OF MY SHIFT WAS UNEVENTFUL. PERHAPS TOMORROW WILL BE MORE EXCITING. SEE YA THEN.

08/26

1800-BRIEFING

1820 - (D) MAN DOWN
A 1Y/O HISPANIC FEMALE WAS UNCONSCIOUS AT A LOCAL HOTEL. SHE HAD BEEN JUMPING ON THE BED WITH HER TWO SISTERS AND FELL OFF. SHE HIT HER HEAD ON THE GROUND AND LOST CONSCIOUSNESS. HER SISTER RAN AND TOLD THEIR MOTHER. WHEN THE MOTHER ARRIVED, SHE FOUND HER CHILD BLUE AND NOT BREATHING. RESCUE ARRIVED SHORTLY AFTER WE DID. BY THAT TIME, A BYSTANDER HAD LAID THE GIRL DOWN AND ELEVATED HER LEGS. THIS APPARENTLY HELPED TO GET HER BREATHING AGAIN. RESCUE ADMINISTERED SOME MOTOR SKILLS TESTS AND THE GIRL SEEMED TO BE FINE. THERE WAS NO BRUISING ON THE GIRL'S HEAD. SHE WAS ABLE TO SQUEEZE THE MEDIC'S FINGER AND WALK TO HER MOTHER WHO WAS SEVERAL FEET AWAY. AFTER CONFIRMING THAT THIS WAS NOT A CASE OF CHILD ABUSE MY PARTNER AND I LEFT THE SCENE. RESCUE STAYED TO ENSURE THE MOTHER TOOK THE CHILD TO THE HOSPITAL TO BE CHECKED OUT. SHE WAS WAITING ON THE CHILD'S FATHER WHO HAD GONE OUT FOR DIAPERS.

1835-I WENT TO MY FAVORITE EATERY FOR DINNER. I WAS SADDENED TO LEARN THAT THEY HAD LOST ONE OF THEIR EMPLOYEES. HE WAS A 27Y/O H/M. HE WAS KILLED INSTANTLY WHEN HIS VEHICLE WAS T-BONED BY A MUSTANG THAT WAS TRAVELLING 90 MPH. THE DRIVER HAD A SUSPENDED LICENSE. (AND YOU WONDER WHY I'M SO HARD ON THE TRAFFIC OFFENSES. OFTEN TIMES, A SUSPENDED LICENSE IS A SIGN OF MORE SERIOUS UNDERLYING DRIVER PROBLEMS.)

1900 - (D) DISABLED MOTORIST
THE DISPATCHER INFORMED ME OF A W/F WITH AN INFANT WHOSE WHITE CHEVY WAS STALLED. I WAS UNABLE TO LOCATE THE VEHICLE AT THE REPORTED SCENE AND CLEARED THE CALL.

1940 - (BU) TRAFFIC STOP

ANOTHER UNIT ATTEMPTED TO CONDUCT A TRAFFIC STOP ON A RED TOYOTA CELICA WITH AN EXPIRED TAG. THE VEHICLE REFUSED TO STOP FOR THE OFFICER. SEVERAL UNITS, INCLUDING MYSELF, RESPONDED TO THE AREA. THE INITIAL OFFICER DECLINED TO PURSUE AND TURNED OFF FROM BEHIND THE CAR. WE WERE UNABLE TO LOCATE IT. MY GUESS IS THAT EITHER THE DRIVER WAS WANTED OR THE CAR WAS STOLEN. AT ANY RATE, NO SENSE IN RISKING THE LIVES OF CITIZENS BY CHASING THE CAR. SAY WE DID, AND SOMEONE GOT HURT ONLY TO FIND THAT THE ONLY OFENSES WERE AN EXPIRED TAG AND FLEEING. THEN WHAT?

2015 - (BU) DISTURBANCE

I WENT TO BACK ON AN UNKNOWN TYPE OF DISTURBANCE AT A RESIDENCE. TWO UNITS ARRIVED ON SCENE PRIOR TO ME AND CLEARED THE CALL.

2044 - (S) TRAFFIC STOP

I STOPPED A CAR FOR A SUSPENDED LICENSE. THE DRIVER WAS DRIVING HIS BROTHER-IN-LAW'S CAR.

2100 - (BU) TRAFFIC STOP

MY AREA PARTNER STOPPED A CAR WHOSE OWNER WAS POSSIBLY WANTED. MY PARTNER DISCOVERED THE WARRANT WAS NEGATIVE AND CANCELLED ME.

2130 - (BU) DISTURBANCE

I WENT TO BACK UP MY PARTNER WHO WAS GOING TO A DISTURBANCE AT A DUNKIN DONUTS BETWEEN A CLERK AND A CUSTOMER. I WAS STUCK IN BUMPER-TO-BUMPER TRAFFIC ABOUT A BLOCK AWAY. MY PARTNER TOOK CARE OF IT AND CANCELLED ME.

(I WASN'T HUNGRY ANYWAY.)

2225 - (S) TRAFFIC STOP

I CONDUCTED A TRAFFIC STOP FOR A POSSIBLE SUSPENDED LICENSE. IT WAS THE DRIVER'S FRIEND WHOSE LICENSE WAS SUSPENDED.

2254 - (S) TRAFFIC STOP

I STOPPED A CAR WHOSE TAG DIDN'T COME BACK TO IT. AT LEAST IT DIDN'T COME BACK TO IT ON MY COMPUTER. THE DRIVER WAS ABLE TO PROVIDE ME WITH A COPY OF THE REGISTRATION.

0115-I STOPPED IN ON A LOCAL HOTEL TO CHECK ON THE PERSONNEL. (PUBLIC RELATIONS ARE VERY IMPORTANT.) AS I STOOD IN THE LOBBY SPEAKING WITH A SECURITY OFFICER FRIEND OF MINE, ONE OF THE FRONT DESK LADIES CALLED HIM. THEY TOLD HIM TO HAVE ME COME OVER WHEN I WAS FINISHED. SHE TOLD ME THAT THE GIRLS AT THE FRONT DESK LIKE THE WAY I WALK. SHE TRIED TO HOOK ME UP WITH HER MANAGER. SHE SAID, "SHE'S REALLY NICE". I TOLD HER I HAD A CALL AND HAD TO GO. (I REALLY DID HAVE A CALL. ASK THE SECURITY, HE HEARD WHEN THE DISPATCHER GAVE IT TO ME.)

0123 - (D) AREA CHECK

I GOT A LOUD MUSIC CALL IN A RESIDENTIAL NEIGHBORHOOD. I MADE CONTACT WITH THE CULPRITS. THEY WERE HAVING A LITTLE DRINKING PARTY IN THEIR GARAGE. I TOLD THEM TO KEEP IT DOWN BECAUSE THEIR NEIGHBORS WERE COMPLAINING. THEY SAID THEY WOULD, AND PROCEEDED TO LET DOWN THE GARAGE DOOR. (WE'LL SHIELD THE NOISE, BUT THE PARTY MUST GO ON...)

0151 - WHILE GETTING GAS, I MADE AN INTERESTING OBSERVATION. A CARLOAD OF HISPANIC MALES WERE LEAVING THE STORE AFTER MAKING SOME PURCHASES. AFTER THEY LEFT THE STORE, THE CLERK, AN ELDERLY W/M, CAME FROM AROUND THE COUNTER AND CHECKED THE DISPLAYS IN FRONT OF THE REGISTER. MY GUESS IS THAT HE WANTED TO SEE IF ANYTHING WAS MISSING. (JUST AN OBSERVATION)

0208 - JUST CRUISIN' AND THINKIN'. MY CELL HASN'T RUNG ALL NIGHT. I'M ALWAYS TELLING GIRLS I'M TOO BUSY AND DODGING THEM THEN WHEN THEY DON'T

CALL I GET ALL WORRIED. WHAT'S UP WITH THAT?

0210 - (D) DISTURBANCE

THIS WAS A CALL AT A 24 HOUR GROCERY STORE. A W/F IN HER THIRTIES HAD COME IN TO BUY BEER. THE CLERK SAID HE COULDN'T SELL IT BECAUSE IT WAS AFTER 2AM. SHE LEFT THE STORE. ENTER A W/M IN HIS THIRTIES. HE WENT BACK AND GOT A 24PK AND A 12PK OF BEER. WHEN THE CLERK TRIED TO STOP HIM, HE SLAPPED A TWENTY DOWN ON THE COUNTER AND WALKED OUT OF THE STORE. HE THEN GOT INTO A VEHCILE WITH THE FEMALE AND DROVE AWAY. INTERESTING SITUATION. BY THE LETTER OF THE LAW, IT'S RETAIL THEFT WHEN NO EFFORT IS MADE TO PAY FOR MERCHANDISE. AN EFFORT WAS MADE, BUT THE COST OF ITEMS TAKEN WAS ABOUT $30.00, NOT $20.00. THE CLERK SAID THE LADY GETS OFF WORK IN THE AREA EVERY WEEKEND AROUND 2 AND TRIES TO PURCHASE BEER. EVERY WEEKEND HE TELLS HER NO. (I GUESS THIS TIME SHE HAD TO HAVE IT AND WASN'T TAKING NO FOR AN ANSWER.)

0316 - (S) TRAFFIC STOP

I CONDUCTED A TRAFFIC STOP OF A VEHICLE WITH A NEW YORK TAG. MY COMPUTER SHOWED "SUSPENDED" AT THE END OF THE VEHICLE'S INFORMATION LISTING. THE YOUNG B/M SHOWED ME A VALID REGISTRATION AND I RECEIVED CONFIRMATION THAT HIS LICENSE WAS VALID. APPARENTLY THE COMPUTER WAS ADVISING HIS INSURANCE WASN'T VALID. HE ASSURED ME THAT IT WAS. I TOOK HIS WORD FOR IT AND RELEASED HIM. I STOPPED THE B/M IN THE LOT OF THE CONVENIENCE STORE WHERE HE IS EMPLOYED. A HAITIAN FEMALE CO-WORKER CAME OUT AND STOOD BY THROUGHOUT THE STOP. AFTER I CLEARED THE B/M, SHE BEGAN TALKING TO ME AS IF SHE KNEW ME. WHEN I TOLD HER SHE DIDN'T, SHE ASKED, "DON'T YOU COME IN HERE WITH ANOTHER COP ALL THE TIME?" I TOLD HER NO AND THAT IF I DID, I WOULD HAVE REMEMBERED HER, I SAID, "ACTUALLY, I MIGHT NOT HAVE REMEMBERED YOU, BUT I WOULDN'T HAVE FORGOTTEN YOU LIPS." (SHE HAD THE MOST GORGEOUS, FULL SET OF LIPS). AFTER MAKING THAT COMMENT, I QUICKLY WALKED BACK TO MY VEHICLE SO AS NOT TO FURTHER ENGAGE.

0359 - (S) SUSPICIOUS VEHICLES

I CHECKED OUT TWO VEHICLES, A HONDA AND A FORD, THAT WERE PARKED IN AN OPEN LOT BETWEEN TWO BUSINESSES. NEITHER WAS STOLEN, SO I CLEARED.

0427 - (D) STOLEN VEHICLE

I WAS DISPATCHED TO A STOLEN CAR CALL IN WHICH THE CAR WAS LOCATED BEFORE IT WAS REPORTED STOLEN. THE VICTIM WAS A 16Y/O, GREEK, GYPSY MALE (BY THE WAY, HE WAS WHITE AS OPPOSED TO THE MORE WIDELY KNOWN BLACK, GREEK GYPSIES.) HE SAID HE WAS BUSY WITH HIS WEDDING AND RECEPTION AND HIS CAR WAS IN AND OUT OF VALET AT THE HOTEL WHERE HE WAS STAYING. WHEN HE WENT TO PICK IT UP, THE CAR WAS THERE, BUT THE KEYS WERE NOT. HE WENT BACK THE NEXT DAY. THIS TIME, THE KEYS WERE THERE AND THE CAR WAS NOT. HOTEL SECURITY LOCATED THE CAR IN THE LOT OF A NEARBY APARTMENT COMPLEX. THE CAR WAS A $50,000.00, TRICKED OUT, PONTIAC TRANS AM CONVERTIBLE. THE W/M SAID HIS $2,200.00 ROLEX WAS STOLEN FROM THE GLOVE BOX AND NOW THE ENGINE RATTLES. NOW TO THE REAL ISSUE. WHAT IN THE "HAYO" IS A 16Y/O KID DOING GETTING MARRIED. BEING THE INQUISITIVE PERSON THAT I AM, I ASKED. HE SAID IT WAS CUSTOMARY IN HIS RELIGION TO GET MARRIED AT A YOUNG AGE, I SAID, "WHAT RELIGION, GREEK OR GYPSY?" HE SAID GYPSY. HE SAID IT WAS AN ARRANGED MARRIAGE. HIS WIFE WAS 18 AND HE ASKED ME IF THAT COULD BE CONSIDERED STATUTORY RAPE. I ASKED HIM HOW LONG HE THOUGHT IT WOULD LAST. HE SAID HOPEFULLY FOR THE REST OF HIS LIFE. BY THE WAY, THERE WAS ONLY ONE VALET WHO WORKED THE LATE SHIFT DURING THE TIME THE THEFT OCCURRED. COINCIDENTALLY, THIS WAS THE SAME PERSON WHO EXPRESSED A GREAT DEAL OF INTEREST IN THE KID'S CAR.

0525 -I WENT TO A 7/11 PARKING LOT TO COMPLETE MY PAPERWORK. MY SERGEANT TOLD ME I COULD TURN IT IN WHEN I RETURNED TO WORK LATER THAT NIGHT. THAT'S WHEN I'LL TALK TO YOU AGAIN.

08/27

2000 - BRIEFING

2016 - (BU) SUICIDE ATTEMPT
  I BACKED MY PARTNER UP ON THIS CALL. THE PERSON ATTEMPTING TO KILL HIMSELF WAS A W/M IN HIS EARLY FORTIES. HE WAS HERE ON VACATION FROM ENGLAND, WITH HIS WIFE AND 12Y/O DAUGHTER. HE TOOK A LARGE QUANTITY OF PILLS AND TOLD US HE SIMPLY DIDN'T WANT TO LIVE ANY LONGER. HIS DAUGHTER WAS ASKING HIM, "DADDY, WHY ARE YOU DOING THIS TO US?" MY PARTNER WAS HANDLING THE CALL, SO I TOOK OFF. I GUESS EVERYONE HAS PROBLEMS THAT NO ONE ELSE KNOWS ABOUT. EVEN SO, ALL I CAN SAY IS, "WAY TO MESS UP VACATION FOR EVERBODY...DAD.")

2036 - (D) ALARM
  I WAS DISPATCHED TO AN ALARM AT A DEPARTMENT STORE IN A MALL. THE MALL HAS SECURITY. I CALLED ONE OF THE OFFICERS AND ASKED IF HE WOULD CHECK IT OUT. HE DID, AND SAVED ME A TRIP.

2045 -I WENT TO EAT AT MY FAVORITE ESTABLISHMENT. (EXCELLENT FOOD - TIPPING DISCOURAGED)

2127 - BACK OUT ON PATROL

2130 - (S) TRAFFIC STOP
  I CONDUCTED A TRAFFIC STOP OF A VEHICLE WHOSE OWNER'S LICENSE WAS SUSPENDED. AS IT TURNED OUT, THAT PERSON WAS NOT DRIVING, BUT IN THE PASSENGER SEAT. I GAVE THE YOUNG H/F A WRITTEN WARNING AND TOOK HER LICENSE. SHE WAS AWARE OF A LAPSE IN HER INSURANCE COVERAGE, BUT DIDN'T KNOW THEY SUSPENDED HER LICENSE.

2147 - (BU) DISTURBANCE
  I RESPONDED TO A LOCAL HOTEL IN RESPONSE TO A DISTURBANCE BETWEEN A YOUNG B/M AND A YOUNG B/F. A VERBAL ARGUMENT HAD OCCURRED BETWEEN THE TWO, OVER WHAT I DON'T KNOW. THE COUPLE WAS ON VACATION

AND IT WAS APPARENTLY ENDING EARLY. THE MALE HAD ALREADY LEFT THE ROOM BY THE TIME WE ARRIVED. HE LEFT TO PREVENT THE FIGHT FROM ESCALATING AND TO GIVE THE FEMALE AN OPPORTUNITY TO PACK HER BAGS. SHE WAS FLYING OUT IMMEDIATELY. I ASKED HER IF THE FIGHT HAD BECOME PHYSICAL AT ALL. SHE SAID IT HADN'T. SHE WAS OBVIOUSLY DISTURBED BY THE WHOLE THING. I TOLD HER, "DON'T YOU JUMP ON HIM WHEN HE COMES BACK, NOW". THAT MADE HER SMILE AND SHE STARTED TO SAY SOMETHING. I LEFT IMMEDIATELY, FEARING THAT SHE MIGHT ASK IF SHE COULD FINISH OUT HER VACATION AT MY PLACE.

2242 - CITIZEN ASSIST
A TOURIST ASKED ME WHERE HE COULD GET COME BEER FROM BECAUSE THE SUPERMARKET WAS CLOSED. I DIRECTED HIM TO THE NEAREST 7/11.

2245 -I CALLED HOME TO CHECK MY MACHINE. FG3 (YOU KNOW, THE 24Y/O P/R F) HAD LEFT A MESSAGE SAYING, "I'M NOT ASKING TO BE YOUR GIRLFRIEND; I JUST WANT TO SPEND SOME TIME WITH YOU".

2305 - (D) ALARM
I RESPONDED TO AN ALARM AT A COMIC BOOK STORE. THE OWNERS ARE AN OLDER W/M W/F COUPLE. THEY RESPONDED TO THE STORE AS WELL. THEY WERE ON THEIR WAY HOME. THE WOMAN WAS A BIG ACTION HERO FAN. SHE SHOWED ME THE BRUCE LEE SHIRT SHE WAS WEARING TO CONFIRM THAT FACT. THE ALARM WAS UNFOUNDED.

2344 - (S) TRAFFIC STOP
I PULLED OVER ANOTHER VEHICLE ON THE INTERSTATE WHOSE OWNER HAD A SUSPENDED LICENSE. THE OCCUPANTS WERE A MIDDLE-AGED, HISPANIC COUPLE, HEADING TO MIAMI. THE MALE, WHO WAS IN THE PASSENGER SEAT, SAID, "I KNOW MY LICENSE IS SUSPENDED, THAT'S WHY MY WIFE IS DRIVING".

2351-(S) TRAFFIC STOP
I STOPPED THE NEXT CAR FOR THE SAME REASON. THIS WAS A HAITIAN MALE IN HIS THIRTIES. HE SAID HE WENT TO

COURT FOR HIS TRAFFIC TICKET, BUT WAS UNABLE TO PAY IT. I ARRESTED HIM, THOUGH HE PLEADED FOR ME NOT TO. HE SAID, "PLEASE SIR, TODAY YOU ARE MY BROTHER, YOU ARE MY FATHER. PLEASE UNDERSTAND". I GAVE HIM MY STANDARD SPEECH ABOUT HAVING HEARD MANY HARD-LUCK STORIES, AND HAVING TO REMAIN CONSISTENT. HE WAS ON HIS WAY TO PICK UP A FRIEND FROM WORK I LET HIM USE MY PHONE TO CALL SOMEONE TO PICK UP HIS CAR, BUT HE GOT NO ANSWER. I THEN WENT TO WHERE HIS FRIEND WAS WAITING. HE TOLD HER WHY HE WAS BEING ARRESTED AND GAVE HER HIS KEYS. SHE HAD NO DRIVER LICENSE.

0041-CITIZEN ASSIST
TWO PEOPLE CAME UP AND ASKED FOR DIRECTIONS WHILE I WAS ARRESTING THE B/M. THEY COULD CARE LESS WHAT I WAS DOING. THEY JUST FIGURED I COULD HELP THEM GET TO THEIR DESTINATIONS. AND I DID, WITH A SMILE.

0114-I WRAPPED UP THE ARREST AND WAS TRYING TO GET TO THE CHOW HALL BEFORE THEY CLOSED AT 0200. (WILL HE MAKE IT, OR WON'T HE?)

0125 - (S) TRAFFIC STOP
I FIGURED I'D DO A QUICK TRAFFIC STOP ON THE WAY. THE VEHICLE'S OWNER HAD AN EXPIRED LICENSE. THE VEHICLE'S OWNER WAS NOT DRIVING.

0130 - (D) TRAFFIC CRASH (WITH INJURIES)
BEFORE I COULD CLEAR THE STOP, A CALL WENT OUT TO A LOCATION JUST UP THE HIGHWAY. IT WAS A CRASH WITH ENTRAPMENT AND INJURIES. FIRE AND RESCUE WAS ALREADY ON THE SCENE. A CAR HAD GONE OFF THE ROAD AND SLAMMED INTO A TREE. THE CAR WAS CRUSHED LIKE AN ACCORDIAN. SECONDS AFTER THAT CRASH, ANOTHER ONE OCCURRED JUST ON THE OPPOSITE SIDE OF THE ROAD. THAT WAS PROBABLY A RUBBER-NECKER WHO LOST IT. THE DRIVER OF THE CAR IN THE FIRST CRASH HAD TO BE MEDIVACED TO THE HOSPITAL. ANOTHER OFFICER AND I HAD TO SET UP A LANDING ZONE FOR THE HELICOPTER TO TOUCH DOWN. THAT ENTAILS BLOCKING OFF TRAFFIC AND ENSURING NO ONE GETS WITHIN RANGE OF THE HELICOPTER PROPELLERS.

FLORIDA HIGHWAY PATROL RESPONDED TO TAKE CARE OF THE ACCIDENT. THE SCENE WAS CLEARED RELATIVELY QUICKLY. HOPEFULLY THAT PERSON WILL SURVIVE, BUT JUDGING FROM THE VEHICLE IT DIDN'T LOOK GOOD.

0215-I WENT TO GAS UP THE CRUISER AND CHECK ON THE ELDERLY W/M WHO WORKS THE GRAVEYARD SHIFT. HE HANDED ME A BUFFALO NICKEL THAT SOMEONE HAD GIVEN HIM AND ASKED IF I COULD SEE THE DATE. HE SAID IT'S NOT WORTH ANYTHING UNLESS YOU CAN SEE THE DATE. I ASKED IF HE WAS A COIN COLLECTOR AND HE SAID HE USED TO BE. HE ALSO COLLECTED STAMPS. HE SAID HE HAD A FULL SET OF VATICAN STAMPS BACK IN THE 60'S. HE PAID $10,000.00 FOR THEM BACK THEN AND THEY'RE NOW WORTH $100,000.00. HE SAID HE UNLOADED ALL OF IT TO PREVENT IF FROM BECOMING AN ISSUE DURING HIS DIVORCE. HE NOW BUYS GOLD. HE'S GOT ABOUT TWENTY OUNCES. HE SAYS THE PRESENT STATE OF OUR ECONOMY CAN'T LAST, BUT IF WE GO BROKE, EVERYONE GOES BROKE. EVERYTHING DEPENDS ON THE U.S. DOLLAR. AS A YOUNG SALESMAN, HE TRAVELLED TO HONGKONG. A MERCHANT TOLD HIM THE PRICE OF AN ITEM WAS 10 DOLLARS WORTH OF HONG KONG CURRENCY, OR 5 U.S. DOLLARS. AS I LEFT, HE OFFERED ME A FOUNTAIN DRINK AND SOME OLD HOT DOGS THAT HE HAD TAKEN OFF THE GRILL BECAUSE THEY WERE TOO OLD TO SELL. I DECLINED AND WALKED OUT THINKING YOU CAN ALWAYS LEARN SOMETHING NEW FROM AN ELDERLY PERSON IF YOU JUST TAKE TIME OUT TO LISTEN TO THEM.

0248 - (D) ALARM
I WENT TO AN ALARM AT POLO JEANS COMPANY. THE BUILDING WAS SECURE AND I CLEARED THE CALL. (AFTER WINDOW SHOPPING THAT IS. WHEN I GET BIG AND GET A JOB, I'M GONNA BUY ALL THAT POLO STUFF.)

0302 - (S) SUSPICIOUS PERSONS
I STOPPED TO CHECK OUT THREE HISPANIC MALES WHO WERE HANGING OUT AT A BUS STOP IN FRONT OF A RESTAURANT. THIS WAS SUSPICIOUS BECAUSE BUSES

DON'T RUN AROUND HERE AT 3AM. THEY TOLD ME THEY WORKED AT THE RESTAURANT AND WERE WAITING FOR THEIR RIDE. BELIEVING THEIR STORY, I LEFT THEM BE.

0309 - (S) TRAFFIC STOP

I STOPPED AN 18Y/O B/M WHO WAS DRIVING A CHEVY MALIBU. THE TAG CAME BACK TO A CHEVY PICK-UP. HE TOLD ME THE TAG BELONGED ON HIS IMPALA THAT WAS AT HOME IN HIS YARD. I ARRESTED HIM FOR ATTACHING A TAG THAT WASN'T ASSIGNED. I DIDN'T CHARGE HIM WITH THE ADDITIONAL CRIME OF FAILING TO REGISTER HIS VEHICLE. I LET HIM CALL HIS UNCLE TO COME PICK UP HIS CAR TO SAVE HIM THE TOWING EXPENSE. AS I WAS MAKING THE ARREST, THE PROPERTY SECURITY OFFICER APPROACHED ME. I THOUGHT HE WANTED TO ASSIST ME. INSTEAD, HE WANTED TO TELL ME ABOUT HIS "BRUSH WITH CRIMINAL ACTIVITY". HE TOLD ME HE CALLED 9-1-1 EARLIER BECAUSE HE SAW A B/M PUNCHING A B/F. AFTER THE ATTACK, THE FEMALE CIRCLED AROUND THE BLOCK, PICKED THE MALE UP, AND TOOK OFF. I SHOWED INTEREST IN HIS STORY (AS MUCH AS I COULD MUSTER), THEN GOT BACK TO MY ARREST. THIS WAS A PLEASANT KID AND HE WAS COOPERATIVE THROUGHOUT. THIS INSPITE OF HIS POPULAR "THUG" APPEARANCE (BIG JEANS OFF THE BUTT AND DO-RAG ON THE HEAD). I DID SOMETHING THAT MANY WOULD PROBABLY DISAGREE WITH. I ALLOWED HIM TO GO TO THE ATM TO GET CASH SO HE COULD BOND HIMSELF OUT OF JAIL IN A FEW HOURS.

0505 - FINALLY, I'M GOING TO GRAB A BITE BEFORE GETTING OFF IN AN HOUR. AS I PULLED INTO THE IHOP PARKING LOT, THE MANAGER APPROACHED MY CAR. HE ASKED IF I COULD GET HIM A SHERIFF STICKER FOR HIS CAR FOR SECURITY PURPOSES. HE SAID HE'D PAY ME ANY AMOUNT OF MONEY. HE THEN ASKED IF I COULD CHECK OUT A VEHICLE THAT HAD HIM SCARED TO DEATH BECAUSE IF HAD BEEN PARKED IN THE BACK LOT ALL NIGHT. I TOLD HIM I WAS HUNGRY SO I HOPE IT'S NOT STOLEN. I RAN THE TAG AND IT CAME BACK TO ANOTHER CAR. (HERE WE GO) I APPROACHED THE VEHICLE TO GET

THE V.I.N. AND RUN IT. THAT'S WHEN I NOTICED A
W/M (30'S) ASLEEP IN THE FRONT SEAT. I ORDERED
HIM OUT OF THE CAR. HE SAID ANOTHER OFFICER
TOLD HIM THAT HE COULD SLEEP IN THE LOT OF
A RESTAURANT AS LONG AS THEY WERE OPEN
24 HOURS. (HE HAD APPARENTLY BEEN RUN OFF
FROM A CLOSED ESTABLISHMENT.) I TOLD HIM THAT
WASN'T'MY CONCERN. MY CONCERN WAS WHY THERE
WAS A TAG ON THE VEHICLE THAT DIDN'T BELONG.
HE SAID, "I DON'T KNOW. LET ME TAKE A LOOK AT
WHAT TAG IS ON THERE". ONCE AROUND THE BACK OF
THE CAR HE SAID, "OH, THAT TAG IS OFF MY TOYOTA
TERCEL". THIS CAR WAS A CAMRY. I PROCEEDED TO
TELL HTM THAT THIS WAS A CRIMINAL OFFENSE AND
THAT HE WAS UNDER ARREST. APPALLED BY THIS,
HE ASKED, "CAN'T YOU JUST WRITE ME A TICKET?"
I TOLD HIM NO. (I JUST ARRESTED SOMEONE FOR
THE SAME THING. I MUST REMAIN CONSISTENT NO
MATTER HOW HUNGRY I AM.) HE TURNED TO MY
PARTNER AND ASKED, "IS THIS RIGHT?" MY PARTNER
TOLD HIM, "YES SIR, YOU'VE BEEN TOLD ONCE BY AN
OFFICER OF THE LAW AND YOU NEED TO DO WHAT
HE SAYS." THE MAN PROCLAIMED THAT HE WASN'T
A CRIMINAL. MY PARTNER SAID, "WELL SIR, YOU ARE
NOW." MANAGEMENT ALLOWED HIM TO LEAVE HIS
VEHICLE IN THE LOT. THE VERY VEHICLE THAT HAD HIM
FRIGHTENED ALL NIGHT. THE W/M WAS CHARGED WITH
ATTACHING A TAG THAT WASN'T ASSIGNED.

0615 - AFTER TURNING IN MY PAPERWORK, I HEADED
HOME. ON THE WAY I GRABBED A BAGEL AND SOME
CRANBERRY JUICE. TALK TO YOU LATER.

08/30

1800-BRIEFING

1825-I WENT TO DINNER AND STUDIED MY PORTUGUESE AS I ATE.

1910-I CALLED FG2 AND FG4, MY BRAZILIAN FRIENDS. I'VE GOT TO MAINTAIN CONTACT WITH THEM. FRIENDS ARE SO IMPORTANT. BESIDES, I THINK MY PORTUGUESE CLASS IS GOING TO BE ROUGH. I GOT BOTH THEIR MACHINES. FG3 CALLED ME IN BETWEEN THE OTHER CALLS. SHE SAID SHE MISSED ME AND WOULD BE THINKING ABOUT ME. "COISTADOS", THAT MEANS "POOR THING".

1927 - (D) ALARM
   THIS WAS AN ALARM AT A BUSINESS THAT HAD GONE FROM BEING A SPORTING GOOD STORE TO A GROCERY STORE. THE ALARM WAS UNFOUNDED.

2000 -I PULLED DOWN A SIDE ROAD TO COMPLETE SOME PAPERWORK. SHORTLY THEREAFTER, I WAS APPROACHED BY THE PROPERTY SECURITY OFFICER. FIRST HE RAN THROUGH A LIST OF ALL THE OFFICERS THAT HE KNEW AND ASKED IF I KNEW THEM AS WELL. I KNEW NONE OF THEM. THEN CAME THE POLICE STORIES. I KNEW I WAS IN FOR IT THEN. IT WOULD HAVE BEEN O.K. NORMALLY, BUT I TOLD THIS GUY (OLDER, W/M) I WAS BUSY. HE WENT ON AND ON. I WANTED TO TRY AND INTERJECT SO I COULD SLIP AWAY, BUT THERE WERE NO BREAKS IN HIS CONVERSATION. ALL OF A SUDDEN SOMETHING STRANGE HAPPENED THE GUY GOT INTERESTING. HE DREW ME IN. WE TALKED ABOUT EVERYTHING FROM VIETNAM TO O.J. THEN I GOT A CALL. COULD THE DISPATCHER HAVE WORSE TIMING, OR WHAT? SHE WAS INTERRUPTING ME AND MY FRIEND WHO I ONLY GOT TO SPEND ABOUT AN HOUR AND A HALF CONVERSING WITH. OH WELL WHAT ARE YOU GONNA

DO?

2123 - (D) DISABLED MOTORIST

I WAS DISPATCHED A CALL ADVISING A MOTOR HOME WAS STUCK IN AN INTERSECTION. ANOTHER UNIT CLEARED THE CALL BEFORE I COULD GET THERE. APPARENTLY THEY GOT IT STARTED AGAIN.

2200 - (D) 9-1-1 HANG-UP

SOMEONE DIALED 9-1-1, SHOUTED SOMETHING IN THE PHONE, THEN HUNG UP. THE CALL CAME FROM A PAY PHONE AT A SHOPPING PLAZA. WHEN I GOT THERE, I MET WITH SECURITY. HE SAID HE RAN SOME KIDS OFF EARLIER WHO HAD BEEN PLAYING ON THE PHONES. HE WASN'T SURE, BUT BELIEVES IT MAY HAVE BEEN THEM. I WAS WITH HIM. I CLEARED THE CALL.

2214 - (D) SUSPICIOUS VEHICLE

A BUSINESS CALLED ADVISING THAT AN UNKNOWN VEHICLE WAS PARKED ON THEIR PROPERTY IN A SUSPICIOUS MANNER. BEFORE I COULD GET THERE, THE BUSINESS CALLED US BACK AND SAID THE VEHICLE HAD LEFT.

2232 - (D) DOMESTIC BATTERY

I WAS DISPATCHED TO A BATTERY THAT OCCURRED AT A HOTEL. THE PARTIES INVOLVED WERE A MARRIED COUPLE, VISITING FROM GEORGIA. THE HUSBAND WAS A W/M, 6'-05" AND ABOUT 300 LBS. THE WIFE WAS A SHORT, HEAVY-SET, W/F. TRAVELLING WITH THE COUPLE WERE THEIR TWO SONS, AGES 8 AND 12. BOTH HAD BEEN DRINKING, (NOT THE KIDS). SHE SAID THEY STRUGGLED OVER THE CAR KEYS AFTER A VERBAL ARGUMENT AND THE ALTERCATION TURNED PHYSICAL. SHE SAID THEY FOUGHT ONE ANOTHER, BUT HE STRUCK FIRST. HE SAID THEY ARGUED OVER AN ISSUE CONCERNING ONE OF THE KIDS. HE SAID SHE GOT ANGRY AND DEMANDED THE CAR KEYS. WHEN HE DIDN'T GIVE THEM TO HER, SHE STARTED STRIKING HIM. HE SAID HE NEVER TOUCHED HER. THE W/F CALLED THE BATTERY IN. THE W/M HAD SOME BRUISING ON HIS JAW AND A LACERATION INSIDE HIS MOUTH. THE W/F HAD NO SIGNS OF INJURY. BELIEVING THE WIFE WAS THE PRIMARY AGGRESSOR, I ARRESTED HER. SHE COULD NOT BELIEVE IT. SHE SAID, "HOW CAN I BE GETTING ARRESTED WHEN I WAS

THE ONE WHO CALLED?" I TOLD HER IT DIDN'T MATTER WHO CALLED FIRST. IT WAS MY RESPONSIBILITY TO DETERMINE IF A BATTERY OCCURRED. IF ONE DID, I MUST DETERMINE WHO THE AGGRESSOR WAS. IF THE COMBATANTS ARE RELATED (DOMESTIC), THE AGGRESSOR MUST GO TO JAIL. SHE SAID, "LOOK HOW BIG HE IS AND YOU'RE TAKING ME TO JAIL?" I TOLD HER HE WAS PRETTY BIG AND THAT SHE WAS CRAZY FOR HITTING HIM. I ASKED HER IF THEY WERE FIGHTING IN FRONT OF THE KIDS AND SHE SAID NO. SHE SAID THEY'RE NOT EVEN HIS KIDS, THEY'RE FROM A PREVIOUS RELATIONSHIP. I TOLD HER, "I BET WHEN YOU HOOKED UP WITH HIM YOU WANTED HIM TO CLAIM THOSE KIDS AS HIS? SHE GOT QUIET THEN. SHE ASKED, "DO I HAVE TO GO TO JAIL LIKE THIS WITH NO SHOES AND NO BRA?" SHE WAS WEARING ONLY SHORTS AND A T-SHIRT. I LET HER HUSBAND BRING HER SOME SOCKS, SHOES AND A BRA. BEFORE HAULING HER AWAY, THE COUPLE GAVE EACH OTHER A BIG HUG AND WERE PROFESSING THEIR LOVE FOR ONE ANOTHER. WIFE: "I'M SORRY BABY." HUSBAND: "THAT'S O.K. BABY, I'LL BE DOWN THERE TO PICK YOU UP AS SOON AS I CAN." (WHY DO THESE PEOPLE WASTE MY TIME?)

2315 - FG3 CALLED. I TOLD HER I COULDN'T TALK BECAUSE I WAS TAKING SOMEONE TO JAIL.

0030 -I WENT TO FEED MY FACE.

0130 –I WENT TO THE PARKING LOT OF A CLOSED ESTABLISHMENT TO COMPLETE MY PAPERWORK.

0223 -I WENT BACK OUT ON PATROL.

0300- (S) SUSPICIOUS VEHICLE
I CHECKED OUT A VEHICLE THAT WAS PARKED BESIDE A CLOSED BUSINESS. THIS WAS SUSPICIOUS BECAUSE THEY WERE CLOSED, IT WAS 3AM, AND THIS WAS THE ONLY CAR THERE. I CHECKED TO SEE IF THE CAR WAS STOLEN AND IT CAME BACK NEGATIVE. PERHAPS THE OWNER CAUGHT A RIDE WITH SOMEONE ELSE.

0449 - (D) ALARM
  THIS WAS AN ALARM IN A RESIDENTIAL NEIGHBORHOOD.
PRIOR TO MY ARRIVAL, THE HOMEOWNER GAVE THE PROPER
CODE, CANCELLING ME.

0505 -I WENT TO GAS UP THE CRUISER.

0512 - IT'S BEEN A LONG AND SLOW NIGHT FOR ME. I'M
GOING TO SLOWLY DRIVE HOME (SO AS NOT TO GET
THERE BEFORE 6) MAYBE TONIGHT WILL BE BETTER.
SEE YOU THEN.

08/31

I HAD SCHOOL TODAY SO I STARTED WORK A LITTLE LATER. I HAD A QUIZ IN MY PORTUGUESE CLASS AND I GAVE MY FIRST SPEECH IN MY SPEECH CLASS. I SURVIVED THEM BOTH.

2130-I WENT ON PATROL.

2141-I WENT TO HAVE DINNER. (PRIORITIES MUST REMAIN IN ORDER.)

2220 - I CALLED MY FRIEND FG4 (21YO BRAZILIAN WHO SPEAKS VERY LITTLE ENGLISH). I WANTED TO IMPRESS HER WITH ALL THE NEW WORDS AND PHRASES I HAD LEARNED IN CLASS. SHE BURST OUT LAUGHING WITH EACH WORD I SPOKE. SHE SAID, "BERRY, BERRY GUD", BUT THOUGHT IT WAS THE FUNNIEST THING.

2240 -I SPOKE TO FG3 AND ALL WAS WELL WITH HER.

2304 - (S) TRAFFIC STOP
   I STOPPED A MIDDLE-AGED, WHITE, H/M THAT RAN A RED LIGHT. HE WAS TURNING RIGHT, BUT THERE WAS A SIGN THAT SAID NO TURNING ON RED. THE W/M SPOKE NO ENGLISH. I TRIED EXPLAINING HIS OFFENSE TO HIM THEN CUT HIM LOOSE WITH A WARNING.

2315 - (S) TRAFFIC STOP
   I STOPPED A YOUNG, ASIAN MALE WHO HAD A SUSPENDED LICENSE. THIS TYPE OF SUSPENSION IS USUALLY DUE TO A LAPSE IN INSURANCE COVERAGE. THE W/M WAS UNAWARE THAT HIS LICENSE WAS SUSPENDED. I ASKED HIM ABOUT HIS INSURANCE. HE SAID HE RECENTLY CANCELLED IT FOR TWO MONTHS WHILE HE WAS OUT OF THE COUNTRY ON VACATION. WHEN HE RETURNED, HE HAD IT REINSTATED. HE SPOKE TO HIS AGENT PRIOR TO LEAVING AND WAS TOLD THIS WOULD BE ACCEPTABLE. I TOLD HIM I DIDN'T THINK IT WAS. IT WAS MY BELIEF THAT AS LONG AS A VEHICLE IS REGISTERED IN FLORIDA, THE OWNER MUST MAINTAIN

CONTINUOUS COVERAGE. I TOOK THE GENTLEMAN'S LICENSE AND ISSUED HIM A CITATION. I GAVE HIM A NUMBER TO CALL TO FIND OUT EXACTLY WHY HIS LICENSE WAS SUSPENDED.

2325 - (D) THEFT
  I WAS DISPATCHED TO HOOTERS ON A THEFT CALL. SIX PEOPLE HAD EATEN THERE AND RAN OUT WITHOUT PAYING THE BILL. ABOUT THREE OF THE HOOTERS GIRLS STOOD AROUND AS THE ONE TOLD ME WHAT HAPPENED. THROUGHOUT TH CONVERSATION MY EYES REMAINED ABOVE THEIR NECK LEVELS. (ARE YOU PROUD OF ME?) THE MANAGER THEN CAME OUT. HE SAID THEY DIDN'T WANT A REPORT TO BE TAKEN. THEY HAD HOPED AN OFFICER WAS IN THE AREA AS THE CALL WENT OUT AND COULD STOP THE SUSPECTS AS THEY DROVE AWAY.

0000 -I CALLED FG2 (26YO BRAZILIAN), WHOM I HAVN'T SPOKEN TO IN A VERY LONG WHILE. SHE SPEAKS ENGLISH, PORTUGUESE, AND SPANISH. I WOWED HER AS WELL WITH MY KNOWLEDGE OF THE PORTUGUESE LANGUAGE. SHE SEEMED TO BE GENUINELY IMPRESSED. SHE HELPED ME OUT WITH SOME OF THE SOUNDS AND PRONOUNCIATIONS. TALKING TO HER AGAIN MADE ME REALIZE I MISSED HER. WE USED TO HAVE A PRETTY GOOD TIME BEFORE SHE DECIDED I WASN'T MAKING ENOUGH TIME FOR HER.

0020 - (D) ALARM I RESPONDED TO A HOTEL ALARM THAT TURNED OUT TO BE UNFOUNDED

0100 -I STOPPED BY ANOTHER HOTEL TO USE THE RESTROOM. THE NIGHT AUDITOR HAD A QUESTION FOR ME. HE WANTED TO KNOW IF HIS COUSIN, WHO WAS DISHONORABLY DISCHARGED FROM THE ARMY, COULD GET A GOOD JOB IN THE STATES. HIS COUSIN LIVES IN ST. CROIX, VIRGIN ISLANDS. THE COUSIN GOT INTO SOME TROUBLE THERE, AND HE WANTED TO BRING HIM HERE TO START OVER. THE COUSIN STOLE HIS BROTHER'S GUN AND WAS STOPPED BY THE POLICE WITH THE STOLEN GUN IN HIS POSSESSION. I

TOLD HIM I WAS SURE HE COULD FIND A JOB HERE, BUT JUST HOW GOOD A JOB I DIDN'T KNOW. I TOLD HIM HE MIGHT BE JUST AS WELL STAYING THERE.

0130-I WENT TO EAT ONCE MORE. (DON'T MAKE ME HAVE TO TELL YOU ABOUT PRIORITIES AGAIN.)

0215 - (S) TRAFFIC STOP

I STOPPED A YOUNG B/F WHO WAS DRIVING A CAR WITH A TAG NOT ASSIGNED TO IT. I CONDUCTED THE STOP IN THE GIRL'S NEIGHBORHOOD AS SHE WAS HEADING HOME. SHE SAID THE FORD THAT SHE WAS DRIVING BELONGED TO HER AUNT. THE TAG ATTACHED TO IT BELONGED ON A DODGE. I ASKED HER WHERE THE DODGE WAS AT AND WHAT TAG WAS ON IT. SHE SAID IT WAS AT THE HOUSE AND SHE DIDN'T KNOW WHAT TAG WAS ON IT. I TOLD HER I WAS GOING TO FOLLOW HER TO THE HOUSE SO I COULD SEE THE DODGE. THE CAR WASN'T THERE WHEN WE ARRIVED. I LET HER GO IN TO FIND SOMEONE THAT COULD EXPLAIN THE SITUATION TO ME. SHE CAME OUT WITH HER GRANDFATHER WHO APPEARED TO BE IN HIS 70'S. HE SAID THAT HE AND HIS WIFE HAD JUST FINISHED PRAYING FOR "THOSE KIDS" ABOUT AN HOUR AGO. HE ADVISED THE AUNT (HIS DAUGHTER, I ASSUME) WAS OUT SOMEWHERE IN THE DODGE. I APOLOGIZED FOR HAVING HIM AWAKENED AT 2A. I ALSO TOLD HIM HOW CLOSE HIS GRANDDAUGHTER HAD COME TO GOING TO JAIL, BUT THAT I DIDN'T BELIEVE SHE PUT THE TAG ON THE CAR. I TOLD THE GIRL I HAD SEEN HER BEFORE AND NOT TO LET ME SEE HER IN VIOLATION OF THE LAW IN THE FUTURE. BOTH THE GIRL AND HER GRANDFATHER THANKED ME AND I LEFT.

0245 - (S) TRAFFIC STOP

I STOPPED A GUY FOR DRIVING WITH A SUSPENDED LICENSE. AGAIN, THE SUSPENSION WAS FOR INSURANCE PURPOSES. HE SEEMED TO BE UNAWARE OF THE SUSPENSION. HE DID SAY HE CHANGED COMPANIES ABOUT A YEAR AGO AND THERE WAS A PERIOD OF A FEW DAYS IN WHICH HE WAS NOT COVERED. I TOLD HIM THAT MAY HAVE BEEN THE CAUSE. I WROTE HIM A CITATION AND CLEARED.

0320 - (D) ALARM

I WENT TO AN ALARM AT A BUSINESS. THE ALARM INDICATED ROOF HATCH. LET'S FACE IT I CAN CHECK THE DOORS AND WINDOWS, BUT I'M NOT CHECKING ANYONE'S ROOF. IF THE HELICOPTER IS OUT AND FLYING, THEY CAN CHECK SUCH THINGS. I ARRIVED AND FOUND A CLEANING CREW IN THE KITCHEN. THEY WERE CLEANING ALL THE STOVES AND VENTS AND HAD GONE ON THE ROOF TO CLEAN SOMETHING UP THERE.

0405 - (D) ALARM

I WAS DISPATCHED TO AN ALARM AT A RESTAURANT. WHILE ENROUTE, I BROKE FOR A TRAFFIC STOP...

0415 - (S) TRAFFIC STOP

I STOPPED A GUY WHO HAD AN EXPIRED TEMPORARY TAG ON HIS CAR. THE DRIVER WAS A YOUNG W/M FROM A FOREIGN COUNTRY. I DON'T KNOW FOR SURE, BUT HE SOUNDED GERMAN. HE POSSESSED AN INTERNATIONAL DRIVER LICENSE. HE SAID HE HAS BEEN WORKING SO MUCH HE HADN'T FOUND TIME TO GET THE PERMANENT TAG. I TOLD HIM THAT WASN'T A GOOD EXCUSE (ALTHOUGH I GUESS IT IS) AND THAT HE NEEDED TO GET A FLORIDA LICENSE IF HE WAS GOING TO BE STAYING HERE. HE WAS GRACIOUS. I HEADED TO MY ALARM. BEFORE I COULD GET THERE, A GUY ON MY SQUAD CLEARED IT FOR ME.

0425 -I TOOK THE CRUISER THROUGH THE CAR WASH ABOUT THREE OR FOUR TIMES.

(IT'S A FREE WASH. I MIGHT AS WELL KEEP IT REAL CLEAN.)

0430 - AREA CHECK/LOUD PARTY

A PARTY AT AN APARTMENT SPILLED OVER INTO THE PARKING LOT AND RESIDENTS WERE COMPLAINING. IT WAS BREAKING UP AS ANOTHER OFFICER AND I ARRIVED. THIS IS DEFINITELY OUR PROBLEM COMPLEX. THERE AREN'T MANY SERIOUS CRIMES THERE, JUST LOUD MUSIC AND LOUD PARTIES. (WHERE'S THE PROBLEM IN THAT, RIGHT?)

0439 - (D) BURGLARY TO A BUSINESS

A NIGHT AUDITOR (YOUNG, B/F) AT A HOTEL CALLED IN A BURGLARY THAT OCCURRED OVER THE LAST 15 MINUTES. SHE ADVISED OVER $300.00 WAS STOLEN FROM THE REGISTER AND OVER $800.00 FROM THE SAFE. THE ENTIRE LOBBY/OFFICE AREA WAS LOCKED UP AND THERE WERE NO GUESTS THEREIN. THERE WAS ALSO NO SIGNS OF FORCED ENTRY INTO THE LOBBY/OFFICE. THE B/F HAD THE ONE KEY THAT OPENS THE REGISTER ON A CHAIN AROUND HER WRIST. WITHIN THAT REGISTER WAS THE KEY TO THE SAFE. THE B/F SAID SHE REMOVED THE REGISTER KEY FROM AROUND HER WRIST AND PLACED IT ON THE DESK ABOVE THE SAFE. SHE DID THIS JUST PRIOR TO LEAVING THE OFFICE AND GOING TO THE RESTROOM. SHE WAS GONE FOR ABOUT TEN MINUTES. WHEN SHE RETURNED, SHE DISCOVERED CASH HAD BEEN REMOVED FROM THE REGISTER. SHE LATER NOTICED THE SAFE DOOR WAS OPEN AND THE CASH DRAWER HAD BEEN REMOVED. THE B/F SAID SHE THINKS SOME OTHER EMPLOYEE IS RESPONSIBLE. SHE SAID THEY ALL KNOW THE COMBINATION TO THE LOCK ON THE DOOR AND SOMEONE MUST HAVE ENTERED WHEN SHE STEPPED AWAY. I SAID, "LET ME GET THIS STRAIGHT SOME OTHER EMPLOYEE CAME UP HERE IN THE MIDDLE OF THE NIGHT. THEY WAITED FOR THE MOMENT YOU WOULD STEP AWAY (NOT KNOWING HOW LONG YOU WOULD BE GONE) AND THEN ENTERED. THEY THEN FOUND THE KEY, WHICH THEY MUST HAVE PRAYED THAT YOU WOULD INADVERTANTLY LEAVE BEHIND. THEY THEN UNLOCKED THE REGISTER AND REMOVED THE CASH AND THE SAFE KEY. THEN THEY OPENED THE SAFE, TOOK THE DRAWER AND THE CASH, THEN SLIPPED BACK OUT PRIOR TO YOUR RETURN." SHE ANSWERED, "THEY MUST HAVE." AT ANY RATE, I GOT A SWORN STATEMENT FROM HER AND WROTE A REPORT. I KNOW IT'S THE 31ST AND ALL, BUT I'M SURE SHE PAID HER RENT WEEKS AGO.

0530 - I WENT BACK TO THE STATION TO COMPLETE MY "SO-CALLED BURGLARY" REPORT. SHORTLY

THEREAFTER I WAS DISPATCHED A CALL.

0545 - (D) DISTURBANCE
   I WAS DISPATCHED TO A FIGHT THAT WAS OCCURRING AT OUR PROBLEM APARTMENT COMPLEX. I RESPONDED WITH ABOUT FIVE OR SIX OTHER OFFICERS. WE WERE UNABLE TO LOCATE ANY OF THE PARTICIPANTS. I CLEARED THE CALL AND WENT BACK TO THE STATION.

0600 - I'M SUPPOSED TO BE GETTING OFF NOW, BUT I'M NOT.

0700 -I COMPLETED MY PAPERWORK AND HEADED HOME. I'LL TALK TO YOU TOMORROW.

09/04

1800-BRIEFING

ONCE WE WERE DONE WITH BRIEFING, I WAITED IN THE STATION LOBBY FOR A WHILE. IT WAS POURING DOWN RAINING OUTSIDE AND I DIDN'T WANT TO GO OUT IN IT. (I COULD MELT) IT DIDN'T SEEM TO BE LETTING UP. I RAN OUT TO MY CAR SO I COULD GO EAT BEFORE GETTING DISPATCHED A CALL.

ON MY WAY TO EAT, I GOT A CALL FROM AN OLD, FEMALE FRIEND OF MINE. SHE'S A B/F (MID 20'S). SHE'S AN AFTER-CARE COORDINATOR AT AN ELEMENTARY SCHOOL. SHE WANTED TO KNOW IF I WOULD COME TO HER SCHOOL ONE EVENING AND SPEAK TO THE CHILDREN. I'M SUPPOSED TO SHOW THEM MY POLICE CAR AND OTHER THINGS OF INTEREST TO THEM. I'M ALSO SUPPOSED TO COUNSEL THE PROBLEM CHILDREN REGARDING THE ERROR OF THEIR WAYS. I AGREED TO DO IT.

STILL ON MY WAY TO EAT I PULLED UP NEXT TO A CAR FULL OF TOURISTS WITH ABOUT THREE SMALL CHILDREN IN THE BACK SEAT. THE CHILDREN WERE POINTING AND WAVING AT ME LIKE CRAZY. I GAVE THEM A HUGE SMILE AND A BIG WAVE. THE MOM (I ASSUME), WHO WAS DRIVING THE CAR, THOUGHT I WAS WAVING AT HER. SHE GAVE ME A BIG WAVE BACK. AS WE MOVED ALONG, THE MOTHER GOT MY ATTENTION AGAIN. THIS TIME, SHE WAS POINTING TO THE BACK SEAT WHERE THE CHILDREN WERE. SHE WANTED ME TO WAVE AT THEM TOO. I SMILED AND WAVED AGAIN, THINKING, LADY, I WASN'T WAVING AT YOU IN THE FIRST PLACE.

1830- I HAD DINNER.

1930-I HEADED TO LOCAL HOTEL. I SPOKE TO A FRIEND OF MINE WHO WORKS THERE. (THE MALE FRIEND). FG3 CALLED ON THE WAY. I SPOKE TO HER BRIEFLY.

2025 - IT WAS STILL RAINY OUT AND VERY SLOW. I PULLED INTO A PARKING GARAGE AND CALLED FG4 (BRAZILIAN.NO INGLES). I GOT HER ANSWERING MACHINE. MY TWO BRAZILIAN FRIENDS ARE LETTING ME DOWN. THEY DON'T HAVE TIME FOR ME ANYMORE. I'M GONNA BE PISSED IF THEY MAKE ME FAIL MY PORTUGUESE CLASS. I SUDDENLY REMEMBERED THIS OTHER BRAZILIAN GIRL THAT I HAD MET A WHILE

BACK AND EXCHANGED NUMBERS WITH. I THINK SHE'S ABOUT 19 OR TWENTY. I CALLED HER AND WE SPOKE FOR A WHILE. AS IT TURNS OUT, WE ATTEND THE SAME COLLEGE. WE MADE PLANS TO MEET ON CAMPUS LATER IN THE WEEK.

2100 - BACK OUT ON PATROL

2107 - (BU) DISTURBANCE
I WENT TO BACK UP ANOTHER UNIT WHO WAS RESPONDING TO A STORE. THERE WAS AN ARGUMENT BETWEEN THE CLERK AND A CUSTOMER. THE OTHER UNIT CANCELLED ME BEFORE I COULD GET THERE.

2115 - (D) PANIC ALARM
I WAS DISPATCHED TO AN ALARM AT A MCDONALD'S. UPON ARRIVAL, MANAGEMENT ADVISED IT WAS ACCIDENTAL.

2128 - (S) TRAFFIC STOP
I CONDUCTED A TRAFFIC STOP OF A VEHICLE WITH AN EXPIRED TAG. THE DRIVER (W/M, LATE 30'S) WAS FROM ENGLAND AND HE DISPLAYED FOR ME HIS UNITED KINGDOM DRIVER LICENSE. HE AND HIS FAMILY WERE IN TOWN ON VACATION AND THE CAR WAS RENTED. I CUT THEM LOOSE.

2130 - (S) SUSPICIOUS VEHICLE
I NOTICED A WHITE CHEVY PARKED IN THE LOT OF A HOTEL WITH SOMEONE INSIDE. THE CAR WAS IN SOMEWHAT OF AN OBSCURE LOCATION WHICH SEEMED SUSPICIOUS TO ME. AFTER APPROACHING THE VEHICLE, I REALIZED IT WAS A PRIVATE SECURITY OFFICER, HIRED BY THE HOTEL. I TOLD THE YOUNG W/F THAT I WAS JUST MAKING SURE SHE WASN'T ABOUT TO ROB THE PLACE. SHE TOLD ME THAT WAS WHAT SHE WAS TRYING TO PREVENT. THERE HAVE BEEN AT LEAST TWO ARMED ROBBERIES AT THAT HOTEL THAT I KNOW OF.

2145 - (D) PANIC ALARM
MCDONALD'S AGAIN. YOU TELL ME IF YOU THINK I RUSHED OVER THERE THIS TIME. YOU'RE RIGHT. UPON ARRIVAL, I WAS TOLD THAT IT TOO WAS ACCIDENTAL. I HOPE THEY DON'T HAVE A REAL ONE TONIGHT.

2205 - (D) BURGLARY TO A CONVEYANCE

I RESPONDED TO A LOCAL DINNER THEATRE WHERE A TOURIST FROM TEXAS HAD HIS VAN BROKEN INTO. UPON ARRIVAL, I MET WITH THE W/M AND HIS WIFE (W/F, BOTH LT 30S OR ERLY 40S). AFTER DINNER, THE COUPLE WALKED OUT TO THE LOT WITH ANOTHER COUPLE AND WERE DISCUSSING HOW MUCH THEY ENJOYED IT. THEY ACTUALLY GOT INTO THE VAN WITHOUT NOTICING THE SMASHED OUT WINDOW.

WHEN THEY SAW THE GLASS ON THE SEAT, THEY REALIZED THEIR VEHICLE HAD BEEN BURGLARIZED. THE PASSENGER SIDE BACK WINDOW WAS SMASHED OUT AND THE LADY'S SUITCASE WAS STOLEN. SHE WAS DUE TO GO BACK TO TEXAS THE FOLLOWING MORNING. THE SUITCASE CONTAINED ALL THE CLOTHING THAT THE LADY HAD BOUGHT FOR THEIR TRIP TO FLORIDA. THE LADY SAID HER HUSBAND DIDN'T LIKE WHAT SHE HAD BOUGHT ANYWAY. THE HUSBAND AGREED, BUT SAID HE WOULD HAVE PREFERRED IT WEREN'T STOLEN.

2255 -I CALLED HOME TO CHECK MY MESSAGES. MY 4Y/ O DAUGHTER HAD CALLED. SHE SAID, "HI DADDY. I JUST CALLED TO SAY HI AND BYE". I SPOKE TO HER BEFORE MY SHIFT STARTED. I TOLD HER THAT I MISSED AND LOVED HER. SHE SAID, "WELL HERE, TALK TO MOMMY AND TELL HER YOU WANT TO MARRY HER". "MOMMY" GOT ON THE PHONE AND JUST GIGGLED.

2259 -I SAT IN THE DINNER THEATRE PARKING LOT AND WORKED ON MY REPORT.

2326 - (BU) RESIDENTIAL ALARM

THIS WAS A RESIDENTIAL ALARM. THE HOMEOWNER WAS AT HOME, BUT DID NOT HAVE PROPER CODE. MY PARTNER AND I RESPONDED WITH LIGHTS AND SIRENS. AS WE ARRIVED AT THE COMPLEX, THE PROPER CODE WAS GIVEN.

2334 -I WENT TO A NEARBY SHOPPING PLAZA TO GET BACK TO MY PAPERWORK.

2335 - FG3 CALLED TO SEE HOW I WAS. SHE WAS GOING TO BED AND WANTED TO KNOW IF I HAD GOTTEN

ANYTHING TO EAT.

0006 - (D) PANIC ALARM
   THIS PANIC ALARM WAS FROM A PONTIAC MONTANA.
THE VEHICLE WAS MOBILE AND I WAS DISPACTED TO THE
LOCATION WHERE THE ALARM WAS ACTIVATED. UPON MY
ARRIVAL, THE VAN WAS GONE. SOME OTHER UNITS AND I
CHECKED THE AREA, BUT DID NOT FIND IT.

0030 -I WENT TO A GAS STATION TO FILL UP. I CHATTED
WITH THE CLERK FOR A WHILE (B/F, 40'S). I GAVE OUT
SOME DIRECTIONS AND PROCEEDED TO LEAVE.

0040 - BEFORE LEAVING, I NOTICED A B/M (40'S)
STANDING NEAR THE BACK SIDE OF THE BUSINESS.
I ASKED HIM WHAT HE WAS UP TO. THE B/M, WHO
SEEMED TO BE A TRANSIENT (HOMELESS), SAID HIS
FRIEND GOT A FLAT TIRE JUST DOWN THE ROAD
   AND HE WAS WAITING FOR HIM. I TOLD THE MAN HE WAS
GOING TO HAVE TO MOVE ALONG IF HE WAS NOT GOING TO
PATRONIZE THE STORE NOR HAD ANY OTHER BUSINESS
THERE. THIS SEEMED TO UPSET HIM. HE WENT ON TO TELL
ME THAT HE'S LIVED BEHIND ONE OF THE 7 ELEVEN'S UP THE
ROAD (THE ADJACENT POLICE ZONE) FOR YEARS AND THE
OTHER OFFICERS KNEW HIM. I TOLD HIM THAT I DIDN'T. I
ASKED FOR HIS PERSONAL INFORMATION. I RAN IT AND TOLD
THE MAN TO LEAVE. HE WAS STILL UPSET AND SAID HE WAS
TIRED OF ALWAYS BEING HARRASSED. I ASSURED HIM IT HAD
NOTHING TO DO WITH HIS RACE. HE POINTED TO A W/M (20'S)
AND SAID HE HAD BEEN THERE LONGER AND WANTED TO
KNOW WHY I DIDN'T MESS WITH HIM. I TOLD THE B/M THAT I
DIDN'T SEE HIM, AND IF I HAD, I WOULD HAVE. I THEN CALLED
THE W/M OVER TO ME. I MADE SURE THE B/M KNEW I WASN'T
DOING IT FOR HIS BENEFIT...

0049 - WHEN THE W/M GOT OVER TO ME HE SAID, "I
HEARD WHAT HE SAID. HE WAS LYING. WHEN I WALKED
UP, I SAW YOU TALKING TO HIM. BUT IT'S COOL. HERE'S
MY I.D." I RAN HIS INFORMAION AND FOUND THAT HIS
LICENSE WAS SUSPENDED. HE WAS WALKING THOUGH.
I TOLD HIM HE HAD TO KEEP MOVING AS WELL. HE SAID

NO PROBLEM. FOR SOME REASON, HE DIDN'T SEEM TO FEEL LIKE HE WAS BEING PERSECUTED BY ME LIKE THE OTHER GUY.

0102 -I WENT TO EAT AGAIN.

0200 -I WENT BACK OUT ON PATROL.

0224 - (S) TRAFFIC STOP
  I STOPPED A CAR IN WHICH THE TAG CAME BACK ON MY COMPUTER AS NOT BEING ASSIGNED. THE YOUNG W/M DRIVER SHOWED ME HIS NEW TAG, WHICH WAS IN THE TRUNK. HE SAID IT WASN'T NOVEMBER YET, SO HE DIDN'T THINK HE WAS SUPPOSED TO PUT IT ON. (BOTH THE OLD AND NEW TAGS HAD NOVEMBER STICKERS) I TOLD HE SHOULD HAVE PUT IT ON WHEN HE FIRST RECEIVED IT. THE OLD TAG WAS CANCELLED WHEN THEY ISSUED THE NEW ONE. HE SAID HE'D CHANGE IT AS SOON AS HE GOT HOME.

0300 - THERE AREN'T MANY PEOPLE ON THE STREETS. IT'S VERY QUIET IN TOWN, NO CONVENTIONS, NOT MANY TOURISTS. I PULLED INTO A DRUG STORE PARKING LOT TO REVIEW MY SCHOOL WORK, I MEAN, MY LEGAL BULLETINS AND AGENCY DIRECTIVES.

0400 -I WENT TO THE STATION TO TURN IN MY PAPERWORK.

0430 -I WENT TO ANOTHER PLAZA TO FINISH MY LEGAL BULLETINS.

0600 - WE COME TO THE END OF ANOTHER BEAUTIFUL SHIFT. I'LL SEE YOU TOMORROW.

09/05

2000 - BRIEFING

2030 -I HAD AN EXCELLENT DINNER; LONDON BROIL, STEAMED RICE AND BROCOLLI, AND CURRIED LAMB. I STUDIED MY PORTUGUESE WHILE DINING.

2105 - (D) AREA CHECK

I WENT TO MY PROBLEM APARTMENT COMPLEX ON A LOUD MUSIC COMPLAINT. WHEN I ARRIVED AT THE SUSPECTED APARTMENT, I MADE CONTACT WITH A W/M IN HIS 40'S. HE WAS IN THERE CRANKIN' SOME ROCK-N-ROLL. I TOLD HIM ABOUT THE COMPLAINT. HE TURNED IT DOWN AND THANKED ME.

2200 -I NOTICED THE CAR OF A PERSON WITH A SUSPENDED LICENSE. I WAS UNABLE TO GET TURNED AROUND IN TIME TO GET THEM.

2210 - (D) 9-1-1 HANG-UP
   SOMEONE CALLED 911 FROM A HOTEL. WHEN I GOT THERE, I MET WITH HOTEL SECURITY. THEY CHECKED THE TELEPHONE PRINTOUTS AND SAID NO ONE CALLED. I CLEARED.

2230 - FG2 CALLED ME (26Y/O BRAZILIAN). WHILE I WAS ON THE PHONE, I WAS APPROACHED AND ASKED FOR DIRECTIONS. THAT'S HAPPENED MANY TIMES WHILE WE'VE TALKED. SHE SAID I'D BE RICH IF I GOT PAID FOR IT. I GUESS I DO GET PAID FOR IT THOUGH IT MOST CERTAINLY HASN'T MADE ME RICH.

2245 - (D) BURGLARY TO A RESIDENCE
   I WAS DISPATCHED TO A RESIDENTIAL BURGLARY. UPON ARRIVAL, I MET WITH A YOUNG W/F. SHE SAID SHE DIDN'T KNOW IF HER HOME HAD BEEN BURGLARIZED OR NOT. HER EX-ROOMMATE HAD CALLED AND THREATENED TO TAKE PROPERTY WHILE THE W/F WAS AT WORK. SHE JUST RETURNED HOME AND WANTED TO WAIT ON AN OFFICER BEFORE CHECKING. SHE SAID SHE KNEW HER ROOMMATE

WAS ON HEROIN AND COCAINE. SHE SAID SHE ACTUALLY SAW SOME COCAINE IN HER ROOM. THAT'S WHEN SHE DECIDED TO KICK HER OUT. SHE CHECKED THE RESIDENCE AND FOUND THAT IT HAD NOT BEEN BURGLARIZED. I TOLD HER SHE BETTER BE GLAD THAT GIRL WASN'T ON CRACK BECAUSE CRACK HEADS WILL STEAL FROM THEIR OWN MOTHERS.

0040 - (D) RECKLESS VEHICLE

I GOT A CALL ABOUT AN 18-WHEELED COMMERICAL VEHICLE. IT WAS DRIVING DOWN THE INTERSTATE WITH ITS REAR DOORS SWINGING OPEN. THE CONCERN WAS THAT THE PALLETS THAT WERE INSIDE WOULD FLY OUT. SOME OTHER OFFICERS AND I TRIED TO FIND IT. WE WERE UNABLE TO.

0128-I WENT TO EAT AGAIN.

0212-(D) STAND-BY

I WAS DISPATCHED TO A LOCAL HOTEL TO MEET WITH A YOUNG W/F WHO HAD NO PLACE TO GO. THE DISPATCHER SAID THEY CONTACTED A HOMELESS COALITION FOR THE W/F. THEY SAID THEY HAD AN AVAILABLE BED, BUT THE W/F HAD NO MONEY FOR A CAB. I PICKED THE W/F UP AND TRANSPORTED HER TO THE SHELTER. I ASKED HER WHY SHE WAS HOMELESS. SHE SAID SHE CAME TO FLORIDA ON VACATION FROM PORTLAND, OREGON. WHILE HERE, SOMEONE STOLE ALL HER MONEY. I ASKED HER IF SHE HAD ANY FAMILY. SHE SAID JUST HER DAD AND HE'S BACK IN PORTLAND. I ASKED HER IF HE COULD SEND HER SOME MONEY TO GET HER BACK HOME. SHE SAID HE HAS NO MONEY. I ASKED HER WHAT SHE PLANNED ON DOING. SHE SAID, "I GUESS I'LL HAVE TO STAY HERE A WHILE".

0250 – (S) TRAFFIC STOP

ON MY WAY BACK FROM THE SHELTER, I STOPPED A BLACK FORD WITH AN UNASSIGNED TAG. THE TAG CAME BACK TO A GREY CHRYSLER. UPON STOPPING HIM, THE H/M (30'S) SHOWED ME HIS REGISTRATION. AS IT TURNED

OUT, I RAN THE TAG INCORRECTLY. I APOLOGIZED TO THE
H/M AND LET HIM GO ABOUT HIS BUSINESS.

0320 -I WENT TO GAS UP THE CRUISER AND USE THE
REST ROOM. I REMAINED AT THAT INTERSECTION
UNTIL THE SHIFT ENDED. I'LL SEE YA IN A FEW DAYS.

09/08

1800-BRIEFING

1853 - I'VE ALREADY EATEN DINNER SO I'M GOING STRAIGHT TO PATROL.

1919 - (S) TRAFFIC STOP
  I STOPPED A MIDDLE-AGED W/ M WHO WAS DRIVING A CADILLAC WITH A TAG THAT HAD BEEN EXPIRED FOR ALMOST 6 MONTHS. THE W/M SAID HE HAD RECENTLY PURCHASED THE VEHICLE AND TRANSFERRED THE TAG FROM ANOTHER CAR. HE THOUGHT HE HAD PAID THE RENEWAL FEE, BUT APPARENTLY HAD NOT. WHILE I WAS WRITING HIM A TICKET, HE TOLD ME ABOUT HIS NEW CADY. HE SAID HE GOT A GREAT DEAL ON IT. IT WAS A '93 AND HE PAID 11 K FOR IT. HE SAID THAT WAS A BIT HIGH FOR A '93, AND THAT IT SHOULD HAVE BEEN AROUND 9, BUT IT ONLY HAD 38K MILES ON IT. AFTER I HANDED HIM THE TICKET, HE THANKED ME FOR LETTING HIM KNOW HE'D BEEN DRIVING FOR ALMOST SIX MONTHS WITH AN EXPIRED TAG. I SAID, "NO PROBLEM, SIR. TAKE CARE".

2027 -I PULLED INTO A BURGER KING PARKING LOT WITH SOME B&J MONKEY WRENCH ICECREAM TO INPUT MY STATISTICS INTO MY COMPUTER.

2000 -I CALLED HOME TO CHECK MY MESSAGES. FG3 CALLED ME AND SAID, "CALL ME, PLEASE". I'M NOT GOING TO BECAUSE WE SPEAK TOO FREQUENTLY. ATTACHMENTS START THAT WAY.

2100 - A YOUNG W/F WALKED UP TO ME AND SAID THAT TWO MEN HAD GOTTEN OUT OF THEIR VEHICLES AT A NEARBY INTERSECTION AND WERE FIGHTING. ROAD RAGE I GUESS. ANYWAY, I WENT TO THE INTERSECTION AND NO ONE WAS FIGHTING.

2107-I WENT BACK TO BURGER KING TO FINISH MY WORK. I THREW MY ICE CREAM AWAY. I DIDN'T LIKE

THAT FLAVOR VERY MUCH.

2120 - (S) TRAFFIC STOP
 I STOPPED A MIDDLE-AGED W/M WHO WAS DRIVING A "72 DODGE WITH NO TAILLIGHTS. HE HAD ABOUT FOUR OR FIVE SMALL KIDS IN THE CAR WITH HIM. AFTER VERIFYING THAT HIS LICENSE WAS VALID, I TOLD HIM I WAS GOING TO GIVE HIM A WRITTEN WARNING. AS I WAS GETTING OUT OF MY CAR, I BANGED MY LEG ON THE DOOR. IT HURT LIKE—. THE GUY ASKED ME IF I WAS O.K. PROBABLY BECAUSE I ONLY GAVE HIM A WARNING. IF I HAD WRITTEN HIM A TICKET, HE PROBABLY WOULD HAVE BEEN LIKE: "THAT'S WHAT YOU GET!"

2210-I GOT A CALL FROM AN OFFICER WHO WAS SCHEDULING SOME OFF-DUTY LAW ENFORCEMENT EMPLOYMENT FOR OCTOBER. I GAVE HIM SEVERAL DATES TO SCHEDULE ME FOR. AN ABSOLUTE MUST WHEN YOU MAKE NEXT TO NOTHING, BUT HAVE RESPONSIBILITIES.

2220 - (D) 9-1-1 HANG-UP
 I WAS DISPATECHED TO A RESORT TO HANDLE A CALL IN WHICH A PERSON HAD CALLED 911, THEN HUNG UP. I CALLED THE RESORT'S SECURITY AND TURNED THE CALL OVER TO THEM.

2226 - (D) PETIT THEFT
 I WAS DISPATCHED TO A THEFT AT A GOLDEN CORAL RESTAURANT, BUT IT WAS PICKED UP BY ANOTHER UNIT.

2240 - *(S)* TRAFFIC STOP
 I STOPPED A CAR OF WHICH THE REGISTERED OWNER'S LICENSE WAS EXPIRED. I GAVE THE GUY A WRITTEN WARNING AND CUT HIM LOOSE.

2250 - (S) SUSPICIOUS VEHICLE
 I PULLED UP ON A COUPLE THAT WAS PARKED IN THE LOT OF A CLOSED BUSINESS. AFTER RUNNING THE TAG AND MAKING SURE EVERYTHING WAS GOOD, I ROLLED OFF. I WANTED TO LEAVE THEM WITH THEIR LITTLE "PRIVATE TIME".

I WAS YOUNG ONCE AND ON MORE THAN ONE OCCASION, A COP HAS CAUGHT ME AND SOMEONE'S DAUGHTER DOING MUCH MORE THAN SITTING AND TALKING, AND LET US SLIDE.

2300 - (S) TRAFFIC STOP

I STOPPED A YOUNG, H/M IN A HONDA. HIS LICENSE WAS SUSPENDED LAST DECEMBER FOR CHILD SUPPORT DELINQUENCY. HE TOLD ME THAT WAS INCORRECT BECAUSE HE HAS HAD CUSTODY OF HIS CHILD FOR SIX YEARS. HE SAID IF ANYTHING, THE MOTHER SHOULD BE CHARGED BECAUSE SHE HASN'T PAID WHAT SHE OWES. I DIDN'T TAKE HIM TO JAIL BECAUSE HE SHOWED ME CUSTODY PAPERS. I DID WRITE HIM A TICKET AND TOLD HIM HE NEEDED TO HAVE THE RECORD CORRECTED. IF HE WAS CORRECT, THE TICKET WOULD BE REMOVED.

2318 - (S) TRAFFIC STOP

I RAN THE TAG ON A BLUE HONDA CIVC AND IT CAME BACK AS BEING ASSIGNED TO A RED ONE. IN THE CAR WERE FOUR YOUNG LATIN AMERICANS; TWO MALES IN THE FRONT AND A MALE AND FEMALE IN THE REAR. THE DRIVER SAID HIS CAR WAS NEVER PAINTED AND HAS ALWAYS BEEN BLUE. I LET HIM GO AFTER CHECKING THE VALIDITY OF HIS LICENSE. AS THEY DROVE OFF, THE FEMALE, WHO HAD BEEN FLIRTING WITH ME THE WHOLE TIME, WAVED GOODBYE.

2330 - (S) TRAFFIC STOP

I STOPPED A CAR OF WHICH THE REGISTERED OWNER'S LICENSE WAS SUSPENDED. THE TYPE OF SUSPENSION WAS FOR FAILING TO MAINTAIN INSURANCE COVERAGE THROUGHOUT THE VEHICLE REGISTRATION PERIOD. THE DRIVER WAS A YOUNG B/M. HE SAID HE HAD CHANGED INSURANCE COMPANIES ABOUT A WEEK AGO. I DID TAKE HIS LICENSE AND WRITE HIM A TICKET. OUR ENCOUNTER WAS A VERY PLEASANT ONE. HE THANKED ME WHEN WE WERE DONE.

*NOTE: BE SURE THAT IF YOU CHANGE INSURANCE COMPANIES, YOUR NEW COMPANY INFORMS THE STATE THAT YOU DO HAVE COVERAGE. YOUR OLD COMPANY WILL

MOST DEFINITELY MAKE THEM AWARE THAT YOU ARE NO LONGER COVERED BY THEM

0016 - IT WAS "LATIN NIGHT" AT ONE OF THE LOCAL CLUBS. AS I SAT IN THE PARKING LOT, A CAR OF FOUR BLACK FEMALES PULLED UP TO MINE. THEY ASKED ME IF I KNEW WHERE A "BLACK CLUB" WAS. I LAUGHED, THEN TOLD THEM OF TWO THAT I KNEW OF. I TOLD THEM IN THE ONE DOWNTOWN THE PEOPLE ARE PACKED IN BUTTHOLE TO BELLYBUTTON (AS THEY USED TO SAY IN THE CORPS), IF YOU LIKE IT LIKE THAT. THEY LAUGHED, THANKED ME, AND DROVE OFF.

0035 - (S) TRAFFIC STOP
    I STOPPED A CAR OF WHICH THE OWNER'S LICENSE WAS SUSPENDED. I FOUND THAT THE OWNER'S FRIEND WAS DRIVING, AND THE OWNER WAS IN THE PASSENGER SEAT.

0045 - (S) TRAFFIC STOP
    SUSPENDED LICENSE STOP. THE DRIVER, A YOUNG B/M, HAD A VALID LICENSE. IT WAS HIS SISTER WHOSE LICENSE WAS SUSPENDED.

0130-I DROPPED BY ANOTHER NIGHTCLUB. IT WASN'T "HAPPENING", SO I LEFT. WHAT I MEAN IS THE PATRONS WERE ALL WELL-BEHAVED, SO MY PRESENCE WAS NOT NECESSARY.

0150 - (D) AREA CHECK FOR ROBBERY SUSPECT
    A ROBBERY OCCURRED IN A NEARBY JURISDICTION. THEY REQUESTED WE CHECK OUR AREA FOR THE SUSPECTS. I DIDN'T COME ACROSS THEM.

0230 - (D) TRESPASSER
    I RESPONDED TO THE AFOREMENTIONED NIGHTCLUB IN RESPONSE TO A DRUNKEN, YOUNG W/M WHO HAD GOTTEN OUT OF HAND. AFTER CAUSING A DISTURBANCE, MANAGEMENT ORDERED THE W/M OFF THE PROPERTY. HE REFUSED. HE WENT SO FAR AS TO YELL RACIAL SLURS AT A BLACK SECURITY OFFICER. UPON MY ARRIVAL, HE BEGAN ACTING IN A MORE CIVIL MANNER. WHEN HE DID BEGAN TO GET

OUT OF HAND, I SHIFTED ROLES FROM ARBITRATOR TO "THE AUTHORITY", AND SETTLED HIM RIGHT DOWN. HIS ARGUMENT WAS THAT MANAGEMENT WAS TRYING TO MAKE HIM LEAVE THE PROPERTY, THEREBY FORCING HIM TO DRIVE DRUNK. I TOLD HIM THAT HE SIMPLY HAD TO LEAVE AND THAT NO ONE SAID HE HAD TO DRIVE. BEING THAT HE WAS SO INTOXICATED, THIS CONCEPT HAD TO BE EXPLAINED TO HIM MANY TIMES. (IT DIDN'T HAVE TO BE, BUT I'M MORE PATIENT THAN MOST COPS, I THINK.) MANAGEMENT OFFERED TO CALL HIM A CAB, BUT HE WASN'T HEARING THAT. FINALLY, I TOLD HIM HE WAS TRESPASSED, AND IF HE REFUSED TO LEAVE, HE WAS GOING TO JAIL. AFTER MAKING MENTION OF HIS ATTORNEY AND THE FACT THAT WE WERE FORCING HIM TO DRIVE DRUNK, HE SAID TO JUST TAKE HIM TO JAIL. TIRED OF TALKING TO HIM, I HOOKED HIM UP (HANDCUFFED HIM) AND PLACED HIM IN MY BACK SEAT. HIS FALSE COURAGE SEEMED TO FLEE FROM HIS BODY AT THAT MOMENT. I THINK HE WAS HALF A HEART BEAT AWAY FROM FLAT OUT BAWLING. BY THE TIME I DROVE AROUND TO THE FRONT OF THE BUSINESS, THE W/M HAD AGREED TO LEAVE THE PROPERTY BY ANY OTHER MEANS BESIDES MY VEHICLE. ONCE I TOOK HIM OUT AND UNCUFFED HIM, HE REGAINED SOME COURAGE AND STARTED TALKING TRASH AGAIN. I ORDERED HIM OFF THE PROPERTY ONE LAST TIME AND HE LEFT.

0310 - (S) DOMESTIC DISTURBANCE

THAT NIGHTCLUB IS ATTACHED TO A HOTEL. NO SOONER THAN THE TRESPASSER WAS BOOTED OFF PROPERTY, I WAS INFORMED OF A DOMESTIC DISTURBANCE UP IN ONE OF THE ROOMS. THE COUPLE WAS AN OLDER W/M AND A YOUNG W/F. THEY WERE BOTH INTOXICATED. (THE KIND OF DISFUNCTIONAL COUPLE FOUND ON "COPS".) HE CLAIMED HE NEEDED TO LEAVE VERY EARLY IN THE MORNING AND DEMANDED SHE GIVE HIM HIS KEYS. SHE REFUSED, CLAIMING SHE FEARED HE WOULD ATTEMPT TO DRIVE THAT NIGHT. FINALLY, HE AGREED TO GIVE THE MANAGER THE KEY TO HOLD UNTIL MORNING. THEY WERE TOLD THEY'D BE KICKED OUT OF THE HOTEL IF THEY CAUSED ANY FURTHER DISTURBANCE.

0346 - (D) SUSPICIOUS VEHICLE/PERSONS

I WAS DISPATCHED TO A SEVEN/ELEVEN. THE YOUNG W/F CLERK CALLED IN ABOUT A VEHICLE THAT WAS PARKED IN THE LOT. INSIDE WERE TWO WHITE MALES AND SHE WAS FRIGHTENED. THE DRUG STORE NEXT DOOR HAD RECENTLY BEEN ROBBED AND THE EMPLOYEES WERE BOUND WITH DUCT TAPE AS THEY WERE HELD AT GUNPOINT. I MADE CONTACT WITH THE CLERKS, THE YOUNG W/F AND W/M IN HIS EARLY 40'S. AFTER COMMENTING ON THE FEMALE'S TONGUE RING, I WENT OUT TO THE CAR. INSIDE WERE TWO TOURISTS SLEEPING. THEY BARELY SPOKE ENGLISH, BUT I WAS ABLE TO COMMUNICATE WITH ONE OF THEM. THE CAR WAS RENTED AND THEY HAD DRIVEN IT FROM A NEARBY TOWN. HE ONLY HAD ENOUGH MONEY TO VISIT A FEW ATTRACTIONS, NOT ENOUGH TO PAY FOR A ROOM. (DAYBREAK WAS ONLY A FEW HOURS AWAY.) I TOLD THEM IT WAS GOING TO BE UP THE CLERKS WHETHER OR NOT THEY COULD CONTINUE TO CRASH THERE. ONCE INSIDE THE STORE, I WAS DRAWN INTO CONVERSATION WITH THE CLERKS AND FORGOT ABOUT THE "SUSPICIOUS PERSONS" IN THE LOT. THE GUY SAID HE USED TO BE A COP IN MISSISSIPPI. HE ALSO SAID HE DIDN'T MISS LAW ENFORCEMENT ONE BIT. I TRIED TO GET AWAY FROM HIM, BUT HE KEPT BOMBARDING ME WITH ONE LAW ENFORCEMENT TALE AFTER THE OTHER. I CERTAINLY COULDN'T TELL THAT HE DIDN'T MISS IT. I WENT UP TO THE FRONT OF THE STORE WHERE THE FEMALE WAS. I TOLD HER TO CALL US BACK IF ANYTHING ELSE SEEMED SUSPICIOUS. THAT'S WHEN SHE SHIFTED GEARS, THREW THE LINE OUT, AND HOOKED ME. SHE ASKED HOW LONG I HAD BEEN DOING POLICE WORK. I SHOULDN'T HAVE ANSWERED, BUT I DID. SHE WENT FROM THAT TO TELLING ME HOW SHE WAS RAISED BY A BLACK WOMAN AND MISSES HER "SOUL FOOD" COOKING. I FINALLY MADE IT OUT OF THE SEVEN/ELEVEN. ONCE OUTSIDE, I REMEMBERED I WAS SUPPOSED TO LET THE TOURISTS KNOW IF THEY HAD TO LEAVE OR NOT. I TOLD THEM THEY COULD STAY AND THEY WERE PLEASED.

0422 -I HEADED TO EAT AGAIN, AND REMEMBERED I HADN'T YET TURNED IN MY PAPERWORK. I WENT TO DO

JUST THAT.

0455 - (D) ALARM I RESPONDED TO COMMERCIAL ALARM. AS PER THE NORM, IT WAS UNFOUNDED.

0510 -I MADE IT TO A RESTAURANT TO HAVE BREAKFAST AND DO SOME STUDYING. ANOTHER OFFICER JOINED ME, A TALKATIVE FELLOW I MIGHT ADD. I WAS UNABLE TO GET ANY STUDYING DONE, BUT THAT OFFICER IS A REALLY GOOD GUY.
   I'LL SEE YOU TOMORROW.

09/09

1800 - DURING BRIEFING WE WATCHED NEBRASKA BEAT NOTRE DAME. NEBRASKA WAS VERY LUCKY.

1815 -I WENT TO DINNER.

1840-OUT ON PATROL

1900 - (S) TRAFFIC STOP
I STOPPED A YOUNG W/F WHO WAS DRIVING A BLACK FORD PROBE. THE TAG CAME BACK AS BELONGING ON A WHITE CHEVROLET. THE VEHICLE BELONGED TO HER FRIEND WHOM SHE WAS ON HER WAY TO PICK UP. I TOLD HER SHE WAS RESPONSIBLE FOR THE VEHICLE THAT SHE WAS DRIVING. I TOLD HER IF HER GIRLFRIEND HAD BEEN DRIVING, SHE'D BE GOING TO JAIL. I GAVE HER A WRITTEN WARNING AND CUT HER LOOSE.

1945 - (D) 9-1-1 HANG-UP
SOMEONE CALLED 911 AND HUNG UP. I GOT OUT TO THE RESIDENCE AND MADE CONTACT WITH AN ELDERLY, W/F. SHE BROUGHT ME INTO HER KITCHEN TO SHOW ME HOW THE PHONE COVER FELL OFF AND SHE ACCIDENTALLY DIALED THE WRONG NUMBER. SHE WAS REALLY APPRECIATIVE OF THE FACT THAT I RESPONDED TO HER HOME SO QUICKLY. SHE SAID HER HUSBAND PASSED AWAY TWO MONTHS AGO, AND THIS MADE HER FEEL VERY SECURE. TO ME, THAT'S WHAT THIS JOB IS ALL ABOUT. IT MAKES ME KNOW THAT THIS WAS THE PROPER CAREER CHOICE EVEN IF I AM BROKE.

2015 - (S) TRAFFIC STOP
I STOPPED A CAR THAT BELONGED TO A PERSON WITH A SUSPENDED LICENSE. THE YOUNG, W/M SAID HE DIDN'T KNOW IT WAS SUSPENDED. I TOOK HIS LICENSE AND WROTE HIM A TICKET.

2045 -I STOPPED IN TO CHECK ON THE EMPLOYEES OF THE DRUG STORE THAT HAD RECENTLY BEEN ROBBED. I

PURCHASED A CRANBERRY JUICE AND LEFT.

2055 -I CALLED HOME TO CHECK MY MESSAGES. MY LITTLE GIRL HAD CALLED. I DECIDED TO GO CALL HER BACK, AND MY SON.

2130 - FG4 CALLED. I HAD CALLED HER EARLIER AND LEFT HER A MESSAGE SAYING HAPPY BIRTHDAY. SHE UNDERSTOOD WHEN I TOLD HER THAT AGAIN, BUT NOT MUCH ELSE.

2145-(S) AREA CHECK
  I RESPONDED TO ASSIST ANOTHER OFFICER. HE HAD CONDUCTED A TRAFFIC STOP OF A YOUNG, W/M. HE HAD FELONY TRAFFIC CHARGES, AND THE PERSON TOOK OFF ON HIM. SEVERAL OF US RESPONDED TO SEARCH THE AREA FOR THE YOUNG, W/M. THE DOGS (K-9) AND THE HELICOPTER WERE BROUGHT OUT. WE DIDN'T CATCH THE GUY, BUT WE KNOW WHO HE IS AND WHERE HE LIVES. THE OFFICER STILL HAD THE MAN'S LICENSE IN HIS POSSESSION. IT'S JUST A MATTER OF TIME.

0000 -I STOPPED BY FG4'S PLACE TO SEE HER ON HER BIRTHDAY. SHE MADE ME EAT SOME OF HER CHOCOLATE CAKE THAT SHE HAD RECEIVED. I WENT OVER ALL THE NEW PORTUGUESE STUFF THAT I HAD LEARNED. SHE WAS EXTREMELY IMPRESSED AND SAT AND LISTENED IN AWE. FOR A MINUTE THERE, I THOUGHT SHE WAS GOING TO CRY. I LEFT AFTER A SHORT WHILE AND SHE ASKED ME TO CALL HER THE NEXT DAY.

0130-I WENT BY TO DO A BUSINESS CHECK OF A SEVEN/ELEVEN AND WAS FLAGGED DOWN BY TWO YOUNG MALES; A BLACK AMERICAN AND A WHITE GERMAN. THE TWO MEN WERE IN A RELATIONSHIP. THEIR COMPLAINT WAS THAT THE B/M'S EX-BOYFRIEND BROKE INTO HIS CAR AND STOLE THE W/M'S TRAVEL BAG. HE SUPPOSEDLY DID THIS **OF JEALOUSY. THE W/M HAS A FRIEND WHO IS A COP AND SHE TOLD HIM THE VEHICLE NEEDED TO BE FINGER PRINTED.**

WHEN I TOLD HIM I WASN'T FINGER PRINTING, HE GOT UPSET AND LOUD. I GOT LOUDER AND TOLD THE W/M THAT PERHAPS HE SHOULD GET HER TO WORK THE CASE IF HE WASN'T SATISFIED WITH ME. THE W/M THEN SAID HOW ABOUT IF THEY CALL SOMEONE ELSE. (THEY WERE ON THE PAY PHONE CALLING THE POLICE WHEN I DROVE UP.) I TOLD THE W/M THAT WOULD BE FINE WITH ME AND HE NEEDED TO DECIDE IF THAT'S WHAT HE WANTED TO DO. THE B/M CALMED HIM DOWN AND CONVINCED HIM TO DEAL WITH ME. (THAT WAS PRETTY FUNNY. I'M SURE THE W/M WAS THINKING, "I DIDN'T CALL YOU ANYWAY".) I EXPLAINED TO THEM BOTH THAT IF I PRINTED THE VEHICLE AND FOUND THAT OTHER GUYS PRINTS, IT WOULD PROVE NOTHING. THE B/M HAD GIVEN THE GUY A KEY AND PERMISSION TO USE THE VEHICLE. IN OTHER WORDS, HIS PRINTS WERE SUPPOSED TO BE ON THE CAR. BESIDES, IT HAD RECENTLY RAINED AND I COULDN'T PRINT THE CAR IF I WANTED TO. I CONDUCTED THE HANDLING OF THE CASE IN A PROFESSIONAL MANNER. AT ONE POINT, THE W/M TOOK TIME OUT TO APOLOGIZE ABOUT HIS BEHAVIOR AND SAID THAT HE WAS JUST UPSET. I TOLD HIM IT WASN'T A PROBLEM AND THAT I HATE WHEN PEOPLE TELL ME HOW I'M GOING TO HANDLE A SITUATION. SUGGESTIONS I DON'T MIND. AT ANY RATE, BOTH MEN WERE HAPPY WHEN WE CONCLUDED AND THEY THANKED ME.

0215-I WENT TO ANOTHER SEVEN/ELEVEN TO DO MY PAPERWORK.

0305 - ANOTHER OFFICER SPOTTED A RED GRAND AM WITH A STOLEN TAG ON IT. SEVERAL UNITS, INCLUDING MYSELF, CONDUCTED A SEARCH OF THE AREA. WE WERE UNABLE TO LOCATE THE VEHICLE.

0315 -I WENT TO THE STATION TO TURN IN MY PAPERWORK. FG3 CALLED ME AND I SPOKE TO HER

BRIEFLY.

0322 - (D) LEWD ACT
I WAS DISPATCHED TO A CALL AT A LOCAL HOTEL. PERSONNEL ADVISED THAT TWO WHITE MALES WERE IN THE POOL ENGAGING IN LEWD ACTS. I BROKE FROM THE CALL TO CONDUCT A TRAFFIC STOP....

0329 - (S) TRAFFIC STOP
I STOPPED A RED ECLIPSE BECAUSE THE OWNER'S LICENSE WAS SUSPENDED. THE DRIVER WAS A YOUNG H/F. SHE GAVE ME A NAME OTHER THAN THAT OF THE OWNER AND SAID THE CAR BELONGED TO HER SISTER. WHEN I ASKED HER FOR HER LICENSE SHE SAID SHE DIDN'T HAVE IT ON HER. I NOTICED A NIGHTCLUB WRISTBAND AROUND HER WRIST. I ASKED HER HOW SHE GOT INTO THE CLUB WITHOUT AN I.D. SHE SAID SHE KNEW THE DOORMEN VERY WELL AND THEY LET HER IN WITHOUT ONE. NOT BELIEVING HER STORY, I TOLD HER SHE'D BE FACING AN ADDITIONAL CHARGE IF SHE WERE LYING ABOUT HER NAME. SHE INSISTED SHE WAS WHO SHE SAID SHE WAS. USING THE NAME SHE GAVE ME, I CHECKED FOR A LICENSE. THERE WAS NONE ISSUED TO THAT PERSON. SHE SEEMED REALLY SHOCKED BY THIS. SHE MUST HAVE THOUGHT SHE HAD PICKED THE NAME OF SOMEONE WHO AT LEAST HAD A LICENSE. I ARRESTED THE H/F FOR DRIVING WITHOUT A LICENSE. AFTER PLACING HER IN MY CAR, I SEARCHED HERS. GUESS WHAT I FOUND BELOW HER DRIVER SEAT. YOU GUESSED IT, A DRIVER LICENSE. THE NAME ON THE LICENSE WAS THE SAME AS THE VEHICLE'S REGISTERED OWNER. THE PHOTOGRAPH LOOKED EXACTLY LIKE THE WOMAN I ARRESTED. THE NERVE OF HER SHE DIDN'T TELL ME THAT SHE AND HER SISTER WERE TWINS. I CHARGED HER WITH DRIVING WITH A SUSPENDED LICENSE AND GIVING ME A FALSE NAME. I THINK SHE WAS HALF DRUNK TOO. SHE SLEPT ALL THE WAY TO JAIL.

0618 - I WRAPPED UP THE ARREST, GOT GAS, AND WENT HOME. SEE YA IN A FEW HOURS.
*OFF-DUTY UPDATE. REMEMBER MY FRIEND WHO RUNS THE AFTER SCHOOL PROGRAM AT THE ELEMENTARY SCHOOL? IF NOT, SHE ASKED ME A WHILE BACK IF I WOULD SPEAK TO THE

CHILDREN IN THE PROGRAM. WELL TODAY WAS THE DAY. I MADE IT OVER TO THE ELEMENTARY SCHOOL BETWEEN COLLEGE AND AN OFF-DUTY JOB I HAD TO GET TO. TO SAY THE LEAST, I HAD ONE OF THE MOST ENJOYABLE TIMES OF RECENT MEMORY. I SPOKE TO A GROUP OF ABOUT FIFTY CHILDREN, GRADES K-5. I SPOKE TO THEM ABOUT OBEYING THEIR PARENTS AND TEACHERS, GOOD BEHAVIOR, AND THE BENEFITS OF HARD WORK. AFTER SPEAKING TO THEM BRIEFLY, I AFFORDED THEM THE OPPORTUNITY TO ASK ME QUESTIONS. 95% OF THE QUESTIONS WERE ABOUT JAIL AND THE OTHER 5% WERE ABOUT THE "TOOLS" ON MY BELT. THEY ASKED ME EVERYTHING FROM, "WHAT DO THE BAD GUYS EAT IN JAIL?" TO "DO YOU SLEEP WITH YOUR GUN?" PRECEEDING EVERY QUESTION WAS AN, "OOH, OOH, PICK ME, PICK ME!" BEING SHOUTED OUT BY A MINIATURE HUMAN BEING ON THE EDGE OF THEIR SEAT WITH ONE ARM STRETCHED TO THE SKY, AND THAT ARM BEING SUPPORTED BY THE OTHER. AFTER THAT, EVERYONE RUSHED OUTSIDE TO SEE MY CRUISER. ONE OF THE INSTRUCTORS SHUTTLED THEM ALL THROUGH THE BACK SEAT, EXPLAINING THAT THIS IS WHERE THEY DID NOT WANT TO END UP. THAT INSTRUCTOR KEPT TURNING ON AND OFF THE LIGHTS AND SIREN AND SEEMED TO BE ENJOYING HERSELF MORE THAN THE STUDENTS. OVERALL A GREAT DAY! IT MADE ME REMEMBER THAT HELPING KIDS IS ONE OF THE PRIMARY REASONS WHY I ENTERED THE LAW ENFORCEMENT FIELD.

09/10

1745 - (S) TRAFFIC STOP

ON THE WAY TO BRIEFING, I STOPPED A CAR BECAUSE THE REGISTERED OWNER'S LICENSE WAS SUSPENDED. THE OWNER, A YOUNG, B/M WAS IN THE BACK SEAT. A YOUNG, B/F WAS DRIVING. HER BOYFRIEND, ANOTHER YOUNG, B/M WAS IN THE FRONT PASSENGER SEAT. THE OWNER SAID HE WAS LETTING THE B/F DRIVE BECAUSE HE KNEW HIS LICENSE WAS NO GOOD. HE SAID HE STRAIGHTENED THE PROBLEM, BUT HADN'T YET GONE TO GET A NEW ONE. I TOLD THEM THEY COULD BE ON THEIR WAY AFTER I VERIFIED THAT THE B/F HAD A VALID LICENSE. I RAN HER NAME AND FOUND OUT SHE WAS WANTED. THERE WAS A WARRANT FOR HER ARREST FOR ILLEGAL USE OF CREDIT CARDS. SHE SAID SHE HAD GONE TO COURT AND A REPAYMENT AGREEMENT WAS ARRANGED. SHE WAS TO PAY MONTHLY INSTALLMENTS UNTIL THE TOTAL AMOUNT WAS COVERED. SHE SHOWED ME A BILL FOR THE UPCOMING INSTALLMENT. I ARRESTED HER ANYWAY. I CAN'T GO BY THAT PAPERWORK BECAUSE IT WAS NOT A COURT ORDERED DOCUMENTATION. I DID, HOWEVER, TAKE THE PAPERWORK SO THAT SHE COULD HAVE IT FOR JAIL PERSONNEL. THEY MAY HAVE BEEN ABLE TO ANALYZE IT AND DETERMINE WHETHER OR NOT THE WARRANT SHOULD HAVE BEEN OUTSTANDING.

2100 - FG3 CALLED. SHE WANTED TO KNOW IF I

GET MAD WHEN SHE CALLS ME. I GUESS MY TONE OF VOICE ISN'T ALWAYS PLEASANT. I TOLD HER, "SOMETIMES I'M BUSY, AND IF I SAY I'LL CALL YOU BACK I WILL. DON'T KEEP CALLING". (NOW THAT I'M WRITING IT, IT SOUNDS REALLY MEAN OF ME. I TAKE IT BACK.) SHE HAD CALLED ME WHILE I WAS MAKING THE ARREST AND I TOLD HER I'D CALL HER BACK. I GUESS I DIDN'T GET BACK TO HER QUICK ENOUGH BECAUSE SHE CALLED AGAIN BEFORE I FINISHED WHAT I WAS DOING.

2136 - (D) MISSING PERSON

A GROWN WOMAN CALLED IN AND SAID HER PARENTS WERE MISSING. SHE SAID THEY HAD BEEN GONE SINCE

THIS MORNING. BEFORE I COULD GET THERE, SHE CALLED IN AND CANCELLED. SHE SAID THEY HAD RETURNED. SHE'S LUCKY. I WAS GOING TO GO OVER THERE AND TELL HER THAT HER GROWN BUTT NEEDS TO BE MISSING FROM HER PARENTS HOUSE. NOT REALLY.

2110-I WENT TO DINNER.

2130 - MY FRIEND (GUY) PAGED ME. I CALLED HIM BACK AND SPOKE A WHILE.

2157-I CALLED FG4 AND REVIEWED MY PORTUGUESE VOCABULARY WITH HER.

2230 - (S) TRAFFIC STOP
   THE OWNER OF THE CAR HAD A SUSPENDED LICENSE. THERE WERE THREE YOUNG, H/M'S INSIDE. THE OWNER WAS IN THE BACK SEAT. I ASKED THE DRIVER, WHOSE LICENSE WAS VALID, "HOW COME YOU'RE DRIVING HIS CAR?" HE SAID, "I'M DRIVING BECAUSE HE'S TIRED." I SAID, "HIS LICENSE IS SUSPENDED SO TIRED OR NOT, HE'S FORTUNATE TO HAVE NOT BEEN DRIVING. THE OWNER SAID HE KNEW THAT AND THAT'S WHY HE WASN'T DRIVING. THE FRIEND THAT WAS DRIVING MUST HAVE THOUGHT HE WOULD GET IN TROUBLE REGARDLESS. GOOD FRIEND LOOKIN' OUT FOR HIS BOY.

2228 - I'M VERY SLEEPY I'VE GOT TO GET BUSY. THAT'S PROBABLY WHY I THINK 10:28 COMES AFTER 10:30.

2326 - (D) DISTURBANCE
   I WAS DISPATCHED TO A RESTAURANT. THERE WAS AN ARGUMENT BETWEEN AN EMPLOYEE AND A CUSTOMER. ON THE WAY THERE, I STOPPED A CAR FOR A SUSPENDED LICENSE.

2333 - (S) TRAFFIC STOP
   ANOTHER OFFICER PICKED UP MY CALL AT THE RESTAURANT. THE DRIVER, WHO'S LICENSE WAS SUSPENDED THREE TIMES, WAS A YOUNG, W/M. HE WAS WITH HIS YOUNG, W/F. HE WAS TAKING HER TO GET SOMETHING TO EAT. INSTEAD OF

IMMEDIATELY TOSSING HIM IN MY BACK SEAT, I LET THE TWO OF THEM TALK WHILE I DID MY PAPERWORK. THEY WANTED TO KNOW IF THEY COULD USE MY HANDCUFFS AFTER IT WAS ALL OVER. I ARRESTED HIM IN THE LOT OF A HOTEL. I CALLED HOTEL SECURITY OVER TO ASK IF THE W/M COULD LEAVE HIS CAR IN THEIR LOT FOR A WHILE. (THE W/F DIDN'T HAVE A LICENSE.) HE SAID HE COULD, THEN PROCEEDED TO GO INTO HIS POLICE STORIES. HE WAS AN ARABIC GUY AND SAID HIS GOAL WAS TO BECOME A LAW ENFORCEMENT OFFICER. I HEARD HIM OUT AND GOT BACK TO MY PAPERWORK. HE LINGERED AROUND UNTIL I HEADED OFF TO JAIL. ON THE WAY THERE I FOUND OUT THE W/M HAD A BASEBALL SCHOLARSHIP TO MARSHALL (I THINK), BUT HURT HIS KNEE. NOW HE'S REHABILITATED AND WANTS TO WALK ON AT THE UNIVERSITY OF FLORIDA.

0040 - (D) DISORDERLY INTOXICATION
AN AREA HOTEL CALLED ABOUT A PATRON WHO WAS CAUSING A DISTURBANCE. MY SUPERVISOR AND I ARRIVED TO FIND A DRUNKEN, BRITISH GUY. WE GOT HIM CALMED DOWN AND GAVE HIM ONE OF OUR OLD FAVORITES: "WE DON'T WANT TO HAVE TO COME BACK OUT HERE TONIGHT..." HE AGREED TO GO IN AND GO TO BED. HIS FRIEND SAID HE'D MAKE SURE HE'D STAY THERE.

0108 - ONE OF OUR HELICOPTER PILOTS ASKED IF THERE WERE ANY OFFICERS IN HIS AREA. HE SPOTTED SOME ACTIVITY IN A WOODED AREA. THE AREA WAS NEARBY AND I HEADED OVER. SO DID ABOUT FIVE OTHERS. WE FOUND AN OLDER, W/M IN A FOUR WHEEL DRIVE AND A HOMELESS, W/M (40'S). THEY WERE IN DIFFERENT AREAS. THE GUY IN THE TRUCK SAID HE WAS DEPRESSED AND WENT OUT THERE TO THINK THINGS OVER. ANOTHER OFFICER DEALT WITH HIM. THE HOMELESS GUY SAID HE LIVES OUT THERE. HE SAID HE USED TO SLEEP ABOUT 20 FEET FROM WHERE WE WERE, WHICH WAS CLOSER TO THE WATER. HE SAID HE HAD TO MOVE BECAUSE THE SNAKES KEPT BOTHERING HIM. ANOTHER OFFICER RAN HIS NAME TO SEE IF HE WAS WANTED. HE WAS NOT. THE W/M SAID HE ENJOYED LIVING OUTSIDE. I TOLD HIM THERE

WAS NOTHING WRONG WITH THAT. AFTER ALL, THAT'S HOW IT WAS DONE IN THE BEGINNING. (THAT'S RIGHT ALL YOU SPOILED BRATS WITH YOUR HOUSES, AND RUNNING WATER, AND FANCY COMPUTERS.)

0145 -I WENT TO FEED MY FACE AGAIN.

0159-(D) ALARM

THIS WAS AN ALARM AT A BUSINESS. IT WAS UNFOUNDED.

0225 - (S) TRAFFIC STOP
  I STOPPED A YOUNG, B/F, AND A YOUNG, B/M IN A BLACK CADILLAC ESCALADE S.U.V. BECAUSE THEY WERE DRIVING AN ESCALADE WHILE BLACK, YOU SAY? NO, BECAUSE THE TAG CAME BACK TO A RED FORD. THEY SHOWED ME THE TEMPORARY REGISTRATION THAT REFLICTED THE TAG BEING TRANSFERRED FROM THE FORD TO THE CADILLAC.

0237 - (S) TRAFFIC STOP
  I STOPPED A CAR BECAUSE THE OWNER HAD A VALID FLORIDA I.D. CARD ONLY. I DISCOVERED THE DRIVER WAS A YOUNG, W/ M FROM THE CZHEK REPUBLIC AND HAD AN INTERNATIONAL LICENSE. HE SAID WAS NOW LIVING IN FLORIDA. I TOLD HIM HE NEEDED TO GET A FLORIDA LICENSE IF HE PLANNED ON STAYING.

0245 - (S) TRAFFIC STOP
  I STOPPED A GUY WHOSE LICENSE WAS SUSPENDED 9 TIMES. REVOKED 4 TIMES AND SHOWED A D.U.I. CONVICTION. HE WAS A YOUNG, JAMAICAN, B/M. I CALLED HIS GIRLFRIEND FOR HIM TO SAVE HIM A TOW FEE. (HE NEEDS TO SAVE HIS MONEY TO PAY FOR HIS TRAFFIC TICKETS.) SHE CAME OUT AND PICKED UP HIS CAR AND WE WERE OFF TO JAIL.

0430 - (D) PETIT THEFT
  I WENT TO MEET WITH THE MANAGER OF A RESTAURANT. TWO BLACK MALES HAD EATEN AND ONE TOOK OFF. THE OTHER WAITED THERE FOR ME TO ARRIVE. THE MANAGER WANTED THE B/M THAT REMAINED TO PAY THE ENTIRE BILL.

THE B/M SAID HE WAS WILLING TO PAY FOR WHAT HE ATE, BUT NOT WILLING TO PAY THE WHOLE THING. I SIDED WITH THE B/M. I TOLD THE MANAGER I WOULDN'T WANT TO PAY FOR SOMEONE ELSE IF THEY RAN OUT ON A BILL. THE B/M SAID THAT WHERE HE CAME FROM (HE WAS VISITING OUR AREA.), THE WAITER ASKS IF THE MEAL WILL BE ON THE SAME, OR SEPARATE TABS. THAT SEEMED REASONABLE TO ME. THE MANAGER WENT AHEAD AND TOOK MONEY FOR THE PORTION EATEN BY THAT B/M. THE B/M HAD SAID HE DIDN'T KNOW THE GUY THAT RAN OUT AND THAT THEY JUST MET. AFTER LETTING HIM KNOW THAT I DIDN'T BELIEVE THAT FOR ONE SECOND, I TOLD HIM HE WAS FREE TO LEAVE. THE MANAGER LATER SAID HE ONLY CALLED TO SCARE THE GUY. HE SAID THEY USUALLY PAY UP WHEN HE THREATENS TO DO THAT.

0509 -I WANTED TO GET OUT AND FIND SOMETHING ELSE BEFORE GOING HOME, BUT MY COMPUTER WAS ACTING UP. I'M LESS MOTIVATED WHEN IT'S FAILING. I'LL GO EAT AGAIN AND STUDY A BIT. GOODBYE.

09/13

1743-(S) TRAFFIC STOP
I STOPPED A YOUNG H/M ON THE INTERSTATE WHILE ON MY WAY TO WORK. HE WAS DRIVING WITH A SUSPENDED LICENSE. BEFORE HAULING HIM IN, I LET HIM HAVE ONE LAST SMOKE AND CALL HIS GIRLFRIEND TO PICK UP HIS VEHICLE. YET ANOTHER WHO WAS GOING TO GET HIS LICENSE TAKEN CARE OF TOMORROW. GO FIGURE I CAN'T WIN THE LOTTERY, BUT CAN CATCH ALL THESE FOLKS THE DAY BEFORE THEY WERE GOING TO GET THEIR LICENSES TAKEN CARE OF.

2030-I WENT TO EAT.

2100-I WENT TO THE HOSPITAL TO DELIVER SOME PAPERWORK TO ANOTHER OFFICER. HE WAS ASSIGNED TO ANOTHER UNIT AND APPARENTLY INFREQUENTLY HANDLED THE TYPE OF CASE THAT HE WAS WORKING. I THINK IT WAS A DOMESTIC BATTERY OR SOMETHING OF THAT NATURE.

2200 - (S) TRAFFIC STOP
I STOPPED A YOUNG, B/F WHO HAD AN EXPIRED LICENSE AND WAS POSSIBLY WANTED FOR AGGRAVATED ASSAULT. SHE WAS ABLE TO PRODUCE AN I.D. CARD ONLY. SHE LOST HER LICENSE A WHILE AGO AND SOMEONE TOLD HER IT WAS SUFFICIENT FOR DRIVING. I TOLD HER I COULD VERIFY THE VALIDITY OF HER LICENSE WITH HER I.D., BUT IT WAS NOT SUFFICIENT FOR DRIVING. WHEN I EXPLAINED TO HER THAT SHE WAS POSSIBLY WANTED SHE BECAME HYSTERICAL. SHE COULDN'T STOP CRYING. SHE SAID SHE WAS A CHRISTIAN AND HAS NEVER BEEN IN TROUBLE A DAY IN HER LIFE.   THE WARRANT WAS CONFIRMED GOING BY JUST HER NAME. THE DESCRIPTION OF THE WANTED PERSON WAS OFF AS FAR AS HEIGHT AND WEIGHT. I LET THE GIRL CALL HER MOTHER AND SHE ARRIVED SHORTLY THEREAFTER. THE GIRL ALSO SAID SHE WAS ON HER WAY TO HER RECENTLY OBTAINED JOB. SHE WAS A COUNSELOR AT A JUVENILE DRUG TREATMENT FACILITY. SHE SAID THEY CONDUCTED A BACKGROUND CHECK AND CLEARED HER BEFORE HIRING HER. AFTER A LENGTHY ROADSIDE INVESTIGATION, INCLUDING TELEPHONING THE

WARRANTS AND RECORDS DIVISIONS, I DECIDED NOT TO ARREST THE B/F. THERE WERE TOO MANY DISCREPANCIES TO CONSIDER. I ALSO LEARNED THE B/F HAD A ROOMMATE A WHILE BACK WHO MATCHED THE WANTED PERSON'S DESCRIPTION. THE ROOMMATE ALSO HAD A POLICE RECORD THAT INCLUDED AGGRAVATED STALKING. THE B/F HAD LOST HER LICENSE WHILE LIVING WITH THE OTHER FEMALE. MY BELIEF WAS THAT THE EX-ROOMMATE HAD BEEN USING HER NAME. THE B/F FOUND IT HARD TO BELIEVE A FRIEND COULD BE INVOLVED. HER MOTHER SAID, "YOU SEE I TOLD YOU ABOUT THOSE SO-CALLED FRIENDS OF YOURS." I DIDN'T ARREST HER, BUT I TOOK ALL HER INFORMATION. IF IT TURNS OUT TO BE HER, I KNOW WHERE TO GO AND GET HER. (WHILE CONDUCTING MY LITTLE ROADSIDE INVESTIGATION, I WAS PLEASED TO HELP A COUPLE WHO PULLED OFF THE ROAD TO ASK ME FOR DIRECTION.)

2233 - I WENT TO A GAS MART TO GAS UP. IT WAS VERY SLOW OUT AND I WAS GETTING SLEEPY. I PURCHASED SOME JUICE AND CRACKER JACK'S WITH HOPES THAT IT WOULD PEP ME UP. MY CRACKER JACK PRIZE WAS A LITTLE STICKER THAT I STUCK ON MY CLIPBOARD.

2341-(D) PETIT THEFT
I WAS DISPATCHED TO A THEFT AT A HOTEL. I HAD TO BREAK FROM THE THEFT TO RESPOND TO AN EMERGENCY CALL...

2345-(D) 9-1-1 HANG UP
THE VICTIM WAS A YOUNG W/M. HIS EX-GIRLFRIEND, A YOUNG W/F, WHOSE APARTMENT THEY WERE AT SAID HE HAD TRIED TO KILL HIMSELF. THE TWO BROKE UP ABOUT THREE WEEKS AGO AND HE WAS APPARENTLY UNABLE TO MOVE ON WITH HIS LIFE. I ASKED HIM WHAT HE WAS STILL DOING HANGING OUT OVER THERE IF THEY WERE BROKEN UP. HE SAID BECAUSE THEY WERE STILL GOOD FRIENDS. HE THEN ASKED ME, "HAVEN'T YOU EVER REMAINED GOOD FRIENDS WITH AN EX-GIRLFRIEND?" I ANSWERED, "NO. WHAT'S THE POINT OF THAT?" (BESIDES, I DON'T HAVE EX'S, JUST GIRLS I'VE LOST CONTACT WITH.) THE W/M, WHO WAS SOMEWHAT INTOXICATED, INSISTED HE HAD NOT TRIED TO KILL HIMSELF. THE W/F SAID THE TWO STRUGGLED AS SHE ATTEMPTED TO

TAKE A KNIFE FROM HIM. THAT WAS WHEN SHE THREATENED TO CALL 9-1-1. SHE DID IN FACT DIAL THE NUMBERS BEFORE HANGING UP THE PHONE. WHEN WE ARRIVED (3 OR 4 OTHER OFFICERS AND MYSELF), THE W/M WAS LOCKED IN THE BATHROOM. HE HAD ABOUT FIVE SLASHES ON HIS WRIST THAT HE INITIALLY REFUSED TO SHOW ME. (INITIALLY, MEANING PRE-YOU GO TO JAIL NOW SPEECH) I ASKED HIM WHAT THAT WAS ALL ABOUT IF HE WASN'T TRYING TO KILL HIMSELF. HE SAID THAT WAS NOTHING. WHILE SITTING IN THE TUB, HE DECIDED TO USE HIS KEY CHAIN TO "PLAY" WITH HIS WRIST. THAT WAS ALL I NEEDED

TO HEAR. I TOOK HIM INTO CUSTODY SO HE COULD RECEIVE A PSYCHOLOGICAL EVALUATION. THE W/M PLEADED FOR ME NOT TO TAKE HIM. HE WAS A MAKE-UP ARTIST. HE SAID HE NEEDED TO BE ON THE SET OF A MOVIE IN THE MORNING. HE SAID HE WAS GOING TO LOSE THE MOVIE IF HE WASN'T THERE BY 6:00 AM. I TOLD HIM I FELT BAD ABOUT THAT, BUT I HAD A RESPONSIBILITY TO GET HIM HELP IF HE PRESENTED A THREAT TO HIMSELF OR OTHERS DUE TO A POSSIBLE MENTAL ILLNESS. HE CONTINUED TO INSIST THAT HE WAS NEITHER MENTALLY ILL, NOR SUICIDAL. I TOOK HIM ANYWAY. HE HAD ASKED IF HE COULD SPEAK TO THE W/F BEFORE WE LEFT. I TOLD HIM HE COULD IF SHE WANTED TO SPEAK TO HIM. SHE DIDN'T WANT TO.

0106-(D) MAN DOWN
I WAS DISPATCHED A CALL ADVISING A W/M WAS PASSED OUT NEAR A CONVENIENCE STORE. MY AREA PARTNER GOT THERE BEFORE I DID AND SAID HE WAS JUST DRUNK.

0108-I WENT TO EAT AGAIN.

0200 - MY SUPERVISOR ASKED ME TO MEET WITH HIM. I HAD NO IDEA WHAT FOR. HE WANTED TO APOLOGIZE FOR HIS LACK OF PATIENCE EARLIER IN DEALING WITH THE MAKE-UP ARTIST. WHILE I WAS CONVERSING WITH HIM AND TRYING TO FEEL HIM OUT, MY SUPERVISOR WAS LIKE, "YOU TRIED TO KILL YOURSELF AND NOW YOU'RE COMING WITH US. END OF DISCUSSION." I IMMEDIATELY KNEW HE WAS GOING WITH ME AS WELL. I JUST WANTED TO EASE HIM OUT MENTALLY TO

MAKE IT AS SMOOTH AS POSSIBLE. ON THE SCENE, I DIDN'T THINK TWICE ABOUT MY SUPERVISOR'S COMMENTS. I KNEW IT WAS, AS WE SAY, "MY SCENE". HE JUST WANTED TO REITERATE THAT THOUGH AND I APPRECIATED IT. GREAT GUY - MORE TIME ON THE JOB - LESS PATIENT.

0247 -I CHECKED IN ON A FEW 24 HOUR ESTABLISHMENTS. THEY WERE ALL FINE.

0300 -I WENT TO THE STATION TO TURN IN MY PAPERWORK AND MAKE A PHONE CALL. MY HIGH SCHOOL SWEETHEART HAD LEFT ME A MESSAGE AND I WAS RETURNING IT.

0330-I PULLED INTO A GAS STATION IN THE HEART OF TOWN FOR SOME HEATED SALTED CASHEWS AND TO STUDY.

0515-(D) ALARM
  I WAS DISPATCHED TO AN ALARM AT A STORE IN A STRIP MALL. I CALLED THE MALL SECURITY AND TURNED IT OVER TO THEM.

0530 - I'M GOING TO EASE IN THE HOMEWARD DIRECTION AND I SHALL SPEAK TO YOU TOMORROW.

09/14

2115-I GOT OUT OF SCHOOL AND HEADED TO WORK. OF COURSE I HAD TO EAT BEFORE GETTING STARTED.

2202 -I WENT TO A NIGHTCLUB IN MY AREA. IT WAS VERY QUIET.

2255 -I WENT TO CRUISE AROUND.

2301 - FG3 CALLED ME AND WE SPOKE BRIEFLY.

2310 -(S) TRAFFIC STOP
  I STOPPED A GREEN TOYOTA WITH A TAG ON IT THAT CAME BACK UNASSIGNED. THE DRIVER, A YOUNG, W/F, SHOWED ME HER VALID REGISTRATION AND I CUT HER LOOSE. IN PARTING SHE SAID TO ME, "I WONDERED WHY YOU WERE STOPPING ME.I SAID TO MYSELF, I KNOW I'M NOT SPEEDING."

2320 - (S) SUSPICIOUS VEHICLE
  WHILE RUNNING TAGS IN A NIGHTCLUB PARKING LOT, I CAME ACROSS A RED CAMARO. THE TAG THAT WAS ON IT BELONGED ON A TURQUOISE SATURN. I WASN'T GOING TO WAIT AROUND FOR THE DRIVER TO COME OUT OF THE CLUB. HE GOT AWAY WITH THAT ONE. HAD IT BEEN STOLEN, IT WOULD HAVE BEEN A DIFFERENT STORY.

2357 - (S) TRAFFIC STOP
  I STOPPED A PURPLE CAR WITH A TAG ON IT THAT CAME BACK TO GREEN ONE. THEY PRESENTED ME WITH A VALID REGISTRATION AND I LET THEM GO.

0026 - (S) TRAFFIC STOP
  I STOPPED A YOUNG, B/F WHO WAS DRIVING A CAR WITH A TAG THAT WASN'T ASSIGNED TO IT. SHE EXPLAINED THE VEHICLE BELONGED TO A FRIEND OF HER'S. HE LET HER USE IT TO PICK UP ANOTHER FRIEND. I GAVE HER A WRITTEN WARNING AND TOLD HER SHE WAS RESPONSIBLE FOR ANY VEHICLE THAT SHE CHOSE TO DRIVE. I THEN SAID, "AFTER I CHECK YOUR NAME AND VERIFY THAT YOU'RE NOT A MURDERER, YOU CAN GO." SHE REPLIED, "DO I LOOK LIKE A MURDERER?

I WOULD BE A FINE MURDERER." I SAID, "OH, SO YOU JUST KNOW YOU'RE FINE, HUH?" SHE SAID THE GUYS IN FLORIDA MADE HER FEEL THAT WAY. SHE'S FRENCH CANADIAN AND RECENTLY MOVED HERE FROM CANADA. SHE SAID THEY GIVE HER SO MUCH ATTENTION THAT NOW SHE JUST THROWS ON SOME SHORT SHORTS AND GOES OUT AND SUCKS IT ALL UP. (SHE WAS WEARING SOME "DAISY DUKES" AND A SPANDEX BLOUSE.) WHILE I WAS WRITING HER THE WARNING, WE HEARD SOMEONE IN THE DISTANCE WHISTLING. SHE SAID, "YOU HEAR THAT? SOMEONE'S WHISTLING AT ME." I SAID, "HOW DO YOU KNOW THEY'RE WHISTLING AT YOU? SHE SAID, "THEY COULD BE WHISTLING AT YOU. YOU'RE FINE TOO." SHE SAID HER EX-BOYFRIEND WAS ABUSIVE AND CONTINUES TO HARASS HER. SHE WANTED TO KNOW IF SHE COULD CONTACT ME LATER FOR ADVICE ON DEALING WITH HIM. SHE SAID SHE DIDN'T WANT ME TO SHOW UP AT HIS HOUSE WITH MY BIG SHERIFF CAR OR ANYTHING, BUT WANTED TO KNOW WHAT OPTIONS SHE HAD. I SAID I'LL GIVE YOU ADVICE AND YOU CAN TEACH ME FRENCH. I GAVE HER MY CARD AND CLEARED THE STOP.

0045 -I PULLED INTO THE LOT OF A POPULAR NIGHTCLUB. THERE WERE SEVERAL OFFICERS FROM ANOTHER DEPARTMENT WORKING THE CLUB. I SPOKE BRIEFLY TO A YOUNG B/F OFFICER WHO WAS STANDING OUT IN FRONT OF THE CLUB.

0109 - (S) TRAFFIC STOP
   I STOPPED A YOUNG W/M FOR HAVING AN UNASSIGNED TAG ON HIS CAR. HE SHOWED ME A VALID REGISTRATION AND CLEARED UP THAT CONCERN. I TOLD HIM TO LET TO ME CHECK HIS LICENSE AND HE COULD BE ON HIS WAY. THE YOUNG MAN'S LICENSE WAS SUSPENDED AND I ARRESTED HIM. I EXPLAINED TO HIM HIS CHARGE AND WHAT IT WOULD TAKE FOR HIM TO GET OUT OF JAIL. I LET HIM GO BACK TO HIS CAR AND TELL HIS FRIENDS (3 OTHER W/M'S) WHAT THE DEAL WAS.   THEY TOOK HIS CAR AND SAID THEY WOULD BAIL HIM OUT SHORTLY. WHILE I WORKED ON MY PAPERWORK, HE CONVERSED WITH ME FROM THE BACKSEAT. WE DISCUSSED THE STATE OF THE ART STEREO SYSTEM THAT HE HAD IN HIS CAR. HE SAID HE INITIALLY

THOUGHT HE WAS BEING PULLED OVER BECAUSE IT WAS CRANKED TOO LOUD. I TOLD HIM I DID HEAR IT, BUT DIDN'T PULL HIM FOR THAT REASON. HE ALSO TALKED ABOUT HIS JOB. HE WORKED FOR A SOFTWARE MANUFACTURER IN A CLEAN ROOM. THE COMPANY FIRED HIM, BUT RECENTLY HIRED HIM BACK. SOMEONE SENT HIM A CHAIN LETTER REFERENCEING A CHILD WITH AN INCUREABLE DISEASE. IT URGED READERS TO CONTRIBUTE AND $1.00 OR $5.00 FOR THE KID'S TREATMENT. THE W/M MEANT TO SEND IT TO A FRIEND OF HIS BUT PUSHED THE WRONG BUTTON. HE INADVERTANTLY SENT IT TO EVERYONE AT HIS COMPANY. HE SAID IT ALWAYS BACKFIRES WHEN HE TRIES TO DO THE RIGHT THING.

0237-TRAFFIC STOP

ON MY WAY BACK FROM JAIL, I STOPPED A YOUNG, B/ F. THE TAG ON THE CAR WAS NOT ASSIGNED AND THE REGISTERED OWNER'S LICENSE WAS SUSPENDED. THE B/ F DRIVER SAID THE CAR BELONGED TO HER FRIEND WHO WAS INSIDE THE NEARBY NIGHTCLUB. SHE SAID SHE JUST LEFT BECAUSE SHE HAD TO GO TO THE RESTROOM. I ASKED HER WHY SHE DIDN'T GO INSIDE THE CLUB. SHE SAID SHE HAD BEEN IN THE PARKING LOT ALL NIGHT BECAUSE SHE DIDN'T FEEL LIKE DEALING WITH THE CLUB SCENE. SHE SAID SHE WAS GOING TO PEE IN THE PARKING LOT, BUT DIDN'T WANT TO GET CAUGHT AND ARRESTED. WHEN I ASKED HER FOR HER LICENSE SHE SAID SHE DIDN'T HAVE ONE. SHE SAID THAT'S WHY SHE COULDN'T GET INTO THE CLUB TO USE THEIR RESTROOM. I RAN HER NAME AND FOUND OUT SHE WAS TELLING THE TRUTH. SHE DIDN'T HAVE A LICENSE. SHE DID, HOWEVER, HAVE A FLORIDA IDENTIFICATION CARD AND IT HAD 5 SUSPENSIONS. THAT'S WHAT HAPPENS WHEN PEOPLE WITHOUT A LICENSE RECEIVE TRAFFIC INFRACTIONS THEY SUSPEND THEIR I.D. CARDS. THOUGH SHE PLEADED WITH ME TO NOT ARREST HER, I DID JUST THAT. SHE SAID ALL SHE WAS DOING WAS USING THE RESTROOM. I CONTACTED HER BOYFRIEND AND HE AND HER STEPFATHER CAME AND PICKED UP THE CAR. SHE HAD TRIED A FEW OTHER DUDES BEFORE THAT ONE. THEY WERE UNWILLING TO GO DOWN TO THE JAIL AND BAIL HER OUT. I THINK EVEN THAT ONE HAD INITIALLY

SAID NO. (LESSON FOR THE LADIES: I'M SURE YOUR MAN LOVES YOU TO DEATH, BUT DON'T BE CALLIN' HIM AT 3AM TALKIN' 'BOUT BAILIN' YOU OUT OF JAIL, ESPECIALLY IF HE'S SLEEPING.) SHE WAS A FUNNY GIRL AND I THINK SHE MAY HAVE BEEN A BIT HIGH. THE DRESS SHE WAS WEARING WAS SLEEVELESS. SHE SAID, "I KNOW IT'S GONNA BE COLD IN THE JAIL CAN I GET A SHIRT OUT OF THE CAR?" HER BOYFRIEND FOUND A "CIRCLE K" SHIRT IN THE TRUNK AND I GAVE IT TO HER. I ASKED WHERE SHE GOT THAT FROM. SHE SAID, "THAT'S WHERE I USED TO WORK." I SAID, "SO YOU JUST KEPT THE PEOPLE'S SHIRT?" SHE SAID, "YEP." AS I WORKED ON MY PAPERWORK, SHE WAS HALF LAID OUT IN THE BACKSEAT. I ASKED FOR HER FOR HER PERSONAL INFORMATION TO FILL IN THE BLANKS. SHE TOLD ME TO STOP ASKING SO MANY QUESTIONS BECAUSE SHE WAS TRYING TO SLEEP. SHE SLEPT ALL THE WAY TO JAIL.

0445 -I WENT TO THE STATION TO TURN IN MY PAPERWORK.

0450 - I WENT TO BREAKFAST.

0458 -I CALLED FG3 BACK. SHE HAD CALLED ME DURING THE LAST ARREST AND I TOLD HER I WAS BUSY. SHE WAKES UP IN THE MIDDLE OF THE NIGHT AND CALLS ME. SHE'S GETTING ACCLIMATED TO MY SCREWED UP SCHEDULE. POOR THING.

0614 – I HEADED TO THE HOUSE. – TALK TO YOU IN A FEW DAYS.

09/18

1800-BRIEFING

1820 -I WENT TO DINNER.

1842 -I WENT OUT ON PATROL.

2100-I WENT TO WASH AND GAS UP THE CRUISER.

2130 - MY COMPUTER'S BEEN DOWN ALL NIGHT. I THINK I'VE FORGOTTEN HOW TO BE A POLICE WITHOUT IT. AS YOU KNOW, IT ACCOUNTS FOR ABOUT 95% OF MY SELF-INITIATED ACTIVITY.

2135 - (S) TRAFFIC STOP
   I STOPPED A YOUNG, W/M WHO WAS DRIVING A BLUE FORD PICK-UP. HIS LICENSE WAS SUSPENDED, BUT HE ACTED AS IF THAT WAS NEWS TO HIM. I GAVE HIM THE BENEFIT OF THE DOUBT AND DIDN'T TAKE HIM IN. I DID, HOWEVER, WRITE HIM A TICKET AND TAKE HIS LICENSE.

2143-(S) TRAFFIC STOP
   I STOPPED A WHITE CHEVY ON THE INTERSTATE BECAUSE IT HAD AN UNREADABLE TEMP TAG. THE DRIVER WAS A YOUNG, W/M AND THE PASSENGER WAS HIS GIRLFRIEND, A YOUNG, W/F. HE HAD NO LICENSE WHATSOEVER. I ASKED HIM WHAT HE WAS DOING DRIVING. HE SAID HIS GIRLFRIEND, WHO WAS EIGHT MONTHS PREGNANT, WAS HAVING PAINS AND THEY WERE ENROUTE TO THE HOSPITAL. I WENT AROUND TO TALK TO THE W/F. SHE WAS VERY PREGNANT AND SAID SHE WAS IN FACT EXPERIENCING SOME PAIN. I ASKED HER IF SHE NEEDED ME TO HAVE RESCUE RESPOND TO TREAT HER. SHE SAID SHE WASN'T IN THAT MUCH PAIN. I TOLD THEM BOTH THAT HE, THE W/M, SHOULD NOT HAVE BEEN DRIVING WITHOUT A LICENSE. A MEDICAL OR OTHER EMERGENCY IS UNDERSTANDABLE. HOWEVER, IF SHE DIDN'T NEED ME TO HAVE AN AMBULANCE RESPOND TO THE SCENE, IT WAS OBVIOUSLY NOT AN EMERGENCY. THE W/F, WHO HAD A VALID LICENSE, DROVE THE REST OF THE WAY.

2150 - (S) TRAFFIC STOP

WHILE STILL ON THE INTERSTATE, I STOPPED A BLUE CHEVY. THE TAG DIDN'T COME BACK TO THE CAR. IT WAS OCCUPIED BY THREE YOUNG, HISPANIC MALES. THE DRIVER SPOKE VERY LITTLE ENGLISH, BUT WAS ABLE TO TELL ME THAT IT WAS HIS FRIEND'S CAR. THE H/M, WHO WAS EXTREMELY POLITE AND COOPERATIVE, SHOWED ME A PIECE OF PAPER THAT INDICATED THE TAG HAD BEEN TRANSFERRED TO THAT VEHICLE FROM ANOTHER ONE. AFTER CHECKING THE VALIDITY OF HIS LICENSE, I LET THEM GO.

2200 - (S) TRAFFIC STOP

I STOPPED A SMALL, WHITE PICK-UP THAT HAD A PARTIALLY OBSURED TEMPORARY TAG. THE OLDER, B/M DRIVER GOT OUT WITH SOMEWHAT OF AN ATTITUDE. HE ASKED ME WHY HE HAD BEEN STOPPED. I POINTED TO THE CRAP IN BACK OF HIS TRUCK THAT WAS BLOCKING THE TAG. HIS ATTITUDE SUDDENLY CHANGED AND HE BEGAN TO READJUST THE "CRAP". AFTER MAKING SURE HE WAS "GOOD-TO-GO" I CUT HIM LOOSE.

2245 - (S) TRAFFIC STOP

I STOPPED A B/F (40'S) FOR DRIVING WITH A SUSPENDED LICENSE. SHE WAS UNAWARE OF THE SUSPENSION. I TOLD HER IT WAS SUSPENDED FOR FAILING TO MAINTAIN INSURANCE COVERAGE ON A REGISTERED VEHICLE. SHE SAID SHE CANCELLED THE INSURANCE ON HER OTHER VEHICLE. SHE SAID SHE DIDN'T HAVE THE MONEY TO MAINTAIN COVERAGE ON TWO VEHICLES, ESPECIALLY WHEN ONE WAS BROKEN DOWN. I WROTE HER A TICKET AND TOOK HER LICENSE.

2305 - I STOPPED BY A CHICKEN RESTAURANT AND GOT SOME WINGS AND "DIRTY RICE".

2331-(D) 9-1-1 HANG-UP

THIS OCCURRED AT A LOCAL RESORT. I TURNED IT OVER TO THEIR SECURITY. I TOLD HIM TO CALL US IF THERE WAS ANYTHING TO THE CALL. (MOST ARE ACCIDENTAL)

0019-(S) TRAFFIC STOP

I STOPPED A SMALL RED PICK-UP WITH A TAG THAT HAD BEEN EXPIRED FOR ABOUT ONE MONTH. THE OCCUPANTS WERE TWO YOUNG, WHITE, FRENCH FEMALES. THE DRIVER, WHO WAS WEARING A LOW BUTTONED SWEATER, SAID THE TRUCK WAS OWNED BY BOTH GIRLS. THEY WERE HERE ON A WORK VISA AND WORKED ALL THE TIME. THEY HADN'T HAD TIME TO RENEW THE REGISTRATION. THE DRIVER EVENTUALLY BUTTONED UP HER SWEATER. EITHER SHE REALIZED HOW LOW IT WAS, OR SHE THOUGHT I WAS LOOKING. THE LATTER COULDN'T BE FARTHER FROM THE TRUTH. YOU GUYS KNOW ME. AFTER GIVING HER A WRITTEN WARNING, I LET THEM GO.

0035 - (S) TRAFFIC STOP

I STOPPED AN OLDER VIETNAMESE LADY IN A GREEN SPORTS UTILITY VEHICLE. HER LICENSE WAS SUSPENDED FOR FAILING TO MAINTAIN INSURANCE COVERAGE. SHE SAID HER DAUGHTER TAKES CARE OF THE INSURANCE PAYMENTS EVERY MONTH. I TOLD HER THAT SHE MUST NOT. I WROTE HER A TICKET AND TOOK HER LICENSE. I GAVE HER MY CARD IN CASE SHE OR HER DAUGHTER HAD ANY QUESTIONS FOR ME.

0100 - (S) TRAFFIC STOP

THE OWNER OF THE VEHICLE HAD A SUSPENDED LICENSE AND THE TAG WAS NOT ASSIGNED TO THE VEHICLE. THE OWNER, A BLACK, HAITIAN MALE (30'S) WAS IN THE PASSENGER SEAT. HIS WIFE, A WHITE, AMERICAN FEMALE (30'S) WAS DRIVING. I TOOK THE MAN'S LICENSE AND GAVE HIM A WRITTEN WARNING. THE WOMAN'S LICENSE WAS VALID. APPARENTLY THEY HAD RECENTLY PURCHASED THE VEHICLE AND THOUGHT THE TAG WAS TRANSFERRED FROM THEIR OLD CAR. THE W/F INSISTED SHE DIDN'T KNOW ABOUT THE TAG. I GAVE THEM A VERBAL WARNING ABOUT THE TAG AND TOLD THEM THEY COULD LEAVE. THE W/F THANKED ME AND SAID AGAIN THAT SHE DIDN'T KNOW ABOUT THE TAG.

0116 - (BU) I ASSISTED MY AREA PARTNER WITH A TRAFFIC STOP. THE DRIVER WAS A YOUNG, DRUNK, W/M. HE HAD DRIVEN AT LEAST A COUPLE OF MILES

THAT WE KNEW OF ON RIMS. THE TIRES ON THE LEFT SIDE OF THE CAR WERE FINE, BUT THE TWO ON THE RIGHT WERE WORN DOWN TO THE RIMS. SPARKS WERE FLYING AS HE DROVE DOWN THE ROAD AND A HORRIBLE METAL SCREECHING SOUND WAS BEING MADE. DRIVING ON THE RIMS LIKE THAT CAUSED DAMAGE TO THE FRONT QUARTER PANEL. HOW WASTED DO YOU HAVE TO BE TO DESTROY YOUR CAR LIKE THAT? IT WAS A NICE AND FAIRLY NEW VEHICLE TOO. THE YOUNG W/M KEPT INSISTING HE WAS A GOOD GUY. HE SAID HE WAS AN ILLUSTRATOR, BUT WORKED AT AN OFFICE SUPPLY STORE. HE SAID HE KNEW HE HAD MADE A MISTAKE AND BEGGED NOT TO BE TAKEN TO JAIL.

0205 - AFTER LEAVING THE D.U.I. SCENE, I WENT TO CHECK OUT A NEARBY NEIGHBORHOOD. THE STREETS WERE BARE WITH THE EXCEPTION OF ONE VEHICLE. IT WAS A COUPLE OF LONG BLOCKS AHEAD OF ME. THE MERE FACT THAT IT WAS THE ONLY VEHICLE CRUISING AROUND THE NEIGHBORHOOD AT THAT TIME OF NIGHT CAUSED ME TO BE SUSPICIOUS. AS I TRIED TO CATCH UP TO THE VEHICLE. THE DRIVER BEGAN TRYING TO ELUDE ME. I CALLED IT IN TO THE DISPATCHER AND ASKED IF THERE WERE ANY OTHER UNITS IN THE AREA THAT COULD RESPOND FOR ASSISTANCE. NO ONE WAS IN THE AREA. I HADN'T ACTIVATED MY LIGHTS OR SIREN, BUT OUR SPEEDS CONTINUED TO INCREASE. MY HEART RATE GREW MORE AND MORE RAPID AND I COULD FEEL THE EXCITEMENT IN MY BONES. THEN REALITY SET IN. IF EITHER HIS OR MY CAR ENDS UP WRAPPED AROUND A PALM TREE OR IN SOMEONE'S LIVING ROOM, I'M SCREWED. SO I BROKE IT OFF AND ACCEPTED THE FACT THAT HE "SHOOK" ME. THAT'S KIND OF HARD TO ACCEPT, BUT WE BOTH LIVE ANOTHER DAY. HIM TO CONTINUE A LIFE OF CRIME (BECAUSE I KNOW THAT EITHER THE CAR WAS STOLEN OR HE HAD JUST PURCHASED DRUGS, WHICH THAT AREA IS KNOWN FOR), AND ME TO DETER OR CATCH HIM.

0225 - (S) TRAFFIC STOP
   I STOPPED A PURPLE DODGE INTREPID WITH CHROME RIMS FOR NOT HAVING A TAG LIGHT. THE DRIVER LIVED IN THE

NEIGHBORHOOD, AND WOULDN'T STOP UNTIL HE PULLED INTO HIS YARD. HE APPARENTLY THOUGHT HE WOULD BE FREE TO DISREGARD ME AND ENTER HIS HOUSE ONCE HE "MADE IT" INTO HIS YARD. HE WAS WRONG. I DEMANDED THE YOUNG, B/M TO STOP AND ADDRESS ME. HE CONTINUED TOWARD HIS FRONT DOOR UNTIL I UNDID MY PEPPER SPRAY HOLSTER (USED WHEN ENCOUNTERING RESISTANCE). THE YOUNG, B/M STARTED CRYING AND YELLING THAT HE WAS TIRED OF US MESSING WITH HIM BECAUSE HE DROVE AN INTREPID WITH RIMS ON IT. HE SAID, "MAN MY DADDY JUST DIED AND I DON'T NEED THIS SHIT!" I TOLD HIM I WAS SORRY ABOUT HIS FATHER, BUT THAT HAD NOTHING TO DO WITH ME. HE REFUSED TO COMPLY WITH MY ORDERS SO I CUFFED HIM AND PUT HIM IN MY BACK SEAT. HE INSISTED HE WAS CONTINUOUSLY STOPPED BECAUSE OF HIS VEHICLE. I TOLD HIM THAT IF HIS TAG LIGHT HAD BEEN OPERABLE, I WOULDN'T HAVE STOPPED HIM. HE CONTINUED TO BE BELIGERENT AND ASKED WHY I WAS TREATING HIM IN SUCH A MANNER. I TOLD HIM I WAS A HUMAN BEING AND AN OFFICER OF THE LAW AND DEMANDED TO BE TREATED WITH RESPECT. I TOLD HIM THAT AS LONG AS HE TREATED PEOPLE IN A DISRESPECTFUL MANNER, THAT'S HOW HE WOULD BE ADDRESSED. AFTER HE SETTLED DOWN A BIT AND BEGAN COMPYING, I UNCUFFED HIM. HE WAS ULTIMATELY GIVEN A WARNING AND TOLD AGAIN THAT IF HIS VEHICLE WERE IN ORDER HE WOULDN'T HAVE TO WORRY ABOUT BEING STOPPED SO MUCH. THROUGHOUT THE INCIDENT, HIS FRIEND, A YOUNG, B/M, INSISTED THAT HE WAS USUALLY NOT LIKE THAT. HE SAID HE HAD GROWN UP WITH THE DRIVER AND HE WAS A NICE GUY. HE SAID HE WAS JUST GOING THROUGH A LOT LATELY. I TOLD HIM I COULD UNDERSTAND THAT.

0249 - (D) SUSPICIOUS INCIDENT
    THIS WAS SOMETHING ABOUT A TOYOTA AT A SHOPPING PLAZA. ANOTHER UNIT PICKED UP THE CALL FOR ME SO I DON'T KNOW THE DETAILS.

0325 - (S) TRAFFIC STOP
    I STOPPED A YOUNG, B/M FOR DRIVING WITH A SUSPENDED LICENSE. THIS GUY WAS EXTREMELY NICE. HE WAS HERE FROM THE WASHINGTON, D.C./MARYLAND/VIRGINIA AREA

LIKE ME. WE TALKED ABOUT THAT A LITTLE AND ABOUT THE SUSPENSION. I TOLD HIM IT WAS INSURANCE RELATED. HE SAID HE HAD RECENT PROBLEMS WITH HIS COMPANY. I WROTE HIM A TICKET AND TOOK HIS LICENSE.

0340 - (S) TRAFFIC STOP
I STOPPED THIS CAR BECAUSE THE REGISTERED OWNER HAD A VALID IDENTIFICATION CARD ONLY. THE DRIVER WAS AN OLDER, BLACK, JAMAICAN MALE WHO WAS TAKING HIS WIFE TO WORK. HE SAID SHE WORKS EARLY AND HE WORKS LATE. HE SAID THEY HAD BAD CREDIT AND THE REGISTERED OWNER MERELY SIGNED FOR THEM TO GET THE VEHICLE. AFTER CHECKING HIS LICENSE I LET THEM GO. VERY NICE MAN.

0349 - (D) DISTURBANCE
THIS WAS A NOISE COMPLAINT AT "THE" PROBLEM APARTMENTS IN MY AREA. IT WAS PICKED UP AND CLEARED BY MY SUPERVISOR.
WE GOT A SECOND COMPLAINT AT THAT LOCATION. I ARRIVED JUST AS THE GROUP OF PEOPLE WAS WALKING AWAY. THEY LIKE TO HAVE LITTLE BLOCK PARTIES OVER THERE ON WEEKENDS... AND ON MONDAY, TUESDAY, WEDNESDAY...

0404 - (D) SUSPICIOUS INCIDENT
A W/F (40'S) WAS HOME WITH HER YOUNG SON AND DAUGHTER. HER HUSBAND WAS OUT OF TOWN ON BUSINESS. SHE HEARD SOME UNUSUAL SOUNDS THAT SEEMED TO HAVE COME FROM THE GARAGE. SHE WAS ESPECIALLY FRIGHTENED BECAUSE SHE HAD BEEN RECENTLY RECEIVING SOME UNUSUAL TELEPHONE SOLICITATIONS. TWO OTHER OFFICERS AND I CHECKED THE HOME VERY WELL, INCLUDING ITS OUTER PERIMETER. WE SEEMED TO HAVE MADE THEM ALL FEEL A LITTLE BETTER. WE TOLD HER NOT TO HESITATE IN CALLING 9-1-1 SHOULD AN EMERGENCY ARISE AND WE LEFT.

0430 - THE GIRL FROM THE CHICKEN RESTAURANT GAVE ME SOME EXTRA FOOD. AT THE TIME I TOLD HER I DIDN'T WANT IT BECAUSE I DIDN'T WANT TO WASTE IT. SHE TOLD ME TO TAKE IT HOME AND EAT IT LATER. I TOLD HER THE BISCUITS ARE NO GOOD WHEN YOU REHEAT THEM. SHE SAID, "YEAH THEY ARE. YOU JUST CAN'T

REHEAT THEM IN THE OVEN AND YOU CAN'T LEAVE THEM IN THE MICROWAVE FOR MORE THAN ABOUT 30 SECONDS." I LEFT HER RESTARUANT WITH MY NEWLY GAINED KNOWLEDGE OF POST BISCUIT PREPARATION THAT HAD PLAGUED ME FOR YEARS. ADMIT IT. YOU KNOW YOU'VE REHEATED LEFT OVER BISCUITS UNTIL THEY WERE LIKE LITTLE BRICKS. I KNOW I'M NOT THE ONLY ONE. (UPDATE: THE CHICKEN NEVER MADE IT TO THE REHEAT STAGE. I KILLED THAT COLD CHICKEN AND BISCUIT WHILE STILL IN FRONT SEAT OF MY CRUISER). THEN I WENT TO AN AREA HOTEL TO WASH MY GREASY HANDS AND USE THE RESTROOM.

0502 -I TRIED VERY HARD TO FIND A BAD GUY TONIGHT, BUT I COULDN'T. I MUST CONCEDE. NOW IT'S TO THE GAS STATION TO PARK AND RIDE THIS THING ON OUT. UNTIL TOMORROW...

09/19

2000 - ON PATROL

2035 - (BU) VEHICLE PURSUIT
  AN ADJACENT DISTRICT WAS CHASING ARMED ROBBERY
SUSPECTS. THE CALL WENT OUT OVER ALL CHANNELS AND
I WENT TO JOIN IN ON THE FUN. BEFORE I COULD GET THERE
THEY HAD THE CAR STOPPED AND TWO INDIVIDUALS IN
CUSTODY. MAN, I NEVER GET TO HAVE ANY FUN.

2130 - (D) DISTURBANCE
  THIS CALL CAME FROM A SECURITY OFFICER AT A
SHOPPING VILLAGE. HE WAS COMPLAINING ABOUT CAB
DRIVERS THAT PARK IN THE FIRE LANES DIRECTLY IN FRONT
AND BEHIND THE VILLAGE. HE SAID HE CONTINUALLY TELLS
THEM THEY MUST KEEP MOVING. I CAUGHT A COUPLE OF
THEM AND TRESPASSED THEM FROM THE PROPERTY. THEY
BOTH KEPT TRYING TO GET ME TO UNDERSTAND THAT THEY
WERE JUST POOR CAB DRIVERS TRYING TO MAKE A LIVING.
I TOLD THEM I WAS SYMPATHETIC, BUT THEY NEEDED TO
PLEAD THEIR CASES WITH THE PROPERTY MANAGEMENT.
I GAVE THEM THE MANAGER'S PHONE NUMBER AND TOLD
THEM THEY COULD NOT RETURN UNLESS INVITED BACK.

2345 - I ATTEMPTED TO GET SOMETHING TO EAT. JUST
AS I STEPPED UP TO THE ENTRANCE I GOT A CALL...

2351 - (D) BURGLARY TO A VEHICLE
  THIS BURGLARY OCCURRED IN A HOTEL PARKING LOT.
THE VICTIM WAS A W/F IN HER FIFTIES. SHE WAS VISITING
HERE FROM MIAMI WITH TWO OTHER W/F'S (FIFTIES). WHILE
CHECKING INTO THE HOTEL, SHE PARKED HER CAR IN THE
FRONT DRIVEWAY. SHE WAS AWAY FROM THE VEHICLE
FOR ONLY ABOUT TEN OR FIFTEEN MINUTES. WHEN SHE
RETURNED, THE INTERIOR LIGHT WAS ON AND HER CELL
PHONE WAS MISSING FROM THE CENTER CONSOLE. I
ASKED HER IF SHE HAD LOCKED THE DOORS. SHE SAID,
"AS A RULE, I ALWAYS LOCK THE DOORS." THERE WERE NO
SIGNS OF A FORCED ENTRY AND SHE COULDN'T REMEMBER
WHETHER OR NOT SHE UNLOCKED THE DOOR PRIOR TO

DISCOVERING HER MISSING PHONE. I BELIEVE SHE OR ONE OF THE OTHER LADIES LEFT THE CAR UNLOCKED. AT ANY RATE, I TOOK THE REPORT AND CLEARED THE CALL.

0136-I WENT TO THE STATION TO FILL UP MY WATER BOTTLES. FREE WATER, CAN'T BEAT THAT.

0140-(D) ALARM
  AN APARTMENT RESIDENT CALLED IN A COMPLAINT OF A CAR ALARM THAT WAS GOING OFF CONTINUOUSLY. I WENT TO THE APARTMENT AND FOUND THE CAR, BUT THE ALARM WASN'T GOING OFF.

0201-I SAT IN THE APARTMENT COMPLEX AND WORKED ON MY PAPERWORK. SHORTLY THEREAFTER, THE CAR ALARM STARTED GOING OFF. IT WAS PRETTY ANNOYING TOO. I RAN THE TAG AND FOUND OUT WHICH APARTMENT THE OWNER LIVED IN. I BANGED ON HIS DOOR FOR ABOUT TEN MINUTES BEFORE HE AWOKE AND ANSWERED IT. (IT'S GOOD THAT AT LEAST HE WAS ABLE TO GET SOME SLEEP, HIS NEIGHBORS SURE COULDN'T WITH THAT ALARM OF HIS.) HE WAS APOLOGETIC AND CAME OUT TO TAKE CARE OF IT. HE COULDN'T SHUT IT OFF AND SAID IT WAS THE FIRST TIME IT'S GONE OFF SINCE HE'S HAD THE CAR. FINALLY, HE JUST DISARMED IT. I WENT TO ANOTHER AREA OF THE PARKING LOT TO FINISH UP MY PAPERWORK. ON MY WAY OUT OF THE COMPLEX, I PASSED THE SPOT WHERE THE GUY'S CAR WAS PARKED. IT WAS GONE. GEE, I HOPE NO ONE STOLE THE MAN'S CAR AS SOON AS HE SHUT THE ALARM OFF. THAT WOULD SUCK IF I HAVE TO GO BACK AND TAKE A STOLEN CAR REPORT FROM THE SAME GUY I TOLD TO DISARM HE BOTHERSOME ALARM.

0248 - I HEADED TO THE STATION TO TURN IN MY PAPERWORK.

0300 -I WENT OUT ON PATROL AND DID SOME BUSINESS AND AREA CHECKS. I FOUND NO PROBLEMS

AND ALL WAS QUIET.

0427 - WHILE I WAS PARKED AT A MAJOR
INTERSECTION, A YOUNG W/M APPROACHED ME
AND ADVISED HIS VEHICLE HAD STALLED ON
THE INTERSTATE. HE WAS TRYING TO REACH HIS
ROADSIDE SERVICE PROVIDER ON HIS CELL AND
ASKED IF I KNEW WHERE THE NEAREST GARAGE
WAS. I TOLD HIM WHERE THE ONE I KNEW OF WAS. HE
SEEMED PRETTY SAD AS HE WALKED AWAY. I FELT BAD
BECAUSE I DIDN'T HELP HIM MORE. I THEN TOLD HIM I
COULD GIVE HIM A RIDE SOMEWHERE IF HE NEEDED.
HE GRACIOUSLY DECLINED AND SAID HE'D RIDE WITH
THE TOW TRUCK DRIVER TO WHEREVER THEY TOWED
HIS VEHICLE.

0503 - GAS - BREAKFAST – HOME, IN THAT ORDER. SAY
IT WITH ME. THAT'S IT. I KNEW YOU COULD. SEE YA IN
TRES DIAS.

09/22/00

*I WAS ASKED IF I HAD ANY ADVICE FOR COPS' WIVES. ANSWER: I HAVEN'T FIGURED OUT A WAY TO JUSTIFY MY LIFESTYLE TO THE FAIRER SEX. THAT'S WHY I'M SINGLE. SERIOUSLY THOUGH, ALL I CAN SAY IS: BE PATIENT WITH HIM AND REMEMBER THAT HE'S FROM "MARS".

1800-BRIEFING

1830 - (S) DISABLED VEHICLE
MY AREA PARTNER AND I HELPED A YOUNG W/F WHOSE VEHICLE WAS STALLED IN RUSH-HOUR TRAFFIC. WE PUSHED HER CAR UP THE STREET UNTIL WE FOUND A GOOD ROADSIDE SPOT TO PUT IT. SHE SAID SEVERAL PEOPLE HAD STOPPED TO HELP HER, BUT SHE DECLINED FOR SAFETY PURPOSES. (THANKS A LOT LADY NOTHING LIKE GETTING ALL SWEATY AT THE BEGINNING OF YOUR SHIFT).

1900 -I WENT TO DINNER

1920 - ON PATROL. IT'S RAINY OUT. I'M NOT GONNA DO MUCH IN THE RAIN.

1944 - (D) PETIT THEFT
ANOTHER CAB DRIVER STORY. A TOURIST WAS CALLING AND COMPLAINING FROM HER HOTEL ROOM. SHE SAID SHE TOOK A TRIP IN A CAB EARLIER. AFTER BEING DROPPED OFF, SHE REALIZED SHE LEFT HER CELL PHONE IN THE TAXI. THE DRIVER BROUGHT THE PHONE BACK, BUT REFUSED TO RETURN IT UNLESS THE TOURIST PAID HIM FOR THE TRIP BACK TO THE HOTEL. ANOTHER OFFICER AND I WENT TO THE SCENE. THE DRIVER WAS TOLD THAT HE'D BE CHARGED WITH THEFT IF HE DIDN'T RETURN THE PHONE. HE WAS VERY DISPLEASED BUT HE RETURNED IT. I COULD SEE WHERE HE WAS COMING FROM, BUT THE LAW IS THE LAW. HE'S A BUSINESS MAN AND IN BUSINESS YOU SOMETIMES TAKE A LOSS, YOU KNOW?

2013 - (D) STOLEN AUTOMOBILE

I RESPONDED TO THE PARKING LOT OF A RESTAURANT TO MEET WITH THE VICTIM OF THE ALLEGED STOLEN AUTOMOBILE. THE VICTIM WAS A W/F IN HER FIFTIES. SHE SAID SHE PARKED HER CAR AT THE RESTAURANT BECAUSE THE CONVENTION CENTER (WHERE SHE WAS ATTENDING A CONFERENCE) LOT WAS FULL. I ASKED HER IF SHE WAS SURE THAT WAS WHERE SHE PARKED. SHE SAID SHE WAS ALMOST POSITIVE, BUT WAS OBVIOUSLY BEGINNING TO DOUBT HERSELF. HER HUSBAND CAME OUT FROM HOME TO MEET HER WHEN SHE INFORMED HIM OF THE STOLEN CAR. MY FIRST THOUGHT WAS THAT SHE SIMPLY FORGOT WHERE SHE PARKED. BEFORE CONDUCTING MY OWN SEARCH OF THE AREA, I DECIDED TO CALL THE COMMUNICATIONS CENTER TO SEE IF A TOW COMPANY REPORTED TOWING HER CAR. THAT WAS NEGATIVE. I THEN WENT TO LOOK FOR THE CAR. I FOUND IT ABOUT A BLOCK AWAY IN THE REAR LOT Of ANOTHER RESTAURANT. THEY WERE BOTH ELATED. I WAS PLEASED TO HAVE HELPED.

2235 - (S) TRAFFIC STOP

I STOPPED A YOUNG, H/M WHO WAS DRIVING WITH A SUSPENDED LICENSE. IT WAS SUSPENDED FOR FAILING TO MAINTAIN INSURANCE COVERAGE. HE SAID THE STATE MAILED HIM A LETTER ADVISING HIM OF THE SUSPENSION. I WROTE HIM A TICKET, TOOK HIS LICENSE, AND ARRESTED HIM. I LET HIM CONTACT A FRIEND AND SHE CAME TO PICK UP HIS CAR. SHE TOLD HIM SHE WOULD BAIL HIM OUT LATER. HE DIDN'T SAY ANYTHING ON THE WAY TO JAIL.

2341 - BACK ON PATROL

0020 -I STOPPED A WHITE LEXUS WITH AN UNREADABLE TEMPORARY TAG. THE DRIVER WAS A YOUNG. H/M AND THERE WERE TWO OTHER YOUNG H/M PASSENGERS. THE DRIVER INITIALLY SAID HE DIDN'T HAVE HIS LICENSE ON HIM. WHEN I RAN HIS NAME I FOUND OUT IT WAS SUSPENDED. I ARRESTED THE H/M AND PLACED HIM IN MY CAR. HE SHOWED ME HIS CONCEALED WEAPONS PERMIT AND TOLD ME HIS GUN WAS IN THE GLOVE BOX. AT THAT POINT

I EVACUATED THE VEHICLE AND RETRIEVED THE
GLOCK AND HOLSTER. MY NEXT PRIORITY WAS
TRYING TO DETERMINE WHETHER OR NOT THE CAR
WAS STOLEN. THE H/M SAID IT WAS A LONER VEHICLE
FROM A PRIVATE DEALER WHILE HIS VOLVO WAS
BEING WORKED ON. HE SEEMED CREDIBLE, BUT I'VE
LEARNED NOT TO BELIEVE EVERYTHING I HEAR. THE
VEHICLE IDENTIFICATION NUMBER THAT WAS IN THE
DOOR WAS INCONSISTENT WITH THE ONE WRITTEN
ON THE TEMP TAG. AND THE ONE IN THE FRONT
WINDOW WAS HOMEMADE. SOMEONE HAD INSCRIBED
SOME LETTERS AND NUMBERS ON A SMALL PIECE
OF METAL AND STUCK IT BETWEEN THE DASH
AND WINDSHIELD. IT DIDN'T EVEN HAVE ENOUGH
CHARACTERS. I RAN BOTH OF THE OTHER NUMBERS
THROUGH COMMUNICATIONS. THEY ADVISED THERE
WAS NO RECORD FOUND. IN THE MEANTIME, THE H/M
ASKED ME IF I COULD LET HIM OUT OF THE CAR FOR
A WHILE BECAUSE HE WAS ILL AND IT WAS VERY HOT
IN THE BACKSEAT. WHEN I LET HIM STAND OUTSIDE
THE CAR HE PUKED. I THANKED HIM FOR THE EARLY
WARNING. (I KNOW A STATE TROOPER
WHO HAD SOME DRUNKEN PRISONER THROW UP WHILE
SITTING IN HIS FRONT PASSENGER SEAT. IT GOT ALL OVER
HIS RADIO EQUIPMENT AND EVERYTHING. BUT I DIGRESS)
I COULDN'T DETERMINE THAT IT WAS STOLEN SO I LET
HIS FRIENDS TAKE IT. ON THE WAS TO JAIL WE HAD A
PRETTY GOOD CONVERSATION. HE OWNED A PRODUCTION
COMPANY AND PRODUCED TRACKS FOR PEOPLE AND
DID PROMOTIONS. HE SAID IT WAS ROUGH OWNING HIS
OWN BUSINESS. WE ALSO TALKED ABOUT PIRATE RADIO
STATIONS HERE IN OUR AREA. I TOLD HIM ABOUT ONE
THAT I USED TO LISTEN TO. THE MUSIC WAS PRETTY
GOOD, BUT I COULD ONLY PICK IT UP FOR ABOUT FOUR
SQUARE BLOCKS. HE SAID HE KNEW ABOUT THAT ONE,
BUT THERE WAS A BETTER ONE. THE DJ WAS SOME RUDE
JAMAICAN WHO TALKED A LOT OF TRASH AND HUNG UP ON
EVERYBODY. FINALLY WE TALKED ABOUT GUNS AND WHY
HE PREFERRED THAT MODEL GLOCK. ONCE AT JAIL, I TOLD
HIM WHERE TO PICK UP HIS GUN THAT I HAD CONFISCATED
FOR SAFEKEEPING. WE PARTED ON PLEASANT TERMS.

0213-I WENT TO GAS UP, USE THE RESTROOM AND CHECK MY MESSAGES. FG3 HAD CALLED AND I CALLED HER BACK. I TOLD HER TO LEAVE ME ALONE, FOR HER BENEFIT, OF COURSE.

0319 - A SQUAD MEMBER AND I WENT TO CRASH A "RAVE" PARTY. THE PARTY WAS FILLED WITH MOSTLY YOUNG TEENAGERS. THERE WERE A FEW OLDER GUYS THERE WHO APPEARED TO BE IN THEIR LATE 30'S, EARLY 40'S. AS YOU MIGHT EXPECT, THEY LOOKED LIKE A BUNCH OF "CHESTERS". WE DIDN'T SEE ANY OPEN USE OF DRUGS. WE KNOW THEY WERE ON THAT "ECSTACY" THOUGH. THEY WERE MASSAGING ONE ANOTHER AND PERFORMING GLOW STICK SHOWS FOR ONE ANOTHER. (ECSTACY ENHANCES THE SCENSES AND THE PEOPLE WHO ARE ON IT LOVE TO BE TOUCHED. SEEING THE DIFFERENT COLORS DANCE BEFORE THEIR EYES ALSO DOES SOMETHING FOR THEM). WE TALKED TO A FEW PEOPLE AND HAD A COUPLE OF LAUGHS BEFORE LEAVING. MANY OF THE KIDS THERE WERE UNDER SIXTEEN. 3:00 IN THE MORNING I WONDER WHERE THESE KIDS' PARENTS ARE AND WHAT THEIR STATES OF MIND ARE.

0410 - MY BUDDY CALLED ME TO TELL ME HOW MANY PEOPLE VISITED OUR WEBSITE THE FIRST DAY ON LINE.

0415 - FG3 CALLED ME AGAIN. SHE WANTED TO KNOW IF I COULD STOP BY WHEN I GOT OFF WORK.

0420 -I WENT TO THE STATION TO TURN IN MY PAPERWORK.

0504 - IN A NEARBY AREA, SOME OFFICERS WERE BEHIND SOME ROBBERY SUSPECTS. THESE CALLS ARE GREAT. YOU GET TO JOIN IN ON ALL THE FUN

WITH NONE OF THAT PESKY PAPERWORK.

0505 - ONCE AGAIN, THE PURSUIT ENDED BEFORE I
COULD GET THERE. THE ROBBERY SUSPECT BAILED
FROM THE CAR AND A K-9 OFFICER WAS LOOKING
FOR HIM. I WENT TO THE STATION TO TURN IN SOME
PAPERWORK.

0530 -I WENT TO GET SOME BREAKFAST.
   SHORTLY AFTER 0600 I HEADED HOME. I'LL TALK TO YOU
LATER.

09/23

1800-BRIEFING

1816-ON PATROL

1825 - FG2 PAGED ME. I CALLED HER BACK AND WE SPOKE BRIEFLY.

1835-I HAD DINNER AT A LOCAL RESTAURANT WITH THREE OTHER OFFICERS ON MY SQUAD. WE CONVERSED ABOUT OUR K-9 OFFICERS AND HOW DIFFICULT IT MUST BE TRACKING DOWN CRIMINALS ON SCENT.

1900-ON PATROL

1928 - (S) TRAFFIC STOP
  I STOPPED A FORTY YEAR OLD B/M FOR RUNNING A RED LIGHT. HIS LICENSE WAS SUSPENDED FOR FAILING TO MAINTAIN INSURANCE COVERAGE. I TOOK HIM AT HIS WORD WHEN HE SAID HE DIDN'T KNOW IT WAS SUSPENDED. HE DID SAY HE HAD SOME PROBLEMS WITH A COMPANY THAT HE UTILIZED IN THE PAST. HE SAID, "THAT'S WHAT I GET FOR DEALING WITH THEM OLD BOOT-LEG INSURANCE COMPANIES." I GAVE HIM A VERBAL WARNING FOR RUNNING THE LIGHT, TOOK HIS LICENSE, AND WROTE HIM A TICKET FOR THE SUSPENSION. HIS EXCUSE FOR RUNNING THE LIGHT WAS THAT HE NEEDLE WAS ON "E" AND HE WAS AFRAID IF HE WAITED ON THE LIGHT HE'D RUN OUT OF GAS.

1949-ON PATROL

2001 - (S) TRAFFIC STOP
  I STOPPED A WHITE ACURA ON THE INTERSTATE WITH AN UNASSIGNED TAG. PASSENGERS IN THE VEHICLE INCLUDED FOUR YOUNG WHITE TEENAGERS; W/M DRIVER, W/F IN PASSENGER SEAT AND TWO W/M'S IN THE BACKSEAT. THE DRIVER WANTED TO KNOW WHY I STOPPED HIM. I TOLD HIM BECAUSE THE TAG ON HIS CAR WAS NOT ASSIGNED TO IT. HE SAID IT WAS THE TAG THAT WAS ON HIS OLD CAR; A

HONDA. HE SAID HE RECENTLY PURCHASED THE ACURA AT A DEALERSHIP WHERE HIS FATHER WORKS AND THEY WERE SUPPOSED TO HAVE TRANSFERRED THE REGISTRATION. I TOLD HIM THEY HADN'T AND ARRESTED HIM FOR FAILING TO REGISTER A VEHICLE AND FOR ATTACHING AN UNASSIGNED TAG. (WHILE I WAS MAKING THE ARREST, TWO TOURISTS FROM MOSCOW PULLED OFF THE ROAD TO ASK ME A QUESTION. THEY WANTED DIRECTIONS TO A LOCATION THAT WAS TWO EXITS DOWN THE INTERSTATE). THE YOUNG MAN WAS TRULY DISAPPOINTED THAT HE WAS GOING TO JAIL. IT WAS HIS GIRLFRIEND'S BIRTHDAY. THEY WERE ON THEIR WAY TO MEET WITH A LIMOUSINE DRIVER WHO WAS GOING TO TAKE THEM OUT TO PARTY. HE WANTED TO KNOW IF I COULD JUST WRITE HIM A TICKET. HE SAID HE WAS SO CLOSE TOO, HE ONLY HAD ONE MORE EXIT TO GO. I EXPLAINED WHAT HE NEEDED TO DO TO GET OUT IN A FEW HOURS. I LET HIS FRIENDS FOLLOW ME TO JAIL. THEY WITHDREW HIS BOND MONEY FROM AN ATM MACHINE OUTSIDE OF BOOKING AND GAVE IT TO ME. THE BOOKING OFFICER SAID IF HE GAVE THEM THE CASH BOND, IT WOULD SPEED THE PROCESS TREMENDOUSLY. ON THE WAY TO JAIL, HE TALKED ABOUT THE HIS HOME TEAM, THE JACKSONVILLE JAGUARS. HE THANKED ME AS I LEFT THE JAIL.

2210-(S) TRAFFIC STOP

I STOPPED A W/M (LATE FORTIES) FOR CROSSING SOME STREET LINES. I FIRST NOTICED HIM PULLING OUT OF THE LOT OF A BAR. I ASKED HIM IF HE HAD BEEN DRINKING. HE GAVE ME THE STANDARD TWO BEER STORY. I CONDUCTED A FIELD SOBRIETY TEST ON HIM. HE PASSED AND I TOLD HIM TO GET HOME SAFELY.

2218-(D) ALARM

I WAS DISPATCHED TO AN ALARM AT A BUSINESS. ANOTHER UNIT THAT WAS CLOSER PICKED IT UP FOR ME.

2228 - (D) BATTERY

A SECURITY OFFICER WAS STANDING AT A BUS STOP WHEN HE WAS BATTERED. HE HAD GOTTEN INTO IT WITH SOME GUY. THE GUY PUNCHED HIM, RIPPED HIS BADGE FROM

HIS CHEST, AND FLED THE AREA IN A VEHICLE. WE CHECKED THE AREA FOR THE SUSPECT'S CAR BUT COULDN'T FIND IT. THE BATTERY TOOK PLACE IN A NEARBY JURISDICTION. HE HAD TO WAIT FOR THAT AGENCY TO ARRIVE TO TAKE HIS REPORT.

2231 - (D) DISTURBANCE

I RESPONDED TO AN ARGUMENT AT A LOCAL RESTAURANT. SOME PATRONS CLAIMED THAT THEIR WAITER WAS EXTREMELY RUDE TO THEM AND USED PROFANITY. THE MANAGER CLAIMED THAT THEY WERE THE PROBLEM. WHEN I ARRIVED, THE PATRONS EXPLAINED WHAT HAD HAPPENED AND AGREED TO LEAVE THE PROPERTY OF THEIR OWN WILL. THE MANAGER, WHO CALLED US, WAS SATISFIED WITH THAT.

2240 - (D) HARASSING CALLS

I WENT TO A RESTAURANT TO MEET WITH THE VICTIM, A YOUNG, B/M. HE SAID HE WAS BEING PURSUED BY A YOUNG, W/M FOR A GAY RELATIONSHIP. HE TOLD THE W/M THAT THEY COULD BE FRIENDS AND HANG OUT SOMETIME, BUT THERE WAS NO CHANCE OF A RELATIONSHIP BECAUSE HE WAS STRAIGHT. HE SAID THE W/M CONTINUOUSLY CALLS HIS JOB AND FOLLOWS HIM. I TOLD THE B/M TO START DOCUMENTING THESE INCIDENTS. ONCE HE HAD ESTABLISHED A DOCUMENTED PATTERN, CHARGES COULD BE FILED AGAINST THE W/M FOR STALKING. HE AGREED TO DO THAT. (MY PERSONAL THOUGHT WAS THAT IT WAS HIS FAULT FOR TEASING THAT POOR GUY, PLAYING WITH HIS EMOTIONS AND STUFF LIKE SAYING WE CAN GO OUT, BUT WE CAN'T KICK IT).

2256 - (S) TRAFFIC STOP

I STOPPED A YOUNG, W/M FOR SPEEDING. AFTER I STOPPED HIM, I REALIZED HIS TAG WAS EXPIRED. I ASKED HIM, "HOW ARE YOU GONNA SPEED WITH AN EXPIRED TAG?" HE SAID HE HAD JUST GOTTEN OFF WORK AND WAS TRYING TO GET HOME. HE SAID HE DIDN'T KNOW IT WAS EXPIRED BECAUSE HIS MOTHER HAD GIVEN HIM THE CAR. IT EXPIRED ON HER BIRTHDAY INSTEAD OF HIS. I WROTE HIM A TICKET AND EXPLAINED THE FINE TO HIM. IT WAS

FOUR MONTHS EXPIRED. I TOLD HIM THAT IN A COUPLE MORE MONTHS IT WOULD BE A CRIMINAL OFFENSE. I TOLD HIM TO HAVE A GOOD NIGHT. HE THANKED ME AND DROVE SLOWLY OFF.

2320 - (S) TRAFFIC STOP
I STOPPED A YOUNG, B/M FOR UNUSUAL DRIVING BEHAVIOR. HE WAS IN THE CAR WITH HIS SISTER, A YOUNG, B/F. I ASKED HIM WHAT HE WAS UP TO AND HE SAID HE WAS VISITING WITH HIS FAMILY WHO LIVED IN THAT NEIGHBORHOOD. I TOLD HIM HE NEEDED TO WATCH HOW HE DROVE AROUND THERE. I TOLD HIM IT WAS A KNOWN DRUG AREA AND THAT I STOP PEOPLE FOR EVERY TRAFFIC OFFENSE THAT I OBSERVE. HE SAID THE CAR WAS RENTED AND HE WOULDN'T BE STUPID ENOUGH TO HAVE DRUGS IT BECAUSE THE CAR WOULD GET TOWED AND A HOST OF OTHER PROBLEMS WOULD FOLLOW. I GAVE HIM A VERBAL WARNING AND TOLD HIM TO WATCH HOW HE DRIVES.

WHILE I WAS OUT WITH THE B/M AND HIS SISTER, ANOTHER YOUNG, B/M WALKED BY. I ASKED HIM WHAT HIS NAME WAS AND HOW OLD HE WAS. HE SAID HIS NAME WAS CURTIS AND HE WAS SIXTEEN. HE SEEMED PRETTY SHORT FOR SIXTEEN. I ASKED HIM IF HE WAS SUPPOSED TO BE OUT THAT TIME OF NIGHT. HE SAID HE JUST LEFT MIDNIGHT BASKETBALL. I SAID, "OH. THAT'S GOOD. BE CAREFUL WALKING HOME, MAN."

2335 - (S) TRAFFIC STOP
I STOPPED A W/M (30'S) WHO WAS DRIVING AN ISUZU AMIGO IN THE SAME DRUG INFESTED NEIGHBORHOOD. HIS TAILLIGHT WAS BROKEN AND THERE WAS WHITE LIGHT SHOWING FROM IT. I ASKED HIM WHERE HE WAS HEADED. HE SAID HE WAS JUST CUTTING THROUGH THE NEIGHBORHOOD TO GO VISIT SOME FRIENDS. I GAVE HIM A WARNING FOR THE TAILLIGHT AND TOLD HIM HE COULD BE ON HIS WAY. AFTERWARDS, I NOTICED HIM TURN AND GO THE OTHER WAY. I GUESS HE DIDN'T WANT TO SEE HIS FRIENDS TOO BADLY.

0000 - (S) TRAFFIC STOP

SAME NEIGHBORHOOD. I STOPPED A BEAT UP VAN FOR STANDING IN THE ROADWAY IN FRONT OF A YARD WHERE SEVERAL GUYS WERE STANDING. (THE DRUG TRADE OUT HERE OPERATES THROUGH A DRIVE-UP SERVICE. THEY DO WHAT THEY CAN FOR THEIR CUSTOMERS). THERE WAS A YOUNG, B/F DRIVING. HER BOYFRIEND, A YOUNG, B/M, WAS IN THE PASSENGER SEAT. THERE WERE TWO MORE YOUNG, B/F'S IN THE BACKSEAT. I HAD THE B/F DRIVER STEP OUT THE VAN WHILE I WAS CHECKING HER LICENSE. HER BOYFRIEND WAS SAYING SOMETHING TO HER. I HEARD HER SAY, "I CAN'T GET BACK IN. THE MAN TOLD ME TO STAND OUT HERE." I SAID, "WHAT'S UP WITH HIM, IS HE JEALOUS OR SOMETHING?" SHE SAID, "YEAH." I TOLD HER, "I UNDERSTAND, YOU CAN GET BACK IN." ONE OF THE FEMALES IN THE BACK OF THE VAN KEPT SAYING SHE HAD TO PEE.   I TOLD HER SHE HAD TO WAIT UNTIL I WAS FINISHED. SHE SAID SHE JUST WANTED TO WALK HOME AND USE IT AND SHE'D COME RIGHT BACK. I TOLD HER SHE COULD GO AFTER I CHECKED OUT HER IDENTIFICATION. SHE DIDN'T HAVE ANY. THE B/M WAS GETTING PRETTY BELIGERENT. I EXPLAINED TO HIM WHY I STOPPED THEM AND TOLD HIM TO GIVE ME HIS IDENTIFICATION. I FINALLY LET THE OTHER B/F LEAVE TO USE THE RESTROOM. AS IT TURNED OUT, BOTH THE DRIVER AND HER BOYFRIEND HAD WARRANTS. THEY BOTH CLAIMED THAT THEY HAD ALREADY BEEN ARRESTED AND RELEASED ON THOSE WARRANTS. THE B/F I LET GO USE THE RESTROOM HAD COME BACK WITH THE ARRESTED B/F'S MOTHER. POOR LADY, SHE SEEMED LIKE SHE WAS JUST WORN DOWN FROM DEALING WITH HER DAUGHTER'S CRIMINAL ACTIVITIES. I WAITED AROUND FOR HER TO GO BACK AND GET SOME COURT PAPERWORK PERTAINING TO THEIR ARRESTS AND TOOK IT WITH US TO JAIL. THE FEMALES PAPERWORK TURNED OUT TO BE LEGITIMATE, BUT THE B/M'S WASN'T. A BOOKING SUPERVISOR CALLED THE WARRANTS SECTION AND THEY ADVISED THE CASE HAD BEEN CLOSED. I TOOK HER BACK TO HER HOUSE BUT HER BOYFRIEND REMAINED IN JAIL. ON THE WAY OUT, SHE YELLED THROUGH HIS IRON CELL DOOR, "HE TAKIN' ME HOME BABY, BUT I'LL BE BACK TO GET

YOU OUT!" WHEN WE GOT TO HER HOUSE SHE TOLD ME SHE UNDERSTOOD THAT I WAS JUST DOIN' MY JOB.

0134-(D) ALARM

I WAS DISPATCHED TO A RESIDENTIAL ALARM. THE HOME APPEARED SECURE AND I CLEARED.

0151-I STOPPED FOR GAS AND TO USE THE RESTROOM AT THE STATION WHERE THE OLDER GENTLEMAN RUNS THE GRAVEYARD SHIFT. AS HE UNLOCKED THE DOOR FOR ME HE SAID, "NO, YOU CAN'T HAVE BEER!" I SAID, "BUT IT'S ONLY 1:55 I'VE GOT 5 MINUTES!"

0206 - (D) MAN DOWN

THIS CALL WAS CONCERNING A W/F (50'S). SHE WAS IN HER HOTEL ROOM FEELING KIND OF DEPRESSED. THERE WAS SOME CONFUSION AS TO HER STATE OF BEING. THERE WAS TALK OF HER ATTEMPTING SUICIDE AND BEING PASSED OUT. NEITHER WAS THE CASE. SHE HAD RUN OUT OF HER PSYCHOTROPIC MEDICATION AND WANTED TO GET TO HER HOSPITAL FOR MORE. WE TOLD HER THAT WE COULDN'T GET HER TO THAT HOSPITAL. WE HAVE CERTAIN ONES WHERE WE TAKE PEOPLE, AND HER'S WASN'T ONE OF THEM. WE FINALLY CAME UP WITH A SOLUTION BEFITTING US BOTH. WE CALLED RESCUE TO TRANSPORT HER TO A NEARBY HOSPITAL FOR A MEDICAL EVALUATION. THEY WOULD INTURN TRANSPORT HER TO HER NORMAL FACILITY.

0243 - *(D)* DISTURBANCE

THIS WAS OCCURRING AT A HOTEL. IT INVOLVED AN UNRULY GROUP OF FOLKS FROM IRELAND. THEY WERE RUNNING BACK AND FORTH BETWEEN THEIR ROOMS DOUSING ONE ANOTHER WITH WATER AND VIDEO TAPING IT. THIS WAS HOW THEY WERE CELEBRATING THEIR LAST DAY IN THE UNITED STATES. I ASKED THEM WHAT TIME IT WAS BACK IN IRELAND. AFTER THEY TOLD ME I SAID, "WELL, IT'S 3:00 O'CLOCK IN THE MORNING HERE, AND YOU'RE BEHAVIOR IS UNACCEPTABLE. OTHER PEOPLE ARE STAYING IN THIS HOTEL AND YOU NEED TO RESPECT THEIR RIGHT TO A

PEACEFUL NIGHTS SLEEP." THEY AGREED TO SETTLE DOWN AND GO TO BED.

0300 -I PICKED UP SOME COMPLETED PAPERWORK FROM AN OFFICER WHO WAS WORKING AN OFF-DUTY JOB AT A HOTEL IN MY AREA. WE FREQUENTLY DO THIS SO THEY CAN GET OFF AT THEIR SCHEDULED TIMES WITHOUT HAVING TO GO INTO THE STATION.

0340 -I PICKED UP SOME MORE PAPERWORK FROM ANOTHER OFFICER WHO WAS WORKING OFF-DUTY AT ANOTHER HOTEL.

0350 - (S) TRAFFIC STOP
 I STOPPED THIS CAR BECAUSE THE OWNER'S LICENSE WAS SUSPENDED THREE TIMES. THE DRIVER WAS A W/M (30'S). HE WAS DRIVING HIS FRIEND'S CAR. AFTER VERIFYING THE VALIDITY OF HIS LICENSE, I LET HIM GO.

0408 -I MET WITH MY SUPERVISOR AT A LOCAL RESTAURANT TO TURN IN MY PAPERWORK AND GET SOME BREAKFAST. WE WERE JOINED BY ANOTHER GUY ON MY SQUAD.

0456 - (S) TRAFFIC STOP
 I STOPPED A CHEVY PICK-UP WITH NO TAG LIGHT IN THE LOT OF A GROCERY STORE. THE DRIVER WAS A YOUNG, W/M WHOSE LICENSE WAS SUSPENDED FOUR TIMES. HIS GIRLFRIEND, A YOUNG W/F WHO WAS FIVE MONTHS PREGNANT, WAS IN THE PASSENGER SEAT. HE SAID THEY ONLY FOUND OUT TWO DAYS AGO THAT SHE WAS PREGNANT. IT LOOKED PRETTY OBVIOUS TO ME. SHE ALREADY HAD THAT LITTLE, SLOW WOBBLE WALK DOWN. I ARRESTED HIM FOR THE OFFENSE. I TOLD THEM THEY COULD HAVE HER MOTHER COME PICK UP THE TRUCK. THE W/F DIDN'T HAVE A LICENSE AND WANTED TO KNOW IF THE W/M COULD PULL THE TRUCK UP NEAR THE PAY PHONE WHILE SHE WAITED ON HER MOM. SHE SAID, "YOU CAN HANDCUFF HIM TO THE STEERING WHEEL." I TOLD HER THAT WOULDN'T BE NECESSARY. I'D LET HIM DRIVE UP TO THE PHONE. AS I UNCUFFED HIM I SAID, "MAKE MY DAY AND LET'S GET INTO

A HIGH SPEED CHASE." I IMMEDIATELY SAID, "I'M KIDDING."
THE YOUNG, W/M SMILED AND SAID, "I'M NOT."   ON THE
WAY TO JAIL WE TALKED ABOUT A LOCAL RAVE CLUB.
HE SAID WE SHOULD SHUT IT DOWN BECAUSE KIDS ARE
DYING. HE ASKED ME WHERE ELSE I WORKED BECAUSE HE
RECOGNIZED ME. I TOLD HIM USUALLY A BIT MORE NORTH
OF WHERE WE WERE. HE SAID THAT I HAD STOPPED HIM A
FEW MONTHS EARLIER AND TOOK HIS LICENSE BECAUSE
IT WAS SUSPENDED. (I KNEW HE LOOKED FAMILIAR AND HE
REFRESHED MY MEMORY OF HIM). HE SAID HE KNEW THAT
WHEN HE SAW ME BEHIND HIM HE WAS GOING TO JAIL. HE
WAS A GOOD KID. HE JUST SIMPLY DIDN'T HAVE THE CASH
TO PAY OFF HIS DEBTS. IT'S GONNA BE EVEN ROUGHER
ONCE HIS CHILD ARRIVES. I'M SYMPATHETIC, BUT I GOT TO
DO MY JOB, RIGHT?

0605 -I WRAPPED UP THE ARREST AND HEADED TO
THE STATION TO TURN IN MY PAPERWORK.
   I WENT TO THE GYM AND WORKED OUT UNTIL 0730.
THEN I WENT HOME AND PLAYED ON THE COMPUTER A BIT
BEFORE GOING TO BED.   LATER.

09/24

1930 - (BU) ARMED ROBBERY

ON MY WAY TO WORK, I STOPPED TO HELP SOME OTHER OFFICERS WHO WERE SEARCHING FOR AN ARMED ROBBERY SUSPECT. A B/M HAD JUMPED OUT OF SOME BUSHES NEAR A RESTAURANT AND ROBBED A W/F AT GUNPOINT. THERE WERE MANY OFFICERS INVOLVED IN THE SEARCH. ONE OF OUR HELICOPTERS AND SEVERAL K-9 OFFICERS ALSO RESPONDED. BEING THAT THERE WERE SO MANY OTHER OFFICERS ON THE SCENE, I LEFT AND HEADED TO BRIEFING. I'M NOT SURE IF THEY CAUGHT THE BAD GUY OR NOT.

2020 -I CALLED AND SPOKE TO MY DAUGHTER AFTER BRIEFING. SHE STARTED CRYING AND TOLD ME, "NO, NO, NO" WHEN I SAID I HAD TO GO TO WORK. HER MOTHER EVENTUALLY PRIED THE PHONE AWAY FROM HER.

2034 - (D) ALARM

I RESPONDED TO A RESIDENTIAL ALARM. UPON ARRIVAL, I FOUND IT TO HAVE BEEN ACCIDENTAL.

2051-(D) FRAUD

MY VICTIM IN THIS CASE WAS A YOUNG MAN WHO WAS ORIGINALLY FROM HONDURAS. HE NOW LIVES IN MIAMI AND WAS ON VACATION IN CENTRAL FLORIDA. HE HAD PURCHASED A TICKET FOR AN AREA THEME PARK. THE SELLER TOLD HIM THAT THE TICKET WAS A LIFETIME PASS TO THAT PARTICULAR PARK. (HINT FOR ALL MY PEOPLES OUT THERE: IF SOMEONE TELLS YOU THEY HAVE A LIFETIME THEME PARK PASS FOR SALE AND YOU PURCHASE IT YOU'VE BEEN SCREWED). THE YOUNG MAN REALIZED THIS AFTER A FUN FILLED DAY AT THE PARK. ON HIS WAY OUT OF THE PARK, HE WAS ASKED TO COMPLETE A SURVEY PERTAINING TO HIS VISIT. HE TOLD THEM HE ESPECIALLY LIKED THE IDEA OF A LIFETIME PASS. THAT'S WHEN PARK PERSONAL CALLED THEIR INVESTIGATORS OVER. THEY CONFISCATED THE TICKET, GAVE HIM A COPY OF IT, AND TOLD HIM THAT THE COMPANY WHO SOLD IT TO HIM WAS

NOT AN AUTHORIZED VENDOR. HE THEN CALLED US. HE
WANTED TO LET US KNOW WHAT THAT COMPANY WAS UP
TO. I TOOK THE REPORT AND TALKED TO THE YOUNG MAN A
BIT. HE SAID IF HE WERE A CITIZEN OF THE UNITED STATES,
HE'D BECOME A POLICE OFFICER, BUT NOT IN MIAMI.

2122-(D) ALARM
I RESPONDED TO A BUSINESS ALARM. THE ALARM WAS
UNFOUNDED.

2048 - (S) TRAFFIC STOP
I STOPPED A YOUNG, DOMINICAN MAN WHO WAS PULLING
HIS GREY HONDA INTO THE LOT OF THE CONVENTION
CENTER. THE TAG ON HIS CAR WAS NOT ASSIGNED TO IT.
AFTER I CALLED HIM OUT OF THE VEHICLE AND ASKED FOR
HIS LICENSE, HE KEPT TELLING ME HE WORKED THERE.
FINALLY, I SAID SIR, I DIDN'T ASK YOU WHERE YOU WORK,
I ASKED YOU FOR YOUR LICENSE. HE DIDN'T HAVE ONE
AND I LATER FOUND OUT IT WAS SUSPENDED. BEFORE
ARRESTING HIM, I LET HIM PARK HIS CAR IN THE REAR LOT
OF THE CENTER. THROUGHOUT THE ARREST, HE BEGGED
AND PLEADED WITH ME NOT TO ARREST HIM. I MEAN IT
WAS NON-STOP, "PLEASE SIR, DON'T TAKE ME TO JAIL -
HAVE TWO KIDS SIR. I SAID, "I DO TOO, AND I MANAGE TO
PAY MY DEBTS". HE SAID, "SIR, JUST GIVE ME A CHANCE."
I SAID, "YOU'RE CHANCES WERE ALL THOSE TICKETS YOU
GOT AND DIDN'T PAY INCLUDING THE TIME WHEN THEY
TOOK YOUR LICENSE. HE CONTINUED TO WHINE AND BEG.
WHILE I WAS DOING MY PAPERWORK IN THE PARKING LOT,
A SUPERVISOR WHO WORKS ON THE SHIFT PRIOR TO MINE
APPROACHED ME. TO MAKE A LONG STORY SHORT HE WAS
CRYING ABOUT THE FACT THAT MY AREA PARTNER AND I
SPEND A LOT OF TIME TAKING PEOPLE TO JAIL. HE SAID WE
ARE SUPPOSED TO BE THEIR RELIEF. INSTEAD WE'RE BACK
AND FORTH TO JAIL. I TOLD HIM THAT HIS SQUAD CAME IN
THREE HOURS PRIOR TO MINE AND ONCE WE CAME IN THEY
DIDN'T DO A THING. HE ALSO SAID WE WORK TOO MUCH
TRAFFIC. I BASICALLY TOLD HIM THE STATE OF FLORIDA GAVE
ME THE AUTHORITY TO ENFORCE THE LAW THROUGH TRAFFIC
AND ANY OTHER LEGAL MEANS THAT I SAW FIT. HE TOLD ME
I DIDN'T HAVE TO YELL AT HIM BECAUSE HE WAS DISCUSSING

IT WITH ME AND ASKING THAT I LOOK AT THE BIGGER PICTURE. THE BIGGER PICTURE WAS THAT HE WAS ASKING ME TO SIT ON MY YOU KNOW WHAT AND DO NOTHING LIKE HE DOES. THE BIGGER PICTURE WAS THAT HE WAS AFRAID HE'D HAVE TO PICK UP A CALL WHILE MY PARTNER AMD I WERE AT JAIL. HE KEPT SAYING HE WASN'T ARGUING WITH ME. BEFORE I GOT TOO BELLIGERENT, I JUST TOLD HIM, "FINE, I HAVE NOTHING MORE TO SAY ABOUT IT. I'VE HEARD WHAT YOU HAD TO SAY AND THAT'S THAT." HE LEFT. I JUST SAT THERE SMOKIN' AND ON TOP OF THAT, THIS GUY BEHIND ME WAS STILL WHINING. I TELL YOU I'M FINDING ALL KIND OF PLAYMATES FOR MY LITTLE DAUGHTER, TWO IN THE LAST FIVE MINUTES. WHY PLAYMATES FOR MY DAUGHTER YOU ASK? BECAUSE THEY'RE ALL FOUR YEAR OLD LITTLE GIRLS.

2330 - ON MY WAY BACK FROM JAIL, I CALLED MY SUPERVISOR TO TELL HIM ABOUT MY LITTLE CONFRONTATION WITH THE SUPERVISOR FROM THE OTHER SQUAD. AFTER RUNNING THE STORY DOWN TO HIM AS I HAVE TO YOU, MY SUPERVISOR SAID, "_ HIM - KEEP DOIN' WHAT YOU BEEN DOIN'!" THAT ME FEEL PRETTY DARN GOOD.

2330 - I WENT TO HAVE DINNER AT A HOTEL CAFETERIA IN MY AREA. THAT SUPERVISOR SHOWED UP. I THOUGHT HE WAS GOING TO COME AND SIT WITH ME AS IF NOTHING HAD HAPPENED. HE DIDN'T, THOUGH. INSTEAD, HE PRETENDED NOT TO SEE ME. I WAS GRATEFUL. I'M NOWHERE NEAR PHONY.

2350 -(S) STAND-BY
  ON MY WAY OUT OF THE RESTAURANT, AN EMPLOYEE STOPPED ME. SHE WAS A WHITE FEMALE IN HER 40'S. SHE WANTED ME TO WALK HER TO HER CAR. YOU KNOW SO SHE WOULDN'T GET MUGGED OR ANYTHING. I WALKED HER, AND SHE THANKED ME. IN HER EYES, I PROVED MYSELF WORTHY FOR I KEPT HER FROM GETTING MUGGED.

0000 - ON PATROL

0025 - (S) TRAFFIC STOP
  I STOPPED A B/M WHO WAS DRIVING A GREY BUICK WITH AN UNREADABLE TEMPORARY TAG. HIS LICENSE WAS GOOD, SO I LET HIM GO.

0034 - (S) TRAFFIC STOP
  I STOPPED A GREEN TOYOTA 4-RUNNER BECAUSE THE OWNER HAD FOUR SUSPENSIONS ON HIS LICENSE. AFTER THE STOP, A YOUNG, W/M EXITED THE VEHICLE AND IMMEDIATELY SAID, "MY LICENSE IS SUSPENDED." HE SAID HE WASN'T GOING TO TRY AND HIDE IT BECAUSE HE KNEW HE WAS WRONG. AFTER PLACING HIM UNDER ARREST, I ALLOWED HIM TO SPEAK WITH THE PASSENGER, ANOTHER YOUNG, W/M WHOM HE HAD JUST PICKED UP FROM WORK. HE TOLD HIS FRIEND TO TAKE HIS CAR AND HE EXPLAINED TO HIM HOW THE BAIL PROCEDURES WORKED. I ASKED HIM HOW HE KNEW SO MUCH ABOUT IT. HE SAID HE HAD JUST GOTTEN HIS GIRLFRIEND OUT OF JAIL FOR THE SAME THING. WE BOTH LAUGHED AT THAT AND HAD A PLEASANT TRIP DOWN TO CENTRAL BOOKING. COOL KID.

0158 - AFTER LEAVING THE JAIL, I WENT TO PICK UP SOME MORE BOOKS OF TICKETS. I KNOW IT'S HARD TO BELIEVE. BUT I RAN OUT.

0239 - (S) TRAFFIC STOP
  I STOPPED AN OLD, BLUE CROWN VICTORIA THAT WAS DRIVEN BY A YOUNG, H/F. THE FRONT PASSENGER WAS ANOTHER YOUNG, H/F AND THE REAR PASSENGER WAS A YOUNG, B/M. THE CAR HAD NO TAILLIGHTS. I CALLED THE H/F DRIVER OUT AND SPOKE TO HER A BIT. I JOKINGLY ASKED HER IF SHE WAS A COP. SHE SAID NO, BUT HER CROWN VIC USED TO BE A COP CAR IN NEW JERSEY, AFTER THAT IT WAS A CAB. (ON THE INSIDE OF HER DOORS, YOU COULD STILL SEE THE BLACK AND YELLOW CHECKER BOARD PATTERN, EVEN THOUGH THE CAR'S EXTERIOR WAS BLUE.) I ASKED HER IF IT STILL HAD A METER IN THERE SO SHE COULD CHARGE HER FRIENDS FOR DRIVING THEM AROUND. SHE DIDN'T THINK THAT WAS TOO FUNNY, BUT HER FRIENDS DID. I GAVE HER A WARNING FOR THE LIGHTS.

0245 - I WENT AHEAD AND SAT IN THE RESTAURANT LOT WHERE I HAD STOPPED THE CROWN VIC. THE RESTAURANT MORNING DELIVERY GUY (W/M, 40'S) CAME OVER TO ME AND SAID, "YOU WOKE ME UP WITH THAT SIREN." THAT WAS HIS INTRO TO TALK TO ME ABOUT THE PATROLLING OF HIS NEIGHBORHOOD. HE SAID THERE WAS A DRUG AREA CLOSE TO HIS HOUSE. HE SAID ALL THE NEW POLICE OFFICERS STOP HIM BECAUSE THEY THINK HE'S OVER THERE BUYING DRUGS. HE KNOWS IT'S BECAUSE HE'S WHITE AND IN THAT NEIGHBORHOOD, BUT HE DOESN'T MIND. HE SAID AFTER THEY GET TO KNOW HIM, THEY DON'T BOTHER HIM ANYMORE.

0320 - (S) SUSPICIOUS VEHICLE
   THIS CALL WAS AT MY PROBLEM APARTMENT COMPLEX. THEY ADVISED A B/F WEARING A YELLOW SHIRT AND DRIVING A GREY S.U.V. WAS DRIVING AROUND THE PARKING LOT LOOKING AT CARS. SHE WASN'T AROUND WHEN I GOT THERE. THE CALLER PROBABLY THOUGHT SHE WAS "SCOPING" OUT CARS TO COMMIT BURGLARY OR SOMETHING. NO, WHAT SHE WAS DOING WAS LOOKING FOR HER OLD MAN'S CAR PARKED UP IN SOME "HOOCHIE'S" APARTMENT AT 3:00 A.M. ON MONDAY MORNING. CAN I GET A WITNESS?

0349 -I WENT TO THE STATION TO TURN IN THE PAPERWORK THAT I HAD COMPLETED AND TO TYPE ANOTHER REPORT. I ALSO HAD TO TURN SOME SEIZED NARCOTICS IN FOR AN OFF DUTY OFFICER WHO HAD TURNED THEM OVER TO ME.
   WHILE I WAS AT THE STATION, I CALLED TO CHECK MY MESSAGES. FG1 CALLED TO SEE HOW I WAS DOING (TRINI, 40'S). FG3 (PR, 20'S) LEFT A MESSAGE SAYING SHE WASN'T GOING TO CALL ME ANYMORE BECAUSE I NEVER CALL HER BACK. SHE SAID SHE BOUGHT ME SOME STUFF FROM THE MALL AND SHE WOULD JUST PASS IT ON TO ME THROUGH A CO-WORKER OF MINE.

0435 - I DID SOME ROBBERY PREVENTION PATROL IN A

FEW OF MY HOTELS.

0526 - I WENT TO BREAKFAST THEN TO MY BED. -
PEACE. (THAT REMINDS ME I'M GONNA LET YOU GO,
BUT I THOUGHT OF SOMEHING. WHENEVER I SAY
"PEACE" TO MY SON (8 Y.O.) TO END A CONVERSATION
HE SAYS TO ME. "PEACE OUT." KIDS NOWADAYS. O.K..
YOU CAN GO NOW.)

09/27

1800-BRIEFING

1848 - (D) ABANDONED VEHICLE
   NEIGHBORHOOD RESIDENTS CALLED IN ABOUT A WHITE, MITSUBISHI PICK-UP TRUCK THAT SEEMED TO HAVE BEEN ABANDONED AND WAS BLOCKING A STREET. THE VEHICLE WAS PARKED ALONGSIDE THE ROADWAY AND NOT BLOCKING THE FREE FLOW OF TRAFFIC. I RAN THE TAG TO SEE IF IT WAS STOLEN AND IT WAS NOT. AT LEAST, IT HADN'T BEEN REPORTED STOLEN. I DIDN'T TOW IT IMMEDIATELY BECAUSE IT WASN'T PARKED ON A PUBLIC ROADWAY AND IT WASN'T BLOCKING TRAFFIC. I DID, HOWEVER, TAG IT WITH 48 HOUR TOW WARNING THAT WE USE FOR ABANDONED VEHICLES.

1920-I CALLED ONE OF MY COLLEGE INSTRUCTORS TO SAY I MIGHT BE LATE THE NEXT DAY BECAUSE MY SQUAD WAS GOING TO BE SHORT-HANDED. I FOUND OUT HE WASN'T GOING TO BE THERE AT ALL. HE WIFE SAID HE WAS IN THE HOSPITAL. SHE HAD RECENTLY RUSHED HIM TO THE EMERGENCY ROOM WHERE HE RECEIVED AN ANGIOPLASTY. APARARENTLY HE HAD A HEART ATTACK. I TOLD HER I HOPED HE WOULD GET WELL. SHE SAID, "HE BETTER." AS FAR AS MY ATTENDANCE, SHE SAID TO DO THE BEST THAT I COULD.

1925 - I HAD DINNER, BUT IT WAS CUT SHORT...

1931 - (D) SUSPICIOUS INCIDENT
   THE COMPLAINANTS WERE A W/M AND W/F COUPLE IN THEIR 60'S. THEY SAID THEIR SON WAS BEHAVING STRANGELY. HE WAS A W/M IN HIS 40'S WHO LIVED WITH THEM. HE HAD SOME SORT OF MENTAL ILLNESS AND THEY WANTED ME TO TAKE HIM AWAY TO A PSYCHOLOGICAL TREATMENT FACILITY. WHEN I ASKED THEM WHAT HE WAS DOING, THEY SAID HE SMOKES SEVERAL CARTONS OF CIGARETTES DAILY AND HE STAYS UP ALL NIGHT LONG. THE MOTHER SAID SHE WAS AFRAID TO GO TO SLEEP AROUND

HIM. (I THINK SHE JUST THREW THAT PART IN TO MAKE ME ACT IN HER FAVOR.) THEY ALSO SAID HE WAS NOT TAKING HIS MEDICATION. (HE HAD A TON OF MEDICATION, LIKE 20 BOTTLES.) AFTER SPEAKING WITH ALL INVOLVED PARTIES, I DETERMINED THAT THE W/M DID NOT FIT THE CRITERIA TO BE TAKEN TO THE HOSPITAL INVOLUNTARILY. THE REASON BEING HE DID NOT POSE A THREAT TO HIMSELF OR ANYONE ELSE. I TOLD HIM THAT HIS PARENTS WERE ALLOWING HIM TO STAY THERE OUT OF THE KINDNESS OF THEIR HEARTS. HE SHOULD RESPECT THEIR WISHES AND TAKE HIS MEDICATION AND GO TO BED AT A DECENT HOUR. HE WAS ADAMANT ABOUT NOT GOING TO THE HOSPITAL AND CLAIMED HE HAD AN APOINTMENT IN A FEW DAYS AND WOULD GO THEN. I ALSO TOLD THE PARENTS THAT EVEN IF HE MET THE CRITERIA FOR ME TO TAKE HIM, THEY COULD ONLY REQUIRE HE STAY FOR A FEW DAYS, THEN HE'D BE FREE TO LEAVE. I TOLD THEM IT WOULD JUST BE A SHORT TERM FIX AS FAR AS THEY WERE CONCERNED. IF THEY HAD A PROBLEM WITH HIM, THEY NEEDED TO MAKE HIM LEAVE THEIR RESIDENCE. THEY SAID THEY LET HIM STAY BECAUSE THEY FELT SORRY FOR HIM AND WOULD FEEL BAD ABOUT KICKING HIM OUT. I TOLD THEM THAT WAS THEIR CHOICE, BUT WE COULDN'T BE OUT THERE EVERYDAY SOLVING THEIR DISPUTES. AFTER TALKING WITH THE W/M AND HIS PARENTS FOR ABOUT AN HOUR, WE CAME TO A SUITABLE CONCLUSION FOR EVERYONE. WE WERE ABLE TO GET HIS DOCTOR ON THE PHONE AND SHE TOLD HIM IT WOULD BE IN HIS BEST INTEREST IF HE GOT SOME IMMEDIATE HELP. HE AGREED TO LET HIS MOTHER AND SISTER TAKE HIM TO A NEARBY FACILITY FOR AN EVALUATION. HOPEFULLY IT WILL WORK OUT FOR THEM ALL. THIS GUY WAS AN ARCHITECT OUT WEST AND BEGAN GOING DOWN HILL AFTER HIS MARRIAGE STARTED TO FAIL.

2050 -I CALLED FG2 AND GOT HER MACHINE. AND SHE SAYS I NEVER CALL. I GUESS I COULD HAVE LEFT A MESSAGE.

2059 - (D) SUSPICIOUS INCIDENT
A B/F IN HER 60'S CAME HOME TO FIND HER PORCH FURNITURE HAD BEEN MOVED AND A PAIR OF SHOES THAT

DIDN'T BELONG TO HER WERE THERE. SHE HAD GONE OUT TO DINNER WITH HER NEXT DOOR NEIGHBOR. HER RESIDENCE WAS EXTREMELY NEAT AND SHE OBVIOUSLY PAID ATTENTION TO DETAIL. ANOTHER OFFICER AND I CHECKED AROUND HER PROPERTY THOROUGHLY AND FOUND NOTHING ELSE OUT OF PLACE. I LEFT HER MY BUSINESS CARD AND TOLD HER NOT TO HESITATE CALLING IN THE EVENT OF ANY OTHER STRANGE OCCURRENCE.

FG2 PAGED ME TWICE. TRYING TO RETURN MY CALL, I GUESS.

2231 - (D) ALARM
I WAS DISPATCHED TO A COMMERCIAL ALARM AT A DEPARTMENT STORE IN A MALL. I CALLED MALL SECURITY AND TURNED IT OVER TO THEM.

2245 -I CALLED FG2 BACK AND WE JUST TALKED ABOUT OUR KIDS MY TWO AND HER ONE.

2300-I WORKED ON SOME PAPERWORK WHILE TALKING TO A GUY ON MY SQUAD , ONE CRUISER FACING ONE WAY , THE OTHER FACING THE OPPOSITE DIRECTION. YOU'VE SEEN IT BEFORE. THAT'S JUST TALKING "GROWN FOLKS" BUSINESS YOU DON'T KNOW NOTHIN' 'BOUT THAT.

0130-I DID HOTEL PARKING LOT PATROLLING. VISUAL PRESENCE IS THE FIRST KEY TO DETERRENCE.

0210 -I WENT TO THE STATION TO TURN IN MY PAPERWORK.

0232 - (D) DISTURBANCE
I WAS DISPATCHED TO A LOUD PARTY IN AN APARTMENT COMPLEX. IT WAS AN AREA CHECK ONLY AND THE CALLER DIDN'T WANT TO MEET. I HAD TO BREAK FROM THAT TO RESPOND TO A BURGLARY IN PROGRESS...

0235 - (BU) BURGLARY
UPON ARRIVING, I FOUND OUT THAT SOMEONE HAD SNATCHED SOME CIGARETTES AND RAN OUT OF THE

GROCERY STORE. AFTER LEARNING THE DETAILS FIVE OTHER
RESPONDING OFFICERS AND I CLEARED OUT AND LEFT THE
INITIAL RESPONDING OFFICER TO HANDLE THE CALL AS A
RETAIL THEFT.

0300 - AFTER HANDLING THE LOUD PARTY CALL, I WENT
TO EAT AGAIN. THE COOK LEAVES AT 2:00 A.M., BUT
THE CAFETERIA REMAINS OPEN. I GOT A TUNA FISH
SANDWICH AND SOME YOGURT.

0342 - IT WAS QUIET OUT. I PARKED AT A GAS STATION
IN THE CENTER OF MY AREA AND WORKED ON SOME
PAPER.

0434 - A YOUNG, W/M IN A HONDA DROVE UP TO ME AND
ASKED IF I KNEW WHERE A 24 HOUR DUNKIN' DONUTS
WAS BECAUSE THE ONE UP THE STREET DOESN'T OPEN
UNTIL 5. THE NERVE OF HIM, ASKING ME SOMETHING
LIKE THAT. ASKING DIRECTIONS IS ONE THING BUT TO
DUNKIN' DONUTS!
    SEE YA NEXT ENTRY.

09/28

2041-I HEADED FROM SCHOOL TO WORK.

2049 - FG3 CALLED ME AND LEFT A MESSAGE SAYING, "HOW COME YOU DON'T CALL ME. ALL I DO IS WORK, GO TO SCHOOL AND MISS YOU."

2102-I WENT TO EAT. I HAD STEAK, SALMON, STRING BEANS, AND MASHED POTATOES.

2120-I GASSED UP THE CRUISER.

2127 -(D) STOLEN CAR
   I WAS DISPATCHED TO A STOLEN CAR AT A THEME PARK IN MY AREA. THEY CANCELLED ME BEFORE I COULD GET THERE. SECURITY HAD FOUND THE CAR. IT'S A BIG PARKING LOT.   PEOPLE THINKING THEIR CAR IS STOLEN WHEN THEY ACTUALLY FORGET WHERE THEY PARKED IS A FREQUENT OCCURRENCE.

2133 - FG2 CALLED ME AND ASKED HOW SCHOOL WENT. I TOLD HER ABOUT MY INSTUCTOR WHO WAS RUSHED TO EMERGENCY. THE SESSION WAS VIDEO TAPED. AT THE END OF CLASS, ALL THE STUDENTS STOOD BEFORE THE CAMERA AND RECORDED A GET WELL MESSAGE. THAT'S GOT TO BE GOOD FOR AT LEAST A FEW EXTRA CREDIT POINTS.

2145 - (D) SUSPICIOUS INCIDENT
   A W/F CALLED AND SAID A CAR FOLLOWED HER HOME AND PARKED IN FRONT OF HER HOUSE FOR A WHILE. WHEN I GOT THERE, SHE SAID, "WHO IS IT?" I SAID, "SHERIFF'S OFFICE." SHE SAID, "OH, DO I HAVE TO OPEN THE DOOR?" I SAID, "AH, NO." SHE SAID, "BECAUSE I DON'T HAVE ANY CLOTHES ON I DIDN'T KNOW THEY WOULD SEND SOMEONE." I SAID, "SO DID YOU JUST WANT US TO CHECK THE AREA?" SHE SAID YES, AND I TOLD HER I'D DO THAT. SHE SAID, "THANK YOU FOR COMING. I CALLED MY HUSBAND AND HE SAID I SHOULD CALL YOU SO I DID." (I'D TELL YOU HER APPROXIMATE AGE, BUT I DON'T KNOW IT. SHE STOOD AT THE WINDOW WITH HER

CURTAINS DRAPED AROUND HER SO I DIDN'T SEE IT I MEAN, HER.

2216-I STOPPED IN ON A LOCAL NIGHTCLUB TO SEE IF ANYTHING EXCITING WAS GOING ON. NOTHING EXCITING WAS GOING ON.

2305-ON PATROL

2323 - (D) DISTURBANCE
   ANOTHER   LOUD   MUSIC   CALL   AT   MY   PROBLEM APARTMENTS.

2325 - MY SERGEANT CALLED ME AND ASKED IF I HAD EATEN. HE WAS EATING AT A RESTAURANT IN MY AREA AND WANTED ME TO JOIN HIM. I TOLD HIM I ATE AFTER SCHOOL. HE SAID, "ANOTHER TIME."
   I CLEARED THE LOUD MUSIC CALL.

2336 - (BU) ALARM
   I BACKED ANOTHER UNIT WHO WAS RESPONDING TO AN ALARM AT A CHURCH. WE FOUND ONE OF THE DOORS OPEN SO WE SEARCHED THE BUILDING. EVERYTHING SEEMED TO BE IN PLACE. THE ALARM RESPONDER LIVED CLOSED TO THE CHURCH AND CAME OUT AND RESET IT.

0005 - FG3 CALLED ME. I TOLD HER SHE SHOULD BE IN BED BECAUSE SHE HAD SCHOOL IN THE MORNING. AFTER WE TALKED A WHILE, I TOLD HER I JUST COULDN'T BE WITH HER, AND SHE STARTED CRYING. I CAN HANDLE A LOT OF THINGS, BUT NOT CRYING.

0010 - (D) AREA CHECK
   ONCE AGAIN, I WAS DISPATCHED TO CHECK THE AREA OF THOSE APARTMENTS FOR LOUD MUSIC.

0030 - (S) TRAFFIC STOP
   I STOPPED A CAR WITH A TAG ON IT THAT HAD BEEN EXPIRED FOR OVER A MONTH. THE OCCUPANTS OF THE VEHICLE WERE TWO YOUNG, H/M'S. THE DRIVER PRODUCED ANOTHER TAG

FOR THE VEHICLE. IT HAD BEEN EXPIRED FOR TWO DAYS. I GAVE HIM A VERBAL WARNING AND LET HIM GO.

0035-I DROPPED INTO THE GAS STATION WHERE THE OLDER W/M WORKS TO USE THE RESTROOM. WHEN I ASKED HIM HOW HE WAS DOING, HE SAID, "O.K., BUT IT'S STILL EARLY." ALWAYS A SOURCE OF OPTIMISM.

0040 -I CALLED FG3 BACK 'CAUSE I FELT BAD FOR HER.

0109 - TRYIN' TO STAY AWAKE. LOOKIN' FOR CRIME. TOO QUIET OUT.
    I SPOKE TOO SOON...

0115 - (BU) ARMED ROBBERY
    A W/M IN HIS 30'S WAS ROBBED IN THE PARKING LOT NEAR HIS VEHICLE. TWO B/M'S WEARING DARK CLOTHING AND MASKS, ONE CARRYING A 38 AND THE OTHER A 45, ATTACKED HIM. THEY PISTOL WHIPPED HIM AND STOLE HIS FANNY PACK. INSIDE HIS FANNY PACK WAS A NEW JERSEY POLICE BADGE AND A FIREFIGHTER SHIELD. AN OFFICER WHO WAS WORKING OFF-DUTY AT THE HOTEL TOOK THE CALL. I SET UP A ROAD BLOCK/CHECK POINT IN THE AREA. WHILE I WAS CHECKING CARS, PEOPLE DIDN'T HESITATE TO ASK ME FOR DIRECTIONS TO WHERE THEY WERE GOING. INSPITE OF THE FACT THAT K-9 AND HELICOPTERS WERE USED TO TRACK THE SUSPECTS, WE WERE UNABLE TO LOCATE THEM. THE VICTIM WAS NOT BADLY INJURED AND SEEMED TO HANDLE THE INCIDENT WELL. I GUESS HE WAS A COP/VOLUNTEER FIREFIGHTER VISITING FROM NEW JERSEY. HECK OF A VACATION, HUH?

0215-(D) ALARM
    I WAS DISPATCHED TO A RESIDENTIAL ALARM. THE HOME APPEARED TO BE SECURE AND I CLEARED.

0235 - (D) VEHICLE BURGLARY
    I WAS DISPATCHED TO A CAR BURGLARY THAT OCCURRED AT A HOTEL. SOMEONE STOLE A CAB DRIVER'S METER FROM HIS VEHICLE WHILE IT WAS PARKED IN THE FRONT DRIVEWAY. HE SUSPECTED A RIVAL CABBIE OF THE OFFENSE, BUT WAS UNSURE. THE HOTEL HAD A CAMERA THAT CONTINUOUSLY

VIDEO TAPED THE FRONT DRIVEWAY, BUT THE MANAGER ON DUTY COULDN'T FIND THE INCIDENT UPON REVIEW OF THE TAPE. I TOOK THE REPORT AND ASKED THE MANAGER TO CONTACT US IF HE CAME UP WITH ANYTHING.

0300 - (S) CITIZEN ASSIST
   WHILE DEALING WITH THE CAB DRIVER, A W/F IN HER 30'S APPROACHED ME. SHE WANTED TO KNOW IF I COULD HELP HER GET INTO HER VEHICLE BECAUSE SHE WAS LOCKED OUT. I TOLD HER I DIDN'T CARRY A SLIM JIM, AND EVEN IF I DID, I DIDN'T KNOW HOW TO USE ONE. I TOLD HER SHE COULD USE MY CELL PHONE TO CALL A LOCKSMITH. THEN I REMEMBERED WE WERE AT A HOTEL. I TOLD HER I WAS SURE THAT THE HOTEL WOULD BE HAPPY TO LET HER USE THEIR PHONE TO CALL ONE. SHE INSISTED ON WAITING FOR ME TO FINISH WITH THE CAB DRIVER SO I COULD HELP HER AND SHE COULD USE MY PHONE. (WHY SHE GOTTA USE UP MY MINUTES?) AFTER CLEARING FROM THE CAB DRIVER, I ASKED HER, "HOW'D YOU MANAGE TO LOCK YOURSELF OUT?" SHE SAID SHE AND HER GIRLFRIEND HAD COME TO THE HOTEL'S NIGHTCLUB TOGETHER. HER FRIEND, WHO'S PURSE CONTAINED HER CAR KEYS, HAD GONE HOME WITH SOME GUY. I KEEP A COUPLE OF TWISTED UP HANGARS IN MY TRUNK FOR SUCH INSTANCES AND I TRIED TO GET IN USING THEM. I CAME VERY CLOSE TO UNLOCKING HER DOOR, BUT NOT QUITE. I TALKED TO THE LADY WHILE I WAS WORKING ON GETTING IN. SHE WAS AN EMERGENCY ROOM NURSE AT A LOCAL HOSPTIAL. WE WERE INTERUPPTED BY AN ALERT TONE FROM MY RADIO ADVISING OF A RESIDENTIAL BURGLARY IN PROGRESS. I TOLD HER, " I HAVE TO GO, BUT I'LL LEAVE MY PHONE WITH YOU, AND GET IT WHEN I COME BACK." I THOUGHT I'D BE BACK SHORTLY AFTER TAKING THE CALL. THAT SHOULD'VE GIVEN HER SUFFICIENT TIME TO CALL A LOCKSMITH AND GET INTO HER CAR. SHE SAID, "I PROMISE I'LL BE HERE WHEN YOU GET BACK."

0345 - (D) RESIDENTIAL BURGLARY
   I RESPONDED TO THE HOME OF A PUERTO RICAN FAMILY. THE HUSBAND ADVISED HIS WIFE'S SCREAMING AWAKENED HIM FROM HIS SLEEP. SHE HAD SEEN A YOUNG, B/M STANDING ON THEIR BACK PATIO. THE B/M WAS PEERING AT THEM THROUGH A SLIDING DOOR THAT LED TO THEIR BEDROOM, ATTEMPTING

TO GAIN ENTRY. WHEN SHE SCREAMED, HE RAN OFF. THEY CHOSE NOT TO CALL THAT TIME, BELIEVING THE B/M WOULD NOT RETURN. THEY WERE WRONG. AFTER GOING BACK TO SLEEP, THEY WERE AWAKENED ONCE AGAIN BY THE B/M PEERING AT THEM. AGAIN HE RAN. THIS TIME THEY CALLED 9-1-1. AS I SAT WITH THE HUSBAND AT HIS DINING ROOM TABLE TAKING THE REPORT, WE LISTENED TO THE RADIO AS MY SQUAD MEMBERS ATTEMPTED TO LOCATE THE B/M. HE KEPT OFFERING ME SOME OF THE COFFEE THAT HE WAS BREWING ON THE STOVE. I KEPT SAYING NO, THANK YOU. (HE WASN'T GOING TO KEEP ME UP ALL MORNING DRINKING THAT STRONG STUFF. MY BEDTIME WAS IN THREE OR FOUR HOURS.) A GUY ON MY SQUAD SPOTTED A B/M ON A BICYCLE IN THE AREA WHO FIT THE DESCRIPTION. WHEN HE SAW THE OFFICER, HE DITCHED THE BIKE AND TOOK OFF RUNNING ON FOOT. SHORTLY THEREAFTER, ANOTHER SQUAD MEMBER SAW THE B/M RUN INTO A SWAMPY, WOODED AREA. I TOLD THE VICTIM IT LOOKED LIKE WE WERE GOING TO CATCH THE SUSPECT. (HIS 16 Y/O DAUGHTER WAS TRYING TO SAY SOMETHING TO HIM, BUT HE KEPT "SHUSHING" HER SO HE COULD HEAR THE RADIO TRANSMISSIONS.) A HELICOPTER AND A K-9 OFFICER RESPONDED TO SEARCH THE WOODED AREA FOR THE SUSPECT. THE DOG TRACKED TO THE WOODLINE, BUT THE UNDERBRUSH WAS TOO THICK FOR HIM TO CONTINUE. THE HELICOPTER PILOT WAS UNABLE TO MAKE VISUAL CONTACT OF THE SUSPECT THROUGH THE TREES. ORDINARILY THEY CAN USE AN INFRARED SYSTEM TO DETECT HEAT PATTERNS, BUT I THINK THAT HELICOPTER'S WAS BROKEN. (GO FIGURE) WE STAYED OUT SEARCHING UNTIL DAYLIGHT. THAT DUDE WAS PRETTY BRAVE HOLDING UP LIKE HE WAS IN THAT WOODED SWAMP. AT THE LEAST, HE WAS EATEN UP BY MOSQUITOS IN THERE. BETTER CASE SCENARIO A FLORIDA 'GATOR GOT HIM. I TOLD THE VICTIM WE'D CONTACT HIM FOR SUSPECT IDENTIFICATION IF WE FOUND THE B/M. IN THE MEAN TIME, WE WERE TURNING OVER THE SEARCH TO THE DAY SHIFT.

0541-I WENT BACK TO THE HOTEL'S FRONT DESK TO SEE IF THE EMERGENCY NURSE HAD TURNED MY PHONE OVER TO THEM SINCE I WAS GONE FOR SO LONG. THEY ADVISED SHE HAD NOT. I DECIDED TO GO BACK AROUND TO WHERE SHE WAS PARKED. TO MY

SURPRISE, SHE WAS STILL THERE. SHE WAS ABLE TO
GAIN ACCESS INTO HER CAR USING THE HANGARS.
I TOLD HER, "SORRY IT TOOK SO LONG, I THOUGHT
YOU'D BE GONE BY NOW." SHE SAID, "I TOLD YOU I'D
WAIT. NOW IT'S TIME FOR BREAKFAST." I ASKED, "YOU
BUYIN?" SHE SAID, "YEAH, I'LL BUY SINCE YOU WERE
SO NICE." I TOLD HER, "MAYBE NEXT TIME. I STILL
HAVE A LOT OF PAPERWORK TO DO." SHE ALREADY
HAD HER NUMBER WRITTEN ON A PIECE OF PAPER
WITH A MESSAGE THAT SAID, "THE WOMAN WHO
WAS LOCKED OUT OF HER CAR NOW YOU'LL NEVER
FORGET ME." SHE'S RIGHT, I PROBABLY WON'T AND
YOU PROBABLY WON'T EITHER.

0641-I FINALLY FINISHED UP THE BURGLARY REPORT
AND GOT IT TURNED IN. NOW I'M GOING TO EAT.
(WHERE'S THE NURSE WHEN YOU NEED HER? I WAS
ALMOST TEMPTED TO CALL HER AND SAY HAVE
BREAKFAST READY I'LL BE THERE IN 15.) REMEMBER,
I ONLY ATE ONCE LAST NIGHT AND YOU KNOW THAT
'AINT RIGHT.
    LATER.

10/02

1800-BRIEFING

1900-I HAD DINNER; SWEET AND SOUR PORK OVER RICE AND MIXED VEGETABLES.

1920 - (D) PETIT THEFT
  I WAS DISPATCHED TO A DEPARTMENT STORE IN A MALL. A CLERK'S PURSE WAS STOLEN FROM BEHIND THE COUNTER. THE YOUNG W/F ADVISED SHE LEFT HER PURSE AND THE STORE UNATTENDED FOR JUST A FEW MINUTES. SHE RAN A COUPLE OF DOORS DOWN TO PICK UP SOME FOOD THAT SHE HAD ORDERED. SHE ASKED THE CLERK FROM THE STORE ACROSS THE WAY TO KEEP AN EYE ON HER STORE. WHEN SHE RETURNED, HER PURSE WAS GONE. THE STORE HAD NO VIDEO SURVEILLANCE AND SHE HAD NO CLUE AS TO WHO WAS RESPONSIBLE. WHILE SHE FILLED OUT HER STATEMENT, I TOOK A LOOK AROUND THE STORE. THOSE LITTLE, SHINY, RAYON MUSCLE SHIRTS WERE $100.00. I THINK IT WAS A "VERSACE" OR SOMETHING. I ASKED THE W/F, "THIS SHIRT COSTS $100.00?" SHE LAUGHED AND SAID, "YEP." NEEDLESS TO SAY, I LOOKED NO FURTHER. MALL SECURITY CHECKED THE GARBAGE CANS IN THE AREA WITH NO SUCCESS.

2030 -I WAS DOING A CHECK OF SOME AREA BUSINESSES WHEN FG2 PAGED ME.

2130-I CALLED FG2 BACK AND SHE HELPED ME WITH MY PORTUGUESE. (YOU KNOW, I'LL PROBABLY END UP CALLING HER FG1 SINCE SHE'S THE ONLY ONE I SPEAK TO ANYMORE, BUT NOT YET. I'LL LET YOU KNOW.)

2210 - (D) DISTURBANCE
  RESTAURANT GUESTS AT A LOCAL RESORT WERE REFUSING TO PAY. I WAS CANCELLED BY ANOTHER UNIT PRIOR TO MY ARRIVAL.

2236 - (D) TRAFFIC STOP
I STOPPED A W/F (40'S) FOR HAVING AN UNASSIGNED TAG
ON HER CAR. SHE HAD THE PROPER TAG IN HER CAR. SHE
SAID SHE WAS WAITING FOR HER BIRTHDAY TO CHANGE
IT. I TOLD HER SHE NEEDED TO SWITCH IT AS SOON AS
POSSIBLE BECAUSE THE OLD TAG BECAME INVALID WHEN
THEY ISSUED HER THE NEW ONE. SHE ASKED ME IF SHE HAD
TO CHANGE IT ON THE SPOT OR IF SHE COULD WAIT UNTIL
SHE GOT HOME. I TOLD HER SHE COULD WAIT. SHE SAID,
"GOOD BECAUSE I'M TAKING MY CAT TO THE EMERGENCY
ROOM. I THANK YOU AND MY CAT THANKS YOU."

**2308 -I GOT FLAGGED DOWN BY A TOURIST WHO
THOUGHT I WAS A TAXI CAB DRIVER "OH, SORRY."**

2345 - (S) TRAFFIC STOP
I STOPPED A COUPLE WHO SPOKE NO ENGLISH.
APPARENTLY RAIN HAD WASHED THE NUMBERS OFF THEIR
TEMPORARY TAG. I CHECKED THE DRIVER'S LICENSE AND
LET THEM GO.

**0005 -I STOPPED AT A CONVENIENCE STORE FOR
SOME CRANBERRY JUICE AND A HEADACHE POWDER.
I HAVE A SLIGHT ONE.**

0030 - (S) TRAFFIC STOP
I STOPPED A B/M (40+) WHO RAN A STOP SIGN. HIS LICENSE
WAS GOOD SO I LET HIM GO WITH A WRITTEN WARNING.

0043- (S) TRAFFIC STOP
I CONDUCTED A TRAFFIC STOP OF A VIHICLE WITH AN
UNREADABLE TEMPORARY TAG. THE DRIVER HAD A VALID
LICENSE AND I CUT HIM LOOSE.

0048 - (D) BUSINESS CHECK
A RESTAURANT MANAGER CALLED IN AND ASKED THAT
WE CHECK THE BUSINESS THROUGHOUT THE NIGHT. THE
ALARM WAS NOT FUNCTIONING PROPERLY.

0110-I PULLED INTO A SHOPPING PLAZA TO WORK ON

SOME HOMEWORK.

0113 - (BU) DISTURBANCE

I WENT TO BACK ANOTHER UNIT WHO WAS RESPONDING TO A FIGHT AT A RESTAURANT/BAR. ONE HALF OF THE DISPUTE (YOUNG W/M AND W/F) HAD LEFT THE RESTAURANT. A RESERVE OFFICER, WHO'S "REAL" JOB IS PASTORING A CHURCH, STOPPED THEM DOWN THE ROAD FROM THE RESTAURANT. I WENT DOWN TO BACK HIM UP. BOTH PARTIES, THE ONE ON THE TRAFFIC STOP AS WELL AS THE HALF AT THE RESTAURANT, CLAIMED THE OTHER WAS THE AGGRESSOR. BOTH WANTED TO PRESS CHARGES AGAINST EACH OTHER. WE GAVE THEM PAPERWORK TO COMPLETE AND TOLD THEM TO RESPOND TO THE STATION ON A LATER DATE IN ORDER TO PURSUE CHARGES. (THIS GIVES THE PARTIES THE OPPORTUNITY TO CALM DOWN. THEY USUALLY CHANGE THEIR MINDS ABOUT PROSECUTING A DAY OR SO LATER. THAT OR THEY'RE TOO LAZY TO GO DOWN TO THE STATION.) AFTERWARDS, A GUY ON MY SQUAD ASKED THE DRIVER IF HE WOULD PASS A FIELD SOBRIETY TEST IF SUBJECTED TO ONE. HE WAS UNSURE. THUS, HE WAS MADE TO LEAVE HIS VEHICLE THERE AND CALL A RIDE FOR HIM AND HIS GIRLFRIEND.

0159-I STOPPED OFF TO WASH THE CAR AND GET SOME GAS.

0239 - (D) SUSPICIOUS INCIDENT

I WAS DISPATCHED TO AN AREA HOTEL IN REFERENCE TO A YOUNG, W/F WHO WAS GRANTED ACCESS TO A ROOM UNDER FALSE PRETENCES. THE W/M WHO HAD OBTAINED THE ROOM GOT ARRESTED EARLIER IN THE DAY AFTER A DRUG STING OPERATION. SHE TOLD HOTEL MANAGEMENT THAT SHE WAS MARRIED TO HIM AND WANTED TO GET INTO THE ROOM TO REMOVE THEIR PROPERTY. MANAGEMENT CALLED US BECAUSE ANOTHER HOTEL GUEST SAID THEY HEARD WHAT SOUNDED LIKE A GUNSHOT FROM THE ROOM WHERE THE W/F WAS. THAT GUEST LATER SAID IT MAY HAVE BEEN A SAFE SLAMMING. MANAGEMENT WANTED ME TO CHECK ON THE POSSIBLE SHOT IN ADDITION TO DETERMINING HER IDENTITY AND WHETHER OR NOT SHE

WAS AUTHORIZED TO BE IN THE ROOM. SHE BECAME BELLIGERENT WHEN I CONFRONTED HER. I TOLD HER SHE HAD NO BUSINESS BEING IN THE ROOM AND HOTEL MANAGEMENT WANTED HER TO LEAVE. SHE REFUSED TO DO SO, STATING SHE WAS GOING TO STAY FOR SEVERAL MORE DAYS. WHEN I TOLD HER SHE'D BE ARRESTED IF SHE DIDN'T LEAVE, SHE SAID, "WELL, DAMNIT, JUST ARREST ME. I'M TIRED OF YA'LL !#*%ING WITH ME, JUST TAKE ME TO JAIL." (SHE OBVIOUSLY HAD A LESS THAN PLEASANT LAW ENFORCEMENT EXPERIENCE EARLIER.) I KEPT TRYING TO GIVE HER A CHANCE TO GO AHEAD AND LEAVE. SHE WOULDN'T SO I 'CUFFED HER. I ASKED HER WHAT SHE WAS ON BASED ON THE WAY SHE WAS ACTING. SHE SAID. "NOTHING, WHAT DO YOU THINK?" I SAID, "I THINK YOU ON CRACK AS CRAZY AS YOU ACTIN'." NEEDLESS TO SAY, SHE REFUSED TO COOPERATE WITH ME IN COMPLETING HER CHARGING PAPERWORK. AND BELIEVE IT OR NOT, SHE DIDN'T CONVERSE WITH ME ON THE WAY TO JAIL.

0530 -I RUSHED TO GET MY PAPERWORK DONE AND TURNED IN BY 0600. I MADE IT.

0600 I WENT TO GET SOME PANCAKES, BACON AND EGGS.   BY-BYE- NOW.

10/03

2000 - BRIEFING

2022 - HEADED TO DINNER, BUT GOT A CALL WHILE ON THE WAY...

2025 - (D) DISTURBANCE
 A B/F CALLED ADVISING THAT IT SOUNDED LIKE A MAN AND WOMAN WERE FIGHTING NEXT DOOR. I KNOCKED ON THE CALLER'S DOOR TO FIND OUT IF IT WAS THE APARTMENT TO HER LEFT OR RIGHT. SHE PEEKED AROUND HER SLIGHTLY OPENED DOOR AND TOLD ME LEFT. SHORTLY THEREAFTER, THE DISPATCHER CALLED ME AND SAID THE CALLER DID NOT WANT TO MEET. (OOPS) ABOUT FOUR OTHER GUYS ON MY SQUAD AND I HAD SHOWN UP. (WE HAD JUST LEFT BRIEFING AND THE APARTMENTS WERE CLOSE TO THE STATION.) WE MADE CONTACT WITH THE OCCUPANTS OF THE APARTMENT WHERE THE DISTURBANCE WAS. THERE WAS ONE YOUNG, W/M, WHOM THE APARTMENT BELONGED TO, TWO YOUNG B/M'S AND A YOUNG B/F. ONE OF THE B/M'S WAS IN THE LIVING ROOM ON THE COUCH. THE OTHER WAS IN THE BEDROOM WITH THE B/F. I TOLD THEM TO COME INTO THE LIVING ROOM. I ASKED THE B/M WHAT WAS GOING ON AND HE SAID NOTHING. I SAID, "THEN HOW COME YOU'RE SWEATING AND WHY'S THE MATTRESS ON THE FLOOR IN THERE." HE SAID, "NO REASON, SIR." I TOLD HIM, "THE NEIGHBORS COMPLAINED OF FIGHTING BETWEEN A MALE AND FEMALE IN HERE." HE SAID, "WE WERE'NT FIGHTING, SIR." AFTER GOING AROUND IN CIRCLES FOR A WHILE, THE B/F SAID, "IF YOU WANT TO KNOW THE TRUTH, WE WERE HAVING SEX." THE B/M AGREED AND SAID TO THE GIRL, "I TOLD YOU, YOU WERE TOO LOUD." I HAD NO CHOICE BUT TO BELIEVE THEM. THERE WERE NO SIGNS OF INJURIES TO EITHER PARTY, JUST THE GUY'S EXCESSIVE HEART RATE. (SHE WAS CALM. SHE APPARENTLY HADN'T BEEN WORKING TOO HARD.) BUT I DIGRESS; I CHECKED EVERYONE'S IDENTIFICATION AND RAN THEM. THE B/M WHO WAS SITTING ON THE COUCH (15 Y/O BY THE WAY) WAS WANTED FOR POSSESSION OF MARIJUANNA. I ARRESTED HIM AND TOOK HIM TO THE JUVENILE DETENTION CENTER.

2153-I LEFT THE FACILITY AND HEADED BACK TO MY AREA, HOPING TO GET SOMETHING TO EAT.

2155-I CALLED HOME TO CHECK MY MESSAGES. FG3 HAD CALLED AND LEFT A MESSAGE SAYING, "I MISS YOU AND I LOVE YOU. CALL ME BACK." NOW I'M DEFINITELY NOT CALLING BACK!

0003 - FOR DINNER I HAD SPAGHETTI WITH MEAT SAUCE, BROCOLLI, SQUASH, AND ITALIAN SAUSAGE.

0034 - (BU) TRAFFIC STOP
  I WENT TO BACK UP ANOTHER UNIT ON A TRAFFIC STOP IN MY AREA. HIS COMPUTER SHOWED THE REGISTERED OWNER OF THE VEHICLE HAD A COUPLE OF DUI'S AND HIS LICENSE WAS REVOKED FOR 10 YEARS. AS IT TURNED OUT, THE DRIVER OF THE VEHICLE WAS A FRIEND OF THE OWNER.

0056 - (S) TRAFFIC STOP
  I STOPPED A VEHICLE ON THE INTERSTATE BECAUSE THE TAG ATTACHED TO IT WAS NOT ASSIGNED. THE DRIVER WAS A W/F (40'S) WHO SAID THE TRUCK BELONGED TO HER BOYFRIEND. I TOLD HER TO TELL HER BOYFRIEND THAT WAS AN ARRESTABLE OFFENSE. AFTER VERIFYING THE VALIDITY OF HER LICENSE, I LET HER GO. SHE THANKED ME AND LEFT.

0120 - (BU) TRAFFIC CRASH
  I RESPONDED TO A POND NEAR AN APARTMENT COMPLEX. A YOUNG W/M HAD DRIVEN HIS SATURN INTO IT. FORTUNATELY HE WAS ABLE TO ESCAPE THE VEHICLE. ALL THAT COULD BE SEEN OF HIS CAR WAS THE VERY TAIL END OF IT TO INCLUDE HIS LICENSE PLATE. HE WAS STANDING ON THE EDGE OF THE POND, WRAPPED IN A YELLOW SHEET THAT THE FIRE/RESCUE GUYS HAD GIVEN HIM. I DON'T KNOW IF HE WAS DRUNK OR JUST DRIVING TOO FAST. THE POND WAS JUST OFF OF A CURVE IN THE ROADWAY. IF HE WAS DRUNK HE WAS SOBER NOW.

0152-(BU) MAN DOWN

I WENT TO BACK A SQUAD MEMBER WHO WAS RESPONDING TO A CALL ADVISING A B/M WAS PASSED OUT BEHIND THE WHEEL AT A GAS PUMP. AS IT TURNED OUT, THE B/M WAS JUST SLEEPING. HE HAD JUST GOTTEN OFF WORK AND WAS EXHAUSTED.

0157- (BU) DISTURBANCE

THIS CALL WAS OCCURRING AT A RESORT. IT WAS AN ARGUMENT BETWEEN A PUERTO RICAN COUPLE, HE WAS 40 AND SHE WAS 19. THEY WERE IN FLORIDA ON VACATION. SHE HAD CALLED 9-1-1, BUT WOULDN'T COOPERATE WHEN ASKED WHAT WAS GOING ON. THE H/M SAID SHE GOT UPSET WITH HIM BECAUSE HE DRANK A LITTLE ALCOHOL AFTER HAVING QUIT SEVERAL MONTHS AGO. THE ALTERCATION SEEMED TO HAVE BEEN VERBAL ONLY. SHE DECIDED TO FLY BACK TO PUERTO RICO FIRST THING IN THE MORNING. IN THE MEANTIME, THE RESORT GAVE HER A SEPARATE ROOM FOR THE NIGHT.

0223 - GOT SOME GAS

0230 - (S) TRAFFIC STOP

I STOPPED A CAR WITH AN UNREADABLE TEMPORARY TAG. THE B/M DRIVER (30'S) HAD A FLORIDA IDENTIFICATION CARD ONLY. HE SAID HE WAS ON HIS WAY HOME FROM WORK. HE TOLD ME HE DID POSSESS A VALID FLORIDA LICENSE, THOUGH HE DIDN'T HAVE IT ON HIM. I RAN HIM TO CHECK. ALL THE WHILE I JUST KNEW THEY WERE GOING TO TELL ME HIS LICENSE WAS SUSPENDED AND HE WAS GOING TO JAIL. THE OPERATOR CAME BACK ADVISING HE DID HAVE A VALID FLORIDA LICENSE. (WELL, WELL, WELL, SOMEONE WAS ACTUALLY TELLING ME THE TRUTH.) I THANKED HIM FOR HIS COOPERATION AND LET HIM GO.

0300 - (S) TRAFFIC STOP

I STOPPED ANOTHER CAR WITH AN UNREADABLE TEMPORARY TAG. ONCE I STOPPED IT, I REALIZED THE TAG HAD EXPIRED. THE OCCUPANTS WERE A YOUNG W/M AND W/F FROM HUNGARY. THEY SPOKE VERY LITTLE ENGLISH. I MANAGED TO COMMUNICATE TO THEM THAT I WANTED

TO SEE A LICENSE. THE W/M PRESENTED ME HIS FOREIGN LICENSE. I TOLD HIM IF HE WAS GOING TO REMAIN IN FLORIDA HE NEEDED TO OBTAIN A FLORIDA LICENSE. THE COUPLE WAS EXTREMELY FRIENDLY. I GAVE HIM A VERBAL WARNING ABOUT THE TAG AND LET THEM GO.

0315-(S) TRAFFIC STOP

I STOPPED A CAR BECAUSE THE TAG ATTACHED TO IT WAS NOT ASSIGNED. ONCE I STOPPED THE CAR, I REALIZED I HAD READ THE TAG WRONG. I RERAN IT USING THE CORRECT INFORMATION. THE TAG WAS THE PROPER ONE AND THE OWNER HAD A VALID LICENSE. WHEN THE YOUNG W/F WALKED BACK TO ME, I ASKED IF SHE WAS THE REGISTERED OWNER. SHE SAID, "YES." I SAID, "O.K., I READ YOUR TAG WRONG. YOU'RE FREE TO GO." SHE SAID, "THANKS."

0325 - IT WAS QUIET AND RAINY OUT. I WENT TO TURN IN MY PAPERWORK AND DID A LITTLE STUDYING.

0417 - (BU) SUSPICIOUS INCIDENT

I RESPONDED TO AN AREA HOTEL TO ASSIST MY PARTNER. HOTEL SECURITY ADVISED THERE WAS A LOT OF TRAFFIC IN AND OUT OF ONE OF THE ROOMS. HE BELIEVED THE TRAFFIC WAS DRUG-RELATED. THE ROOM OCCUPANTS WERE THREE YOUNG, B/F'S AND ONE YOUNG B/M. THEY ALLOWED US TO SEARCH THE ROOM AND WE DID NOT LOCATE ANY DRUGS. THE OCCUPANTS PROMISED TO KEEP THE NOISE AND TRAFFIC DOWN. SECURITY WARNED THEM THAT THEY'D BE KICKED OUT IF THEY DIDN'T. (HOTELS HERE CAN DO THAT AT WILL.)

0445 - I WENT TO BREAKFAST AND HAD PANCAKES, EGGS, BACON, ORANGE JUICE, AND WATER.

0553 - I HEADED TO THE HOUSE. PEACE.

10/06

1800 - MY SQUAD HAD TO ATTEND SOME TRAINING AT ANOTHER STATION IN THE COUNTY. THE TRAINING COVERED USE OF FORCE OPTIONS AND WHAT WE MIGHT CONSIDER AS OPPOSED TO "BUSTING A CAP" INTO SOMEONE. (THE INSTRUCTOR DIDN'T USE SUCH ARCHAIC TERMINOLOGY THOUGH AS I'M SURE YOU KNOW.)

2030 - BRIEFING

2106-(D) ALARM
  I RESPONDED TO A COMMERCIAL ALARM. THE BUILDING APPEARED SECURE AND I CLEARED THE CALL.

2200 - MYFRIEND (B/M, 30) CALLED AND I SPOKE TO HIM BRIEFLY.

2215 - FG3 CALLED, BUT I DIDN'T ANSWER THE PHONE.
  THERE'S ABSOLUTELY NOTHING GOING ON TONIGHT.

2341 - (D) DISTURBANCE
  I RESPONDED TO A RESIDENCE IN REFERENCE TO A PUERTO RICAN COUPLE THAT WAS ARGUING. THE H/F WAS 37 Y/O AND THE H/M WAS 47 Y/O. THEY WERE BOTH TEACHERS AND THEY EACH HAD AN ADDITIONAL PARTTIME JOB. THEY HAD TWO DAUGHTERS. ONLY THE YOUNGEST DAUGHTER HAD THEM IN COMMON. THE ELDEST WAS FROM THE H/F'S PREVIOUS MARRIAGE. SHE HAD CALLED ADVISING HE WAS HARASSING HER. SHE SAID HE CAME UP TO HER PARTTIME JOB ARGUING WITH HER. HE CLAIMS HE ONLY WENT UP THERE TO CHECK HER CAR DOORS. HE SAID SHE'S FORGETFUL AND SOMETIMES LEAVES THE DOORS UNLOCKED. (YEAHHH) THE TWO WERE BICKERING BACK AND FORTH LIKE CHILDREN. ANOTHER OFFICER ASKED THEM WHAT KIND OF EXAMPLE THEY WERE SETTING FOR THEIR CHILDREN AND THEY DIDN'T RESPOND. WE TOLD THEM WE WERE'NT GOING TO FORCE THEM, BUT IT WOULD PROBABLY BE A GOOD IDEA IF ONE OF THEM LEFT FOR THE NIGHT. SHE REFUSED AND HE GRUDGEDLY AGREED. HE REALIZED THAT STAYING AND RISKING A FALSE ALLEGATION OF

DOMESTIC BATTERY WAS NOT WORTH LOSING HIS TEACHING JOB.

FG4 CALLED ME. (SHE SPEAKS LITTLE ENGLISH.) SHE SAID, "I MISS YOU, BUT WORK I WORKEE, WORKEE, WORKEE, SO NO TELEFONEE." (HOLD UP A MINUTE THAT'S MY LINE!)

FG3 ALSO CALLED ME. I'M NOT CALLING HER ANYMORE THOUGH.

0050 -I HAD DINNER. IT CONSISTED OF VEGATABLE LASAGNA AND STIR-FRY BEEF.

0135-(S) TRAFFIC STOP
I STOPPED A YOUNG, B/M IN THE PARKING GARAGE OF A MALL. HIS LICENSE WAS SUSPENDED, BUT HE CLAIMED HE DIDN'T KNOW IT. ALSO, HIS TAG WAS EXPIRED. HE IMMEDIATELY ADMITTED NOT HAVING INSURANCE. HE SAID HE DIDN'T HAVE THE MONEY TO RENEW IT. (HE DIDN'T HAVE THE MONEY FOR INSURANCE, BUT HE DID HAVE THE MONEY FOR A NIGHT OUT ON THE TOWN. IT APPEARED THAT HE WAS ON A DATE. HE WAS ACCOMPANIED BY A YOUNG, B/F.) I WAS GOING TO TAKE HIM TO JAIL. I WAS GOING TO, BUT MY SERGEANT SAID JUST WRITE HIM A TICKET. I WROTE HIM THREE.

ANOTHER OFFICER WAS WORKING OFF-DUTY AT THAT MALL. HE HAD STOPPED A YOUNG, W/M WHO WAS DRIVING A BLACK CAMARO. THE PURPOSE OF THE STOP I DON'T KNOW. HE ENDED UP ARRESTING HIM BECAUSE HIS LICENSE WAS SUSPENDED AND HE HAD A BAG OF MARIJUANNA IN HIS POCKET. THE OFFICER WAS DRIVING AN UNMARKED PICK-UP TRUCK WITHOUT A CAGE IN THE BACK. THEREFORE, I TRANSPORTED HIS PRISONER TO JAIL FOR HIM.

FG3 KEPT CALLING ME AND LEAVING MESSAGES. FINALLY I HAD TO TURN MY CELL OFF.

0327 -I HAD TO GO BACK TO THE JAIL. I FORGOT THAT OTHER OFFICER'S HANDCUFFS THERE.

MY SERGEANT CALLED ME AND ASKED IF I'D MEET HIM AT A RESTAURANT IN MY AREA. HE WANTED TO TELL ME THAT HE DIDN'T MEAN ANYTHING NEGATIVE ABOUT A COMMENT THAT HE MADE IN BREIEFING. (IT WAS SOMETHING THAT COULD BE PERCEIVED AS OFFENSIVE.) HE DIDN'T WANT

ME TO THINK HE WAS THAT KIND OF PERSON. I TOLD HIM, "SARGE, I'VE ALREADY FORMED MY OPINION OF YOU. THERE'S NOTHING NEW THAT YOU CAN SAY TO CHANGE IT." HE SAID, "YEAH, YOU'VE KNOWN MR A WHILE. SOMETIMES I SAY STUPID THINGS." (HE WAS MY SERGEANT WHEN WE BOTH WORKED ANOTHER PART OF THE COUNTY, A PART THAT WASN'T "TOURISTY", OR QUITE AS NICE. IT WAS FULL OF DRUGS AND PROSTITUTION, AND A HOST OF OTHER UNSAVORY THINGS. I BOUNCED FROM CALL TO CALL OVER THERE. FROM ARMED ROBBERY, TO BURGLARY, TO HOME INVASION, TO YOU NAME IT. (I'M SURE IT WOULD HAVE MADE FOR MORE INTERESTING READING, BUT TO TELL YOU THE TRUTH, I GOT SICK OF IT. THERE WAS NEVER ANY TIME FOR SELF-INITIATED ACTIVITY. EVERYTHING WAS REACTIVE AS OPPOSED TO PROACTIVE.) MY SERGEANT LEFT LONG BEFORE I DID. HE REQUESTED I JOIN HIM ON THE OTHER SIDE OF TOWN AND I DID.

0400 -I SPOKE TO MF (B/M, 30) ABOUT THE WEBSITE. FYI HE'S THE OTHER HALF OF THIS THING. HE UPLOADS THE JOURNALS AND DOES MOST EVERTHING ELSE. HE ESPECIALLY LIKES PLAYING WITH THAT SIREN ON THE CRUISER AT THE FRONT OF THE SITE.

0430 - TRYIN' TO STAY AWAKE FOR ANOTHER HOUR AND A HALF

0500 - (D) DISTURBANCE
  I WAS DISPATCHED TO AN ESTABLISHMENT THAT HOLDS "RAVE" PARTIES EVERY WEEKEND. SECURITY CALLED ADVISING OF A FIGHT IN THE PARKING LOT. IT WAS OVER BY THE TIME WE ARRIVED. JUST AS WE WERE PULLING UP, ONE HALF OF THE INVOLVED PARTIES WAS DRIVING OFF. MY AREA PARTNER AND I MADE CONTACT WITH THEM AT A NEARBY GAS STATION. IT WAS A CAR FULL OF JUVENILES. THEY WERE BETWEEN 17 AND 20. THEY ALL LOOKED ABOUT 14 OR 15. (WHERE ARE THESE KIDS' PARENTS? AT THESE RAVES THERE ARE HUNDREDS OF KIDS MOST ARE UNDER 18 AND THEY LAST ALL NIGHT AND INTO THE DAY. IF I WOULD HAVE STAYED OUT LIKE THAT WHEN I WAS A YOUNG BUCK,

MY MOTHER WOULD HAVE RAVED ME.) WHILE WE WERE TALKING TO THEM, TWO MORE CARLOADS PULLED UP. THEY WERE ALL IN TOWN FROM A NEIGHBORING CITY. WE CHECKED TO MAKE SURE NONE OF THEM WERE WANTED AND LET THEM GO.

0600 -I GOT OFF ON TIME. I HEADED HOME.

10/07

1728 - AS SOON AS I WALKED OUT MY APARTMENT ON MY WAY TO WORK, I WAS APPROACHED BY A LITTLE BLACK BOY OF ABOUT SEVEN OR EIGHT. HE SAID, "HEY". I WAVED. HE THEN SAID, "ARE YOU GOING TO TAKE SOMEBODY TO JAIL?" I SAID, "MAYBE, IF THEY ARE BAD." HE SAID, "IF THEY'RE BAD, HUH?" I NODDED AND LEFT.

1800-BRIEFING

1822 -I WENT TO DINNER. I HAD BBQ RIBS, MASHED POTATOES, AND SUCCATASH. I UTILIZED THE LITTLE KNOWN 2-FINGER TECHNIQUE WHEREIN THE BONE IS PLACED BETWEEN THE THUMB AND INDEX FINGER OF THE NON-SHOOTING HAND. THIS DECREASES THE AMOUNT OF BBQ SAUCE TRANSFERRENCE. SUBSEQUENTLY, ONLY TWO FINGERS SMELL LIKE BBQ FOR THE REST OF THE NIGHT, AS OPPOSED TO ALL 10, PLUS WHAT'S LEFT ON THE FOREHEAD, ELBOWS AND HALF THE TOES.

1850-(D) ALARM
  I RESPONDED TO A BUSINESS PANIC ALARM. AFTER CONFIRMING IT WAS UNFOUNDED, I CLEARED THE CALL.

1928 - FG3 KEEPS CALLING ME, BUT I'M NOT ANSWERING THE PHONE. SHE'S GETTING TO BE ALMOST OBSESSIVE. SHE KEEPS BUYING ME THINGS AND THE GIFTS GET INCREASINGLY MORE EXPENSIVE. I MEAN IT, AFTER SHE GETS ME A CAR, WE ARE FINISHED!

1943 - (D) DISTURBANCE
  I WAS DISPATCHED TO A 9-1-1 HANG-UP AT AN OUTLET MALL. I TELEPHONED MALL SECURITY AND TURNED IT OVER TO THEM.

1947-I HAVE TO GO BY AND SEE MY FRIEND TONIGHT WHO WORKS AT A HOTEL AROUND HERE. I THINK I

WAS CALLING HER FG5. SHE'S A 30+Y/O FEMALE FROM TRINIDAD. IT'S BEEN SO LONG SINCE I'VE SPOKEN TO HER I CAN'T REMEMBER. SHE SENT ME AN E-MAIL SAYING SHE MISSES ME BECAUSE I MAKE HER LAUGH.

2023 - A SERGEANT IN ANOTHER AREA CAME UP ON THE RADIO AND STATED HE NEEDED RESCUE TO RESPOND IN EMERGENCY MODE REGARDING A W/F. HE SAID HE COULDN'T GET MUCH OUT OF HER OTHER THAN, "HE'S IN MY BLUE CAR." THE DISPATCHER ASKED WHAT KIND OF INJURIES TO INFORM RESCUE OF. THE SERGEANT SAID SHE WAS HALF NUDE AND WAS COVERED FROM HEAD TO TOE IN BLOOD. THE SERGEANT TOLD EVERY UNIT IN THE AREA TO STOP ALL BLUE CARS.

2043 - THE SERGEANT CAME UP ON THE RADIO AND SAID IT WAS POSSIBLY A RAPE AND THAT THE W/F'S THROAT WAS CUT. THE WOMAN HAD APPARENTLY WALKED TO THAT LOCATION. AFTER A BRIEF WHILE, THE SERGEANT AGAIN CAME UP AND SAID THE CHARGE WOULD BE AN ATTEMPTED MURDER AND TOLD THE DISPATCHER TO GET THE HELICOPTER UP TO DO AN AREA CHECK FOR THE SUSPECT.

2100 - THE SERGEANT SAID TO HAVE THE RESCUE WORKERS USE PRECAUTIONARY MEASURES REGARDING THE VICTIM. THAT MEANT SHE WAS POSSIBLY A CARRIER OF AN INCUREABLE VIRUS.

2116 - A NEIGHBORING AGENCY SAID THEY HAD A B/M STOPPED IN A BLUE VEHICLE. HE WAS COVERED IN BLOOD AND UNDER ARREST. THE SERGEANT CANCELLED THE 'BE ON THE LOOKOUT" (BOLO) FOR THE VEHICLE ONCE IT WAS CONFIRMED THAT THE CAR BELONGED TO THE INJURED FEMALE.

2201-I CALLED FG1 (26 YO, BRAZ). SHE ANSWERED THE PHONE, " OI, EU AMOR." THEN SHE ASKED, "WHAT'S GOING ON?" I TOLD HER ABOUT THAT WOMAN WHO

WAS INJURED. SHE WAS DISTURBED BY IT AND ASKED ME IF THE WOMAN WAS GOING TO LIVE. I TOLD HER I DIDN'T KNOW. WE SPOKE BRIEFLY. I TOLD HER IT WAS GOOD TO HEAR FROM HER. SHE SAID IT WAS ALWAYS GOOD TO HEAR FROM ME. SHE SAID SHE WAS GOING TO CHURCH TOMORROW, SO CALL HER TOMORROW NIGHT. I TOLD HER I WOULD. SHE SAID, "BOA NOITE (GOOD NIGHT)." AND SO DID I.

2221 -I RECEIVED ANOTHER CALL FROM FG3. I DIDN'T ANSWER THE PHONE. SHE'S A VERY SWEET GIRL. I JUST DON'T WANT TO CONTINUE PLAYING THE ENABLER ROLE, ENABLING A USELESS CAUSE. USELESS ONLY BECAUSE IT'S BEYOND FRIENDSHIP IN HER EYES.

2252 - (BU) ALARM
  I WENT TO BACK ANOTHER OFFICER WHO WAS RESPONDING TO ANOTHER ALARM AT A DEPARTMENT STORE IN AN OUTLET MALL. HE WAS CLOSER AND CLEARED THE CALL BEFORE I GOT THERE. IT WAS UNFOUNDED.

2316-(D) ALARM
  ANOTHER ALARM. THIS ONE WAS AT A BUSINESS. TWO UNITS GOT TO THAT ONE BEFORE I DID AND CLEARED IT. (UNFOUNDED)

2350 -I STOPPED BY A 24-HOUR DRUG STORE FOR A SNACK. I GOT A PROTEIN BAR AND SOME CRANGRAPE JUICE.

0009 - (D) ALARM
  I WAS DISPATCHED TO A RESIDENTIAL ALARM. I GOT THERE AND FOUND AN ELDERLY W/F WHO SET THE ALARM OFF BY MISTAKE. SHE SUFFERED FROM ALZHEIMERS AND DIDN'T REMEMBER THE CODE TO DISARM IT. HER NEXT DOOR NEIGHBOR, AN ASIAN W/F (40'S), WAS THERE AND WAS TRYING TO FIND THE TELEPHONE NUMBER OF THE ALARM COMPANY. SHE SAID IT WAS A FREQUENT OCCURRENCE AND SHE WAS PLEASED TO HELP. THE ELDERLY W/F'S

HUSBAND WAS RECENTLY ADMITTED TO THE HOSPITAL. HE POSSIBLY HAD LUNG CANCER.

0025 - (D) CRIMINAL MISCHIEF

THIS CALL WAS AT AN AREA HOTEL. IT INVOLVED TWO DRUNKEN, YOUNG W/M'S FROM PHILADELPHIA. ONE WAS LOCKED OUT OF THEIR ROOM AND THE OTHER WAS PASSED OUT INSIDE. THE ONE THAT WAS LOCKED OUT DECIDED TO KICK THE HOTEL DOOR IN. THE HOTEL CHARGED THEM $250.00 FOR THE DOOR AND EVICTED THEM. AFTER THE CALL, I WENT DOWN TO THE LOBBY AND WAS APPROACHED BY A WOMAN FROM ENGLAND AND HER TWO SONS. THEY WANTED TO KNOW WHAT HAPPENED. I TOLD THE LITTLE BOY, "THEY GOT DRUNK, DAMAGED THEIR ROOM, AND GOT KICKED OUT. SO DON'T DRINK!" THE BOY'S MOM SAID, "THAT'S RIGHT!" THE BOY THEN SAID TO HIS MOM, "SO YOU SHOULDN'T GET DRUNK ALL THE TIME!" HIS MOM SAID, "I DON'T. I HAVE TWO LAGERS EVERY NIGHT." THE BOY SAID, "SHE GETS DRUNK!" FULLY BELIEVING THE BOY WOULD SAY NO, I ASKED HIM, "SO DO YOU WANT ME TO ARREST HER?" HE SAID. "YEAH. AND SHOOT HER!" I SAID. "THAT'S TERRIBLE! THIS IS YOUR MOM." HE SAID, "SHE'S MY FOSTER MOM." SHE SAID, "IT SHOULD BE REVERSED AND HE SHOULD GO TO JAIL." THE BOY NODDED HIS HEAD "YES" AND SMILED REALLY BIG.

0111-I WENT TO THE STATION TO PRINT SOME "STUFF" OFF.

0124-I STOPPED BY THE HOTEL/NIGHTCLUB WHERE MY FRIEND (B/M 31 YO) WORKS. HE WASN'T THERE AND THINGS WERE PRETTY QUIET.

0130-I CHECKED MY CELL PHONE AND SAW THAT FG3 HAD CALLED AGAIN. IT'S GONE FROM CUTE TO FRUSTRATING. I DON'T EVEN LISTEN TO THE MESSAGES ANYMORE. I JUST CLEAR THEM OUT.

I FOUND OUT THAT MY FRIEND HAD GONE HOME EARLY. THE CLUB SEEMED TO BE LETTING OUT SMOOTHLY, SO I LEFT.

0136-I WENT TO EAT AGAIN.

0205 - YOU KNOW WHO CALLED AGAIN. I TURNED MY PHONE OFF AND WENT TO SEE FG5 (B/F, 30+ YO, TRINI). SHE TOLD ME THE STORY OF HOW SHE TOOK THE VIRGINITY OF A 35 YO MAN WHILE SHE WAS ON VACATION IN NEW YORK. THAT'S WHERE SHE AND HER YOUNG SON AND DAUGHTER MOVED TO FLORIDA FROM. SHE WAS THERE FOR ABOUT A WEEK. SHE SAID IT TOOK HER THAT LONG TO GET HIM PROPERLY TRAINED, THOUGH HE STILL NEEDED A BIT MORE WORK. SHE SAID SHE WAS GOING BACK IN A COUPLE OF WEEKS AND WOULD TAKE CARE OF IT THEN.

0300 - (D) AGGRAVATED BATTERY
THIS OCCURRED AT ANOTHER HOTEL IN MY AREA. THE VICTIM WAS A YOUNG W/F AND I MET WITH HER AND HER HUSBAND. THE HUSBAND WAS EXTREMELY INTOXICATED AND ON THE VERGE OF BEING ARRESTED FOR DISORDERLY INTOXICATION. THE COUPLE BECAME ACQUAINTED WITH A HISPANIC COUPLE THAT THEY WERE SHARING THE JACAZZI WITH. THE H/M ASKED THE W/M FOR A BEER AND WAS GIVEN ONE. LATER, THE H/M ASKED FOR ANOTHER BEER AND WAS TOLD NO. THE W/M TOLD HIM HE ONLY HAD A FEW LEFT. APPARENTLY THE H/M WASN'T SATISFIED WITH THAT ANSWER AND PROCEEDED TO REACH INTO THE W/M'S COOLER AND TAKE A BEER. THIS CAUSED A VERBAL ALTERCATION AND THE FEMALES GOT INVOLVED. THE H/F HIT THE W/F IN THE HEAD WITH A CAN OF BEER AND STARTED PUNCHING HER. SECURITY SHOWED UP AT THAT POINT AND THE HISPANIC COUPLE FLED. THE W/F WAS TAKEN TO THE HOSPITAL AND WAS TREATED FOR HEAD INJURIES. I FOLLOWED HER THERE TO GET SOME ADDITIONAL INFORMATION. THE SUSPECTS WERE FROM QUEENS, NEW YORK AND THE VICTIMS WERE FROM REDBANK, NEW JERSEY. AFTER OBTAINING THE INFORMATION THAT I NEEDED, I ADVISED THE COUPLE AS TO THE PROPER COURSE OF ACTION. (I TOLD THEM TO WORK WITH HOTEL SECURITY IN DETERMINING WHETHER OR NOT THE SUSPECTS WERE ALSO HOTEL PATRONS AND GETTING THEM IDENTIFIED.) ABOUT AN HOUR EARLIER I

WAS THREATENING TO TAKE THE W/M TO JAIL. NOW, HE WAS SHAKING MY HAND AND THANKING ME. (THAT'ALCOHOL.)

0419-I WENT TO THE STATION TO WORK ON SOME PAPER.

0451-I WAS DISPATCHED TO AN ALARM WHILE WORKING ON MY AGGRAVATED BATTERY PAPERWORK, BUT MY AREA PARTNER PICKED IT UP FOR ME.

0505 - (D) ARMED ROBBERY

THIS ALLEGED ARMED ROBBERY OCCURRED AT THE SAME HOTEL AS THE AGGRAVATED BATTERY. A YOUNG W/M HAD BROKEN A WINDOW, ENTERED A ROOM, AND WAS SLEEPING INSIDE. A FRIEND OF HIS WHO WAS NOT PRESENT RENTED THE ROOM. HE CLAIMED A CARLOAD OF HISPANIC MALES HAD FOLLOWED HIM FROM A NIGHTCLUB DOWNTOWN. ONCE AT THE HOTEL, THE H/M'S SHOUTED OBSCENITIES AT HIM. FEARING FOR HIS LIFE, THE W/M RAN AND DOVE THROUGH THE WINDOW TO ESCAPE THE H/M'S. (DID I MENTION THIS GUY WAS HEAVILY INTOXICATED?) I DON'T HAVE A PROBLEM TELLING YOU I DRILLED THIS GUY DURING QUESTIONING. THE SCENE WAS NOT CONSISTENT WITH HIS STORY. THE ONLY INJURIES HE HAD WERE ON HIS RIGHT HAND. HAD HE DOVE THROUGH THE WINDOW, HE WOULD HAVE RECEIVED SOME UPPER BODY INJURIES. WHAT I BELIEVED WAS THAT HE GOT TO HIS FRIEND'S ROOM AND HIS FRIEND WASN'T THERE. NOT HAVING A ROOM KEY, BUT DESPERATELY NEEDED TO "CRASH", HE DECIDED TO GAIN ENTRY BY BREAKING THE WINDOW. THE W/M LATER CONFIRMED MY SUSPICIONS AND AGREED TO THE FOLLOWING: (1) PAY THE HOTEL FOR THE BROKEN WINDOW (2) GET OUT OF MY FACE AND STOP WASTING MY TIME!

0545 - I DID A QUICK CHECK OF A COUPLE HOTELS.

0556 -I STOPPED BY THE STATION ONE LAST TIME TO TURN IN SOME PROPERTY.
   I'LL TALK TO YOU LATER.

10/08

2000 - BRIEFING

2022 -I WENT TO HAVE DINNER WITH MY FRIEND (F, 26 Y/O, BRAZ). ON MY WAY, I BROKE FOR A CALL...

2030 - (D) SUSPICIOUS INCIDENT
  A RESIDENT OF A GATED COMMUNITY OBSERVED THREE KIDS JUMPING OVER THE WALL. HE SAW THEM WALKING AROUND THE NEIGHBORHOOD.   ONCE INSIDE THE NEIGHBORHOOD I MET WITH ANOTHER RESIDENT WHO ALSO SAW THE KIDS. WE BOTH DROVE AROUND FOR A WHILE, BUT WERE UNABLE TO LOCATE THEM.

2100 - BACK TO DINNER

2200 (S) TRAFFIC STOP
  I STOPPED A CAR THAT DISPLAYED AN UNASSIGNED TAG. AFTER THE STOP, I REALIZED I HAD READ IT WRONG. I PULLED UP TO THE DRIVER AND TOLD HIM HE COULD PROCEED.

2205 -I WENT TO GET SOME GAS.

2210-I STOPPED BY MY FRIEND'S (B/M, 31 Y/O) HOTEL TO CHECK ON HIM AND THE PROPERTY.

2325 - BACK ON PATROL

2330 - (S) TRAFFIC STOP
  I STOPPED A CAR BECAUSE THE TAG WAS EXPIRED. THE CAR BELONGED TO THE YOUNG, W/F THAT WAS IN THE PASSENGER SEAT. THE DRIVER WAS HER BOYFRIEND, A YOUNG, W/M. HE WAS A DECENT GUY. I FOUND OUT THE W/F WAS FROM FAIRFAX, VIRGINIA LIKE ME. (I WASN'T BORN THERE, BUT I WAS AN OFFICER THERE FOR 3 YEARS) I TOLD THEM TO TAKE CARE OF THE PROBLEM AND I GAVE THEM A VERBAL WARNING. A GROUP OF BRAZILIAN GIRLS CAME UP AND WATCHED ME CONDUCT THE TRAFFIC STOP. I SAID, "HELLO." THEY SAID, "HI, WE'RE FROM BRAZIL." I

SAID, "TUDO BEM? (IS EVERYTHING GOOD?)" THEY SAID, "TUDO BEM? (EVERYTHING IS GOOD." AS I GOT INTO MY CAR, THEY SAID, "BOA NOITE (GOODNIGHT)."

2315 - (BU) DISTURBANCE
  I RESPONDED TO AN EMERGENCY ALARM AT A STORE IN A MALL. AN EMPLOYEE HAD ACCIDENTALLY HIT THE 9-1-1 BUTTON.

0000 - A PROBATIONARY (WITHIN HIS FIRST YEAR) OFFICER CALLED AND WANTED ME TO MEET WITH HIM. IT WAS REGARDING A TRAFFIC STOP THAT HE HAD MADE. HE ASKED MY OPINION OF WHETHER OR NOT HE HANDLED IT PROPERLY. THE MOTORISTS DIDN'T IMMEDIATELY STOP FOR HIM. ONCE HE DID STOP, HE WOULDN'T GET OUT WHEN HE WAS ORDERED TO. THE OFFICER DREW HIS WEAPON AND APPROACHED THE VEHICLE. THE DRIVER WAS A B/M. HIS WIFE, A B/F, WAS IN THE PASSENGER SEAT. SHE WANTED THE OFFICER'S BADGE NUMBER. HE EXPLAINED TO THEM WHY HE HAD DONE WHAT HE DID. HE ALSO SPOKE TO THE LADY'S SON. THE SON WAS IN THE BACKSEAT CRYING. THE SITUATION ENDED PEACEFULLY. THE OFFICER HAD CLOCKED THE CAR SPEEDING. I TOLD THE HIM HE WAS TOTALLY JUSTISFIED IN DRAWING HIS WEAPON. HIS PERSONAL SAFETY IS PARAMOUNT. WHEN THE DRIVER DID NOT COMPLY WITH HIS ORDERS, HE HAD REASON FOR CONCERN. (I THINK HE FELT A LITTLE BETTER ABOUT TRAUMATIZING THAT POOR FAMILY.)

0020 - ANOTHER UNIT CAME UP ON THE RADIO ADVISING THAT HE WAS FOLLOWING A CAR WITH A STOLEN TAG. I WOULD HAVE LOVED JOINING IN ON THE FUN, BUT I WAS TOO FAR AWAY.

0036 - (D) ALARM
  THIS ALARM WAS A CONVENIENCE STORE NEAR THE STATION. I CHECKED IT OUT AND IT WAS ALL SECURE.

0036 -I WENT INTO ANOTHER CONVENIENCE STORE

TO USE THE RESTROOM. BEFORE I COULD GET IT
PUT AWAY, AN ARMED ROBBERY WENT OUT. AFTER
WASHING MY HANDS I RUSHED OUT OF THE STORE...

0130 - (D) ARMED ROBBERY

TWO W/M TOURISTS FROM IRELAND WERE WALKING
DOWN THE SIDEWALK TOWARD THE HOTEL WHERE THEY
WERE STAYING. A COMPACT CAR PULLED UP ALONGSIDE
THEM. A B/M JUMPED OUT OF THE PASSENGER SEAT
AND POINTED A HANDGUN AT THE MEN. ONE OF THE W/M
TOOK OFF WHEN HE SAW THE GUN DISPLAYED. THE B/M
ORDERED THE REMAINING W/M TO THE GROUND. THE B/
M BEGAN REACHING INTO THE W/M'S POCKETS. WHEN
THE B/M GOT TO THE POCKET WHERE THE W/M KEPT HIS
MONEY HE BEGAN RESISTING. ANGERED BY THIS, THE B/
M STARTED KICKING THE W/M IN THE FACE AND STRUCK
HIM ACROSS THE TOP OF HIS HEAD WITH THE BUTT OF
THE GUN. WHEN THE W/M THAT HAD FLED SAW HIS FRIEND
BEING BEATEN, HE RETURNED. THE B/M THEN JUMPED
BACK INTO THE CAR AND IT SPED OFF. I FOLLOWED THE
W/M TO THE HOSPITAL TO OBTAIN SOME ADDITIONAL
INFORMATION. HE WAS TREATED FOR MULTIPLE INJURIES
TO INCLUDE A ONE-INCH LACERATION ON HIS HEAD FROM
THE PISTOL AND A BROKEN NOSE. THE VICTIM SEEMED TO
HANDLE THE ATTACK VERY WELL. HE WAS BLEEDING ALL
OVER THE PLACE, BUT SEEMED VERY RELAXED. I MIGHT
ADD THAT THE TWO IRISH MEN HAD RECENTLY LEFT AN
IRISH PUB WHERE THEY HAD A FEW DRINKS. THAT MAY BE
WHY HIS DEMEANOR WAS CALM AND RESERVED.

0319 -I WENT BACK TO THE HOTEL WHERE THE VICTIM
WAS STAYING TO PICK UP HIS FRIEND'S STATEMENT.
I ASKED THE FRIEND, "DID YOU RUN WHEN YOUR
FRIEND WAS BEING ATTACKED?" HE SEEMED
SLIGHTLY EMBARRASSED AND SAID, "NO. I DIDN'T
RUN. I JUST SORT OF SHUFFLED STEPPED TO THE
SIDE A BIT." I SMILED AND SAID, "O.K."

0331 -I WENT BACK TO THE CONVENIENCE STORE
FOR SOME JUICE AND A BOOK OF STAMPS. I NEED TO
SEND OFF SOME BILLS. I NEED TO PAY OFF MY BABIES'

MOMMAS FOR DOING SUCH A SPECTACULAR JOB
WITH MY BABIES.

0530 -I WENT TO TURN IN MY PAPERWORK.

0545 -I GOT SOME BREAKFAST AND HEADED TO THE
HOUSE. TALK TO YA' IN A FEW.

SCHEDULED DAY OFF. -I TOOK MY FRIEND (F, 26YO, BRAZ) WITH ME TO MY PORTUGUESE CLASS. I HAD MY MID-TERM EXAMINATION. MY INSTRUCTOR HAD HER CONDUCT THE ORAL PORTION OF THE TEST. EVEN THOUGH IT WAS A TEST DAY, WE BOTH HAD A GREAT TIME.

I GOT TO MAKE A FEW PHONE CALLS, WHICH I RARELY DO. I CALLED BOTH MY SON AND DAUGHTER. NEITHER WAS HOME. MY SON'S MOM HAD ASKED IF I COULD SPEND THANKSGIVING WITH HIM. I TOLD HER I WAS WORKING ON THANKSGIVING, BUT I'D LIKE TO HAVE HIM FOR CHRISTMAS. I SPOKE TO MY GRANDMOTHER. SHE TOLD ME HOW MY DAD WAS DOING (HE LIVES WITH HER AND WAS DOING O.K.) SHE TOLD ME SHE'S BEEN RUNNING AROUND A LOT AND WAS VERY TIRED. SHE SAID SHE RECENTLY WENT TO A PRAYER BREAKFAST AND HAD A GREAT TIME. THE HOTEL WHERE IT WAS HELD WAS PACKED AND THE PASTOR WHO SPOKE WAS REALLY GOOD. I ALSO SPOKE TO MY MOTHER BRIEFLY. (MY PARENTS ARE DIVORCED. SHE LIVES IN MIAMI AND HE LIVES NEAR ORLANDO.) SHE TOLD ME THAT SHE LOVES ME AND I SHOULD REMEMBER THAT EVEN THOUGH WE DON'T SPEAK TOO OFTEN. WE SPOKE BRIEFLY BECAUSE SHE WAS ON THE OTHER LINE WITH MY GODMOTHER. I TOLD HER TO TELL MY GODMOTHER THAT I SAID HELLO. I ALSO SPOKE TO A FRIEND THAT I FORGOT I HAD YET ANOTHER BRAZILIAN GIRL. THIS ONE IS 23 AND HAS A YOUNG, PUERTO RICAN BOYFRIEND. HE'S EXTREMELY JEALOUS, SO SHE DOESN'T CALL ME MUCH. SHE DOES TELL ME WHERE SHE'S WORKING SO I CAN VISIT AND TALK TO HER. (HER JOB KEEPS HER FLOATING.) SHE SAYS HER BOYFRIEND DOESN'T UNDERSTAND THAT SHE CAN HAVE MALE FRIENDS. I ASSURED HER THAT HE HAS NOTHING TO WORRY ABOUT WHERE I AM CONCERNED. THAT'S AS LONG AS SHE HAS A MAN AND IS NOT SWAYED BY MY HARMLESS FLIRTING, BECAUSE I CAN RESIST ANYTHING, BUT TEMPTATION (REGARDING THE OPPOSITE SEX).

I LATER WENT TO AN OFF-DUTY JOB. AS PREVIOUSLY STATED, THESE OFF-DUTY JOBS ARE MANDATORY FOR MANY OFFICERS TO MAKE ENDS MEET.

*NOTE - YOU GUYS SHOULD HAVE PITY ON ME. I MOVED HERE FROM VIRGINIA BECAUSE I CAN'T STAND THE COLD. I GUESS IT'S WINTER IN FLORIDA NOW AND IT'S FREEZING. IT'S BEEN LIKE 60'S LATELY EVEN 50'S. POOR ME. RIGHT?

10/11

1800-BRIEFING

1830-I "SHOT THE CRAP" IN THE PARKING LOT WITH A COUPLE OF GUYS ON MY SQUAD ABOUT DERERRED COMPENSATION. WE ALL AGREED THAT WE'LL STILL BE BROKE WHEN WE RETIRE.

1900 - OUT ON PATROL - SURPRISE. I'M NOT HEADING TO DINNER. I GOT UP EARLY AND HAD SOME BREAKFAST, SO I'M NOT HUNGRY. I STOPPED BY MY FRIEND'S (F, 26Y/O, BRAZ) HOUSE AND GAVE HER SOME PHOTOS THAT HER MOM, HER SON, AND I HAD TAKEN A WHILE BACK. HER MOM'S GOING BACK TO BRAZIL SOON. SHE'S BEEN HERE FOR ABOUT FOUR MONTHS. SHE LOVED THE PHOTOS AND SAID I SHOULD HAVE THE ONE OF HER DAUGHTER AND I BLOWN UP.

1915 - (S) SUSPICIOUS PERSONS
    I STOPPED AND CHECKED OUT A YOUNG W/M AND A YOUNG, W/F. THEY WERE STANDING IN FRONT OF THEIR VEHICLE, WHICH WAS PARKED ALONGSIDE A ROADWAY. THE COUPLE WAS HOMELESS AND ALL THE AREA SHELTERS WERE FULL. THEY HAD A PIT BULL PUPPY THAT WAS SLEEPING ON THE BACKSEAT OF THEIR RED FORD. THE W/F WAS DUE TO START WORKING AT A FAST FOOD RESTAURANT THE FOLLOWING WEEK. BOTH THE W/M AND W/F WERE VERY NICE. I GATHERED ALL THEIR PERSONAL INFORMATION AND COMPILED IT ON A COUPLE OF INTELLIGENCE REPORTS. WHEN THEY ASKED, I TOLD THEM THE PURPOSE OF THE REPORTS. (IT WAS SO WE'D HAVE THEIR INFORMATION ON FILE IF IN THE FUTURE THEY WERE SUSPECTED OF CRIMINAL ACTIVITY.)

1935-(S) AREA CHECK
   I DID A NEIGHBORHOOD PATROL. RESIDENTS OF A PREDOMINATELY ELDERLY COMMUNITY REQUESTED INCREASED PATROL. I OBLIGED.

2015-I TALKED TO MY FRIEND (F, 26Y/O, BRAZ). SHE SAID HER MOM FEELS SHE SHOULD NOT GO TO NIGHTCLUBS IF SHE CLAIMS TO BE A CHRISTIAN. HER MOM SAID SHE WAS GOING TO TALK TO ME AND TELL ME NOT TO TAKE HER DAUGHTER THERE IF SHE ASKS ME TO. SHE SAID IT'S WRONG TO GO TO THE NIGHTCLUB THEN TURN AROUND AND GO TO CHURCH. SHE SAID YOU'RE WORSHIPPING THE DEVIL WHEN YOU GO TO NIGHTCLUBS AND ARE IN THAT DRINKING ATMOSPHERE. MY FRIEND DISAGREED WITH HER MOM AND ASKED WHAT I THOUGHT ABOUT IT. I TOLD HER, "YOUR MOM HAS A POINT. THE PEOPLE IN NIGHTCLUBS AREN'T ENGAGED IN THE WORSHIPPING OF CHRIST AND I BELIEVE THE BIBLE STATES THAT YOU'RE EITHER FOR HIM OR AGAINST HIM. ON THE OTHER HAND, WHO AMONGST US IS WITHOUT SIN?" (PERSONALLY, I'D LIKE TO BELIEVE THAT I'M A WORK IN PROGRESS AND I'M CONTINUALLY TRYING TO IMPROVE AS A PERSON AND CHRISTIAN.) I TOLD HER, "I USED TO BE A LOT WORSE THAN I AM NOW". SHE ASKED, "HOW BAD WERE YOU?" I TOLD HER, "I DIDN'T USE DRUGS OR ANYTHING I WAS JUST BAD AS FAR AS GIRLS ARE CONCERNED." SHE SAID, "I'M GLAD YOU CHANGED."

2048 -I HAD BEEN SITTING IN FRONT OF THE PUMPS AT A GAS STATION FOR A WHILE BEFORE GOING IN TO USE THE RESTROOM. THE CLERK, AN ASIAN WOMAN IN HER 50'S, ASKED, "CAN YOU STAY OUT THERE JUST A LITTLE WHILE LONGER, JUST AN HOUR?" SHE SAID SHE FELT SAFE WITH ME OUT THERE.

2049 - (D) AGGRAVATED ASSAULT
  I WAS DISPATCHED, BUT MY PARTNER PICKED THE CALL UP FOR ME. A B/F CLAIMED HER HUSBAND TRIED TO RUN HER OVER WITH A CAR. (MY PARTNER LATER SAID HER CLAIM WAS UNFOUNDED.)

2241 – (D) AGGRAVATED ASSAULT
  THREE WHITE MALES IN A BLUE MAZDA MPV POINTED A SHOTGUN AT THE CALLER THROUGH AN OPEN DOOR.

AFTER BRANDISHING THE WEAPON, THE MPV SPED AWAY. THE INCIDENT OCCURRED WHILE AT A STOPLIGHT. THE VICTIM TURNED OFF TO A RESTAURANT AND CALLED 9-1-1. - WE SEARCHED THE AREA, BUT THE SUSPECT VEHICLE WAS LONG GONE.

2337 - (D) BURGLARY TO A VEHICLE
   A YOUNG, W/M SAID HIS SPORTS UTILITY VEHICLE WAS BURGLARIZED WHILE THEY VISITED A THEME PARK. HE AND HIS FAMILY WERE IN TOWN FROM NORTH CAROLINA. HE SAID $720.00 WAS STOLEN FROM THE CENTER CONSOLE. THERE WAS NO FORCED ENTRY TO THE VEHICLE, BUT MONEY WAS MISSING. YEAH! AT ANY RATE, I TOOK A REPORT AND GAVE THE W/M A CASE NUMBER. I GUESS THAT'S ALL HE NEEDED TO MAKE A FALSE, I MEAN, AN INSURANCE CLAIM.

0033 -I HAD A VERY FLAVORFUL MEAL OF GRILLED CHICKEN BREAST, RICE, CARROTS, AND MACARONI AND CHEESE. YES, TWO STARCHES.

0245 - ANOTHER OFFICER HAD RECENTLY TAKEN AN ARMED ROBBERY REPORT AT AN AREA HOTEL. THE SUSPECTS WERE DRIVING A WHITE TOYOTA TERCEL.
   MY SERGEANT CAME UP ON THE RADIO AND ADVISED HE WAS CONDUCTING A TRAFFIC STOP OF A WHITE TERCEL. THE DRIVER WAS A YOUNG B/F. A B/M GOT OUT OF THE CAR JUST PRIOR TO THE STOP. MY SERGEANT ASKED ME TO COME AND CHECK OUT THE B/M WHILE HE DEALT WITH THE FEMALE. I STARTED HEADING HIS WAY, BUT BROKE FOR A SIGHTING OF ANOTHER WHITE TOYOTA TERCEL...
   ANOTHER OFFICER CAME UP ON THE AIR AND SAID, "I THINK I HAVE THE CAR!" I WENT RIGHT BY THE B/M AND HEADED TOWARD THE OTHER OFFICER.
   MY PARTNER STOPPED THE B/M NEAR MY SERGEANT'S TRAFFIC STOP. WE DETERMINED THIS VEHICLE WAS NOT THAT OF THE SUSPECTS.
   I WENT BACK TO MY SERGEANT'S SCENE AND TOOK CUSTODY OF THE B/F. AT THE LEAST SHE WAS GOING TO JAIL FOR DRIVING WITH A SUSPENDED LICENSE. SHE DID NOT HAVE ONE IN HER POSSESSION. SHE DID GIVE THE NAME OF AN INDIVIDUAL WHOSE LICENSE WAS INVALID.

AFTER A WHILE, WE DETERMINED THAT THESE WERE MOST LIKELY THE SUSPECTS. THE DESCRIPTION OF THE SUSPECTS, THEIR ATTIRE AND THE VEHICLE MATCHED. WE HAD EVERYTHING EXCEPT THE WEAPON. ANOTHER ARMED ROBBERY HAD OCCURRED EARLIER IN ANOTHER AREA. WE FOUND THE PROPERTY OF THE VICTIM OF THAT ROBBERY IN THE POCKET OF THE B/M (HIS DRIVER LICENSE).

ONCE IN MY BACKSEAT, I MIRANDIZED (YOU HAVE THE RIGHT TO REMAIN SILENT...) THE B/F AND STARTED TALKING TO HER. I TOLD HER WE KNEW EXACTLY WHAT HAD HAPPENED. I TOLD HER SHE WAS FACING SOME SERIOUS CHARGES AND SHE NEEDED TO COME CLEAN. I SAID IF THE B/M WAS PRIMARILY RESPONSIBLE, SHE NEEDED TO TELL ME THAT. SHE ENDED UP WRITING OUT A SWORN STATEMENT SAYING SHE DROPPED THE B/M OFF AT THE HOTEL WHERE THE ROBBERY OCCURRED AND PICKED HIM UP AFTER A FEW MINUTES. AFTER THE ROBBERY DETECTIVE GOT A HOLD OF HER, SHE CONFESSED TO THAT AND SEVERAL OTHER ROBBERIES. I TOOK HER AND MY PARTNER TOOK THE B/M. THE VICTIM OF THE OTHER ROBBERY CAME OUT TO OUR SCENE. HE IDENTIFIED THE B/M AND WE TURNED HIS PROPERTY BACK OVER TO HIM.

AFTER I GOT TO THE JAIL, I FOUND OUT THE B/F HAD GIVEN ME THE WRONG NAME. SHE LIED BECAUSE SHE WAS ALSO A FUGITIVE FROM JUSTICE. I CHARGED HER WITH ARMED ROBBERY, DRIVING WITH A SUSPENDED LICENSE, AND THE WARRANT. (REMEMBER WHAT I SAID ABOUT THOSE SUSPENDED LICENSES, MANY TIMES THEY ARE JUST THE ROOT OF MORE SERIOUS PROBLEMS.')

0800 -I LEFT THE JAIL AND HEADED TO THE STATION TO TURN IN MY PAPERWORK. (KEEP IN MIND MY SHIFT SUPPOSEDLY ENDS AT 0600.) WHILE AT A STOPLIGHT, I NOTICED TWO WOMEN AND THEIR VEHICLES IN THE MEDIAN. THEY HAD JUST HAD AN ACCIDENT AND WANTED ME TO WORK IT FOR THEM. I TOLD THEM THAT I WAS WITH THE SHERIFF'S OFFICE AND THAT ANOTHER AGENCY WORKED TRAFFIC CRASHES. THEY SAID O.K. AND THAT THEY HAD ALREADY CALLED IT IN. THANK THE LORD FOR THE HIGHWAY PATROL!

LET ME START OFF BY SAYING I GOT NO SLEEP. I WORKED UNTIL 08:00 THIS MORNING. I WAS ATTEMPTING TO GET AT LEAST AN HOUR OF SLEEP BEFORE HAVING TO GET UP AND GO TO SCHOOL. THAT PLAN WAS RUINED WHEN AN OFFICER ON THE FUGITIVE SQUAD CALLED ME ABOUT A HOMICIDE SUSPECT. (IF YOU CAN RECALL I ARRESTED A PUERTO RICAN, W/M WHO WAS DRIVING A WHITE LEXUS LS400 FOR DRIVING WITH A SUSPENDED LICENSE. HE WAS IN THE CAR WITH TWO OTHER YOUNG, HISPANIC MALES. HE TOLD ME HE OWNED A RECORDING STUDIO AND ON THE WAY TO JAIL, WE TALKED ABOUT UNDERGROUND RADIO STATIONS. REMEMBER? AT ANY RATE, THE DETECTIVE SAID HE IS AN ASSOCIATE OF A H/M WHO IS SUSPECTED OF MURDER. HE WANTED TO KNOW IF THAT PERSON WAS ONE OF THE H/M'S IN THE CAR AT THE TIME OF ARREST. I HAD TO GET UP AND PULL UP THE FUGITIVE WEB SITE AND LOOK AT THE GUY. THEN I CALLED THE DETECTIVE BACK AND TOLD HIM HE WASN'T THERE AND I GAVE HIM ALL THE ADDITIONAL INFORMATION I HAD ON THE GUY I ARRESTED. AFTER GOING TO SCHOOL WITH NO SLEEP, I CAME HOME WITH HOPES OF GETTING IN AT LEAST THREE HOURS BEFORE WORK. IT DIDN'T HAPPEN. JUST AS I BEGAN TO DRIFT OFF, THE APARTMENT COMPLEX MANAGER CALLED ME. SHE SAID THERE WAS SOME DRUG ACTIVITY GOING ON IN THE COMPLEX AND SHE WANTED ME TO CHECK IT OUT. AFTER HARRASSING THE DEALERS FOR A WHILE, I WENT BACK AND GOT MAYBE AN HOUR OF SLEEP. (HARRASS IS ALL YOU CAN DO BECAUSE THEY STASH THE GOODS WHEN THEY SEE YOU COMING.) KEEP THIS IN MIND AS YOU READ THE FOLLOWING ENTRY:

1800-BRIEFING

1823- I WENT TO SCHOOL. MY CLASS EARLIER WAS MY FOREIGN LANGUAGE CLASS. 7PM IS WHEN MY SPEECH CLASS STARTS. I GAVE A SPEECH ON MY FAVORITE BOOK, "THE CATCHER IN THE RYE."

2135-I WENT TO EAT. I HAD CHICKEN AND NOODLE STIRFRY, ROAST PORK, AND CABBAGE.

2200 -I DID A BUSINESS CHECK AT THE HOTEL WHERE MF (B/M, 31 YO) WORKS.

2242 - I STOPPED BY ANOTHER HOTEL TO USE THE TELEPHONE. I HAD MY CELL PHONE TURNED OFF BECAUSE IT STILL GIVES ME HEADACHES. I CHECKED MY MESSAGES AND MY MOTHER, MY DAUGHTER'S MOM, AND FG (F, 40+ YO, TRINIDAD), WHOM I USED TO DATE, HAD CALLED. I COMMENTED TO MY DAUGHTER'S MOM THAT I WOULDN'T BE SINGLE FOREVER. SHE CALLED MY MOM IRATE, ASSUMING I MEANT I WAS GOING TO MARRY FG (TRIN). FG (TRIN) CALLED MY MOM OUT OF THE BLUE BECAUSE SHE HAPPENED TO BE IN THE AREA WHERE MY MOM LIVES. (MY MOM LIVES IN MIAMI AND TRINIDAD CARNIVAL WAS GOING ON DOWN THERE.) MY MOM MENTIONED THE CALL TO FG (TRIN). THEN FG (TRIN) CALLED ME TO FIND OUT WHAT MY DAUGHTER'S MOM WAS TALKING ABOUT. BEING THE LESS THAN DRAMATIC TYPE, I REFUSED TO COMMENT ON THAT, APOLOGIZED TO HER FOR THE CONFUSION, AND TOLD HER I WOULD RESOLVE THE MATTER. I THEN ASKED MY MOM TO REFRAIN FROM ENTERTAINING SUCH DRAMA AND SHE AGREED TO. THEN I CALLED MY DAUGHTER'S MOM AND TOLD HER NOT TO BE CALLING MOM WITH SUCH NONSENSE. SHE ULTIMATELY AGREED. (I'D DIVULGE OUR CONVERSATION, BUT THIS SITE IS RATED G.)

2355 - AS I WALKED OUT OF THE HOTEL, THE CLERK FOLLOWED ME OUT. HE ASKED ME, 'HOW LONG HAVE YOU BEEN AN OFFICER?" AFTER ANSWERING HIM, HE SAID, "I RESPECT WHAT YOU DO. IF THESE WERE TIMES PAST, YOU WOULD HAVE BEEN A WARRIOR IN A DIFFERENT FIELD. ALSO, IN THE FUTURE, YOU'D BE A WARRIOR AS WELL." (THAT MADE ME FEEL PRETTY GOOD AND I THANKED HIM. HE SAW THROUGH TO THE REAL ME, AND I DIDN'T EVEN HAVE TO DO MY QUICK-

CHANGE IN A PHONE BOOTH.)

0110 - (D) NOISE COMPLAINT

THIS CALL WAS REGARDING A LOUD PARTY IN AN APARTMENT COMPLEX. I ARRIVED TO FIND ABOUT TWO YOUNG, W/MS AND FOUR YOUNG, W/FS HAVING A PICNIC. THEY HAD A BLANKET SPREAD ACROSS THE LAWN IN BETWEEN SOME BUILDINGS. THE MUSIC WAS CRANKED AND THERE WAS BUD LIGHT, WHISKEY SOURS, AND DAQUARIES ALL OVER THE PLACE. I STEPPED BRIEFLY OUT OF MY NORMAL CALM AND RELAXED CHARACTER AND WENT OFF ON THEM. IT'S EXTREMELY UPSETTING TO ME WHEN PEOPLE DEMONSTRATE A BLATENT DISREGARD AND DISRESPECT FOR OTHERS. FOR CRYING OUT LOUD, IT WAS 1:00 IN THE MORNING AND THESE GUYS WERE OUT THERE ACTING LIKE IT WAS 12:00 NOON. THERE MUST BE SOME EXPECTATION OF PEACE AND QUIET AT SOME POINT. THEY ALL AGREED AND WRAPPED UP THEIR LITTLE MIDNIGHT PICNIC. TWO OTHER OFFICERS HAD BACKED ME ON THE CALL. AFTERWARDS, WE ALL HEADED UP TO THE HOTEL/NIGHTCLUB WHERE FM (B/M, 31) WORKS. THE CLUB WAS ABOUT TO CLOSE AND THERE'S SOMETIMES A BIT OF ACTION.

0220 - THERE WAS NO ACTION AT THAT CLUB. I WENT TO CHECK ON SOME OTHER HOTELS IN MY AREA.

0228 - (S) SUSPICIOUS VEHICLE

I CRUISED THROUGH THE LOT OF A "HOPPING" NIGHTCLUB THAT CLOSES AT THREE. I LIKE TO RUN THE TAGS. THAT CLUB IS FREQUENTED BY A LOT OF "BIG BAWLERS." MANY TIMES THE SO-CALLED "BIG BAWLERS" STEAL CARS TO GO OUT AND PARTY IN. I NOTICED A CAR WITH AN UNREADABLE TAG. IT HAD A PLASTIC COVER OVER IT THAT WAS ALL FOGGED UP. IT WAS OCCUPIED BY A YOUNG, B/M AND A YOUNG, B/F. THEY WERE ENGAGED IN SOMETHING SEXUAL, WHAT I DON'T KNOW. I WAS IMPRESSED BY THE FEMALE'S ABILITY TO RECOVER SO QUICKLY UPON MY APPROACH. (WHEN I WAS A TEENAGER AND USED TO GET CAUGHT BY COPS, NEITHER MY DATE NOR I WERE ABLE TO MASTER THAT QUICK RECOVERY.) I CHECKED THEIR IDENTIFICATION AND TOLD THEM THEIR TAG WAS NOT VISIBLE. I LEFT THEM ALONE SHORTLY THEREAFTER.

0243 - (S) TRAFFIC STOP

I STOPPED A BEIGE TWO DOOR HONDA ACCORD BECAUSE ITS TAG WAS UNASSIGNED. THE OCCUPANTS WERE TWO B/MS. THE DRIVER HAD ONLY AN ARIZONA IDENTIFICATION CARD. THE PASSENGER HAD AN ARIZONA LICENSE THAT HAD BEEN CANCELLED. I ARRESTED THE DRIVER. MY PARTNER, WHO SHOWED UP TO BACK ME, FOUND A BAG OF MARIJUANA IN THE DRIVER SIDE DOOR COMPARTMENT. WHEN ASKED, THE ARRESTED B/M SAID, "I DON'T KNOW NOTHING ABOUT THAT." WHEN I ASKED THE PASSENGER WHOSE IT WAS, HE SAID, "WHAT DID HE SAY?" I TOLD HIM NOT TO WORRY ABOUT WHAT HE SAID AND TO ANSWER THE QUESTION. HE SAID HE DIDN'T KNOW WHOSE IT WAS. I TOLD THE PASSENGER HE COULD BE GOING AS WELL FOR PRESENTING ME WITH THE CANCELLED LICENSE. HE PROMPTLY ASKED ME WHERE THE NEAREST PAY PHONE WAS AND BEGAN WALKING IN THAT DIRECTION. (WE WERE ON THE INTERSTATE.) I CHARGED THE DRIVER WITH DRIVING WHILE HIS LICENSE WAS CANCELLED AND FOR POSSESSION OF MARIJUANA.

A PUERTO RICAN NURSE AT THE JAIL WANTED TO KNOW IF I WAS MARRIED AND IF SHE COULD CALL ME. SHE WAS PUFFING ON A CIGARETTE WHEN SHE ASKED ME, BUT I GAVE HER MY CARD ANYWAY.

0457 -I WENT TO THE STATION TO TURN IN MY EVIDENCE AND PAPERWORK.

0600 - I WENT TO BREAKFAST. BY 0643 I WAS PULLING UP TO THE HOUSE. I'LL TALK TO YOU NEXT WEEK.

10-16

1809 -I WENT TO DINNER. I HAD BEEF STROGANOFF AND MIXED VEGETABLES WHILE STUDYING FOR A MID-TERM EXAM.

1849-I STOPPED BY THE HOTEL WHERE MY FRIEND (B/M, 31) WORKS AND CHATTED WITH HIM A BIT.

2150-(D) BATTERY
   A W/M (40'S) ADVISED HIS SON GOT INTO A FIGHT WITH HIS PRINCIPAL AT SCHOOL. AS A RESULT, HIS SON WAS ARRESTED AND TAKEN TO THE JUVENILE DETENTION FACILITY. ONCE HIS SON CAME HOME FROM THE FACILITY, INJURIES TO HIS PERSON WERE NOTICED. THE FATHER NOW WANTED TO PRESS CHARGES AGAINST THE PRINCIPAL. I TOLD THE FATHER HE NEEDED TO VOICE HIS CONCERNS TO THE SCHOOL RESOURCE OFFICER THAT ARRESTED HIS SON. HE DIDN'T WANT TO HEAR THAT AND DEMANDED I ASSIST HIM IN FILING CHARGES. I REFUSED, EXPLAINING THAT THE OFFICER ON THE SCENE LIKELY HAD REASON TO CHARGE ONLY HIS SON. HE SAID THAT IT WAS HIS RIGHT AS A CITIZEN TO BE ABLE TO PRESS CHARGES. WE WERE OBVIOUSLY GOING AROUND IN CIRCLES. I GAVE HIM THE ADDRESS TO HEADQUARTERS. HE COULD GO DOWN THERE AND HAVE HIS REQUEST DENIED BY SOMEONE ELSE.

2200 - (BU) TRAFFIC STOP
   I WENT TO BACK UP AN OFFICER WHO WORKS MY AREA ON A TRAFFIC STOP. THE DRIVER, A YOUNG, B/M, WAS A CONVICTED ARMED ROBBER. THE PASSENGER WAS ALSO A YOUNG, B/M. THE TRAFFIC STOP WENT SMOOTHLY. WE GOT SOME INTELLIGENCE INFORMATION FROM THEM AND LET THEM GO.

2244 - I WENT TO GET SOME GAS AND A SNACK, CRANBERRY JUICE AND ANIMAL CRACKERS.

2255 - (BU) ARMED ROBBERY

 I ASSISTED ANOTHER OFFICER WITH AN ARMED ROBBERY. THE VICTIMS WERE TWO TOURISTS VISITING FROM BOGATA, COLUMBIA, A YOUNG W/M AND A YOUNG, W/F. THEY WERE WALKING BACK TO THEIR HOTEL WHEN THE INCIDENT OCCURRED. TWO YOUNG, B/MS JUMPED OUT OF SOME BUSHES, THREW THE MALE ON THE GROUND, AND POINTED A BLACK HANDGUN AT THEM. THE B/MS SHOUTED SOMETHING IN ENGLISH THAT THE TOURISTS DIDN'T UNDERSTAND. (THEY SPOKE VERY LITTLE ENGLISH.) THE FEMALE REMOVED THE WALLET FROM THE MALE'S POCKET AND GAVE IT TO THE B/MS. IT CONTAINED $400.00 AND SOME CREDIT CARDS. THE B/MS ALSO RIPPED THE GOLD CHAINS FROM THE NECKS OF THE TOURISTS. THEY WERE EXTREMELY SHAKEN BY THE INCIDENT. THEIR STATEMENTS HAD TO BE WRITTEN BY SOMEONE ELSE. THE SUSPECTS WERE NOT LOCATED.

0000 - WHILE LEAVING THE HOTEL, I WAS APPROACHED BY AN ENGLISH HEALTHCARE WORKER (W/F 50'S). SHE AND HER PARTY HAD A FLAT TIRE ON THEIR RENTED CAR. SHE WANTED TO KNOW IF THEIR HOTEL WAS CLOSE ENOUGH TO WALK TO OR IF THEY NEEDED TO CALL A CAB. THE W/M THAT WAS WITH HER WAS UNABLE TO LOCATE THE TIRE CHANGING EQUIPMENT IN THE TRUNK. I RECOMMENDED THEY CALL THE RENTAL COMPANY. THE LARGER COMPANIES USUALLY PROVIDE A 24-HOUR ROADSIDE SERVICE. WHILE THE W/M WAS MAKING THE CALL, I CHATTED WITH THE W/F. WE TALKED ABOUT THE ROYAL FAMILY. I SAID, "I HAVE A PROBLEM WITH THE ROYAL FAMILY, ALTHOUGH I KNOW EVERYONE THERE LOVES THEM. I DON'T BELIEVE IN HAILING TO SOMEONE BECAUSE OF THE FAMILY THAT THEY ARE BORN INTO." SHE FELT THE SAME AND SAID, 'I DON'T BELIEVE IN BOWING TO ANY MAN BECAUSE THE LORD CREATED US EQUALLY." I SAID, "MY SENTIMENTS EXACTLY." - AFTER MAKING SURE THEIR RENTAL CAR COMPANY WAS SENDING SOMEONE, I LEFT.

0030 -I PATROLLED SOME OF THE OTHER HOTELS IN MY AREA TO LOOK OUT FOR THE ROBBERY

SUSPECTS.

0100 -I CALLED HOME TO CHECK MY MESSAGES. I HAD EIGHT OF THEM, BUT THE ONLY GOOD ONES WERE FROM MY DAUGHTER (4 Y/O) WHO CALLED TWICE. THE FIRST TIME SHE SAID, "CALL ME BACK RIGHT NOW. I LOVE YOU BETTER THAN ANYTHING IN THIS WORLD. NOW, IF YOU DON'T CALL ME BACK, I'M GOING TO TICKLE YOU." THE SECOND TIME SHE JUST SAID, "DADDY, I STILL WAITING FOR YOU TO CALL ME!"

0131-(D) ALARM
  I RESPONDED TO AN ALARM AT A RESTAURANT. I CHECKED IT OUT AND IT APPEARED SECURE.

0230 – AN OFFICER FROM A NEARBY DISTRICT HAD A MISSING PERSON WHO WAS LAST SEEN AT A RESTAURANT IN MY AREA. HE WANTED ME TO CHECK THE RESTAURANT. IT WAS CLOSED AND THE PARKING LOT WAS EMPTY.

0250 -I DID ANOTHER CHECK OF SOME HOTELS.

0251-(D) ALARM
  I WAS DISPATCHED TO THE SAME RESTAURANT I RESPONDED TO EARLIER IN REFERENCE TO AN ALARM. THIS TIME, I CLEARED IT WITHOUT GOING THERE. MY SERGEANT THEN ADVISED THE DISPATCHER TO DISREGARD IT IF IT CAME UP AGAIN. (THERE WAS OBVIOUSLY A PROBLEM WITH THE ALARM AND I BELIEVE IT WENT OFF WHENEVER THE SPRINKLER SYSTEM CAME ON.)

0300 -I SAT IN A HOTEL PARKING LOT AND DID SOME STUDYING.

0320 - (D) ALARM
  SAME RESTAURANT. CLEARED IT IMMEDIATELY.

0332 - (S) SUSPICIOUS VEHICLE
  I NOTICED A WHITE OLDSMOBILE PARKED IN THE LOT OF A CLOSED NIGHTCLUB. THE IGNITION WAS PUNCHED AND IT

HAD AN OHIO TAG. IT HAD NOT BEEN REPORTED STOLEN AT THAT TIME. I HAD THE DISPATCHER CONTACT THE PROPER OHIO POLICE AGENCY. THEY WERE GOING TO GO TO THE RESIDENCE AND CHECK WITH THE REGISTERED OWNER. THEY GOT BACK WITH US AND ADVISED THE REGISTERED ADDRESS WAS NO GOOD. I HAD NO CHOICE BUT TO LEAVE IT THERE.

0400 - (BU) SUSPICIOUS INCIDENT

I WENT TO BACK UP MY PARTNER AT A GAS STATION IN OUR AREA. SOME GUY LEFT SOME POWDER COCAINE THAT WAS WRAPPED UP IN A TOWEL ON THE COUNTER BY MISTAKE. THE CLERK CALLED US WHEN SHE INITIALLY FOUND IT. MY PARTNER RECOVERED IT FROM HER AND PLACED IT INTO EVIDENCE AS FOUND PROPERTY. LATER, THE YOUNG, W/M RETURNED TO THE STORE AND BEGAN WALKING AROUND, OBVIOUSLY LOOKING FOR SOMETHING. THIS FRIGHTENED THE YOUNG, W/F CLERK AND SHE CALLED US BACK. THE W/M HAD ALREADY LEFT. TO MAKE HER FEEL SAFE, MY PARTNER, MY SERGEANT AND I ALL HUNG OUT IN THE LOT FOR A WHILE.

0445 - (S) TRAFFIC STOP

I STOPPED TWO YOUNG, H/MS AND A YOUNG W/F WHO WERE IN A BLUE CHEVY PICKUP. THEY WERE ON THE INTERSTATE GOING ABOUT NINETY. I ASKED THE DRIVER, 'WHY WERE YOU GOING 90?" HE DIDN'T SEEM TO SPEAK ENGLISH VERY WELL. BUT KEPT SAYING, "NO, NO, NO." I SAID, "WHAT DO YOU MEAN, NO? DO YOU WANT A TICKET?" THAT'S WHEN HE SAID, "I'M GOING TO WORK." I TOLD HIM TO GO BACK TO HIS TRUCK AND I RAN HIS INFORMATION THROUGH THE SYSTEM. HE WASN'T WANTED AND HIS LICENSE WAS GOOD. I TOLD HIM TO SLOW DOWN AND LET HIM GO WITH A WARNING.

0455 -I DROVE THE CRUISER THROUGH A CAR WASH.

0513-I HAD AN INTERESTING BREAKFAST, CHICKEN FINGERS, ONION RINGS, FRENCH-FRIES AND CHEESE STICKS. (YOU HAVE TO TAKE MY WORD ON THIS, BUT IF I WEREN'T IN PRETTY GOOD SHAPE, I WOULD

NEVER TELL YOU GUYS ABOUT ALL THE GARBAGE I EAT.

0614-I WENT TO THE STATION TO DROP OFF SOMETHING, THEN HEADED HOME. GOOD MORNING.

10/17

2025 - BRIEFING - MY SERGEANT PRESENTED ME WITH THE OFFICER OF THE MONTH AWARD AND MY AREA PARTNER GOT IT FOR THE FOLLOWING MONTH. EXCELLENT GESTURE, IT'S GOOD TO KNOW YOU'RE BEING RECOGNIZED FOR "STEPPING IT UP" A BIT IN REGARDS TO YOUR ASSIGNED DUTIES.

2027 - (BU) DISTURBANCE
   I WENT TO BACK UP ANOTHER UNIT AT AN INDIAN CONVENIENCE STORE. THE OWNER AN INDIAN MALE (40'S), WAS COMPLAINING ABOUT A CUSTOMER, INDIAN MALE (40'S) ALSO. THE CUSTOMER WAS REFUSING TO LEAVE THE PREMISES. THE OWNER WANTED HIM GONE BECAUSE HE HAD URINATED IN THE BATHROOM SINK. AFTER HEARING THAT, I WAS ON THE VERGE OF BECOMING IRATE. I TOLD THE CUSTOMER HIS BEHAVIOR WAS TOTALLY UNACCEPTABLE AND I WANTED TO KNOW WHETHER OR NOT HE HAD ANY HOME TRAINING. (THE WORDS I USED WERE SIMILAR TO THE AFOREMENTIONED.) HE CLAIMED HE OWNED THREE RESTAURANTS OF HIS OWN IN THE UNITED STATES AND CANADA. I ASKED HIM, "HOW WOULD LIKE IT IF SOMEONE PISSED IN YOUR SINK?" HE SAID THE STORE'S RESTROOM WAS SO DIRTY THAT HE WOULDN'T EVEN LET HIS DOG USE IT. I SAID, "THEN YOU'RE APPARENTLY LOWER THAN A DOG!" THE CUSTOMER CONTINUED TO BEHAVE IN A BELLIGERENT MANNER AND WAS BUT A HALF-A-HEART BEAT AWAY FROM GOING TO JAIL. HE LEFT AFTER I TRESPASSED HIM AND TOLD HIM HE WAS NOT PERMITTED TO EVER RETURN.

2104-I HEADED TO DINNER - TACO NIGHT - UMMM! 2109 -I MADE SOME CALLS.

2219 - (D) AREA CHECK
   I WAS DISPATCHED AN AREA CHECK FOR A W/M WHO WAS LAID OUT ACROSS THE HOOD OF A CAR. MY SERGEANT GOT TO THE AREA BEFORE I DID AND SAID HE WAS UNABLE TO LOCATE THE MAN.

2240 - (BU) SUSPICIOUS INCIDENT

I ASSISTED ANOTHER OFFICER WHO WAS RESPONDING TO AN APARTMENT COMPLEX. THE CALLER ADVISED TWO PEOPLE WERE WALKING AROUND THE NEIGHBORHOOD LOOKING INTO CARS WITH FLASHLIGHTS. WE CHECKED THE ENTIRE COMPLEX AND CAME ACROSS NO ONE. WHILE CHECKING, AN EMERGENCY CALL (SUSPICIOUS INCIDENT) WENT OUT AND I BROKE FOR IT...

2247 - (D) SUSPICIOUS INCIDENT / DOMESTIC BATTERY

I RESPONDED TO AN AREA HOTEL. THE CALLER ADVISED A YOUNG, W/F WAS LYING ON THE GROUND IN THE PARKING LOT CRYING AND SCREAMING. THEY THOUGHT A VEHICLE HAD STRUCK HER. WE CHECKED ALL AROUND THE PARKING LOT BUT COULDN'T FIND HER. JUST AS WE WERE ABOUT TO CLEAR THE CALL, SECURITY LOCATED THE W/F. SHE HAD GONE BACK TO HER ROOM. SHE SEEMED TO BE UNDER THE INFLUENCE OF ALCHOHOL OR A CONTROLLED SUBSTANCE. SHE KEPT SAYING SHE WAS SEXUALLY BATTERED BY HER FATHER AND SISTER WHEN SHE WAS A CHILD. SHE ALSO SAID HER PARENTS HAD BROUGHT HER TO FLORIDA FROM MASSACHUSETTS AND ABANDONED HER. THE W/FS PARENTS WERE LOCATED AND WE GOT THEIR SIDE OF THE STORY. THE DAUGHTER, WHO WAS IN HER MIDDLE TO LATE TWENTIES, TOLD HER PARENTS SHE WANTED TO MOVE TO FLORIDA TO GET AWAY FROM HER ABUSIVE BOYFRIEND AND START OVER. THE PARENTS AGREED TO BRING HER DOWN HERE. WHEN IT CAME TIME FOR THE PARENTS TO LEAVE, THE DAUGHTER ATTACKED THE MOTHER, PREVENTING HER FROM LEAVING THE HOTEL ROOM. THE MOTHER AND FATHER, WHO WERE IN THEIR 60'S, MANAGED TO GET OUT OF THE ROOM AND OUT TO THEIR CAR. THE WHOLE TIME THE DAUGHTER WAS GRABBING THEM AND SCREAMING FOR THEM NOT TO LEAVE. AFTER THE PARENTS DROVE OFF, THE DAUGHTER COLLAPSED IN A HEAP ON THE PAVEMENT. THE CALLER MUST HAVE OBSERVED HER AT THAT POINT. THE MOTHER AND FATHER BOTH SAID THE DAUGHTER HAD PUSHED AND HIT THE MOTHER DURING THE STRUGGLE IN THE HOTEL ROOM. I HAD RESCUE TRANSPORT THE W/F TO THE HOSPITAL BECAUSE SHE WAS CONPLAINING OF PAIN. AFTERWARDS, I TOOK HER TO JAIL FOR DOMESTIC BATTERY. SHE WANTED TO KNOW WHY SHE WAS GOING

TO JAIL. I TOLD HER IT WAS BECAUSE SHE BATTERED HER MOTHER. SHE SAID HER PARENTS SHOULD BE GOING TO JAIL BECAUSE THEY BATTERED HER. I TOLD HER IT WAS UP TO ME TO DETERMINE WHO INITIATED THE PHYSICAL ALTERCATION. SHE KEPT TELLING ME WHAT I WAS SUPPOSED TO DO AND HOW THEY DID IT BACK IN MASSACHUSETTS. I TOLD HER, "WELL THIS AIN'T KANSAS, AND IN FLORIDA WE TAKE THE PRIMARY AGGRESSOR!" (I KNEW SHE WAS FROM MASSACHUSETTS, BUT SAYING KANSAS SOUNDED MUCH COOLER- YOU KNOW, THAT WHOLE DOROTHY - WIZARD OF OZ THING.) ON THE WAY TO JAIL I EXPLAINED THINGS TO HER MORE AND SHE SETTLED DOWN A BIT. I TOLD HER THE FACT OF THE MATTER WAS THAT I BELIEVED HER PARENTS WERE MORE CREDIBLE THAN SHE WAS. I FURTHER TOLD HER THAT HER BEING INTOXICATED AND ACTING IRRATIONAL HADN'T HELPED EITHER. SHE SAID, "YOU'D BE IRRATIONAL TOO IF YOU'RE PARENTS HIT YOU AND SEXUALLY ASSAULTED YOU ALL YOUR LIFE." SHE HAD A POINT THERE, BUT SHE WAS STILL GOING. I TOLD HER I COULDN'T DO ANYTHING ABOUT HER PAST, I HAD TO DEAL WITH WHAT HAPPENED TODAY.

0200 -I DID A CHECK OF SOME HOTELS IN MY AREA.

0216-I WENT TO THE STATION TO TURN IN SOME PAPERWORK AND FILL MY BOTTLES WITH SOME FREE WATER.

0248 - I WENT TO PATROL MY PROBLEM APARTMENT COMPLEX. IT'S BEEN QUIET THERE LATELY - TOO QUIET.

0312 - AFTERWARDS, I PATROLLED A RETIREMENT COMMUNITY IN MY AREA.

0359 -I DID A BUSINESS CHECK OF THAT RESTAURANT WITH THE PROBLEM ALARM. UNFORTUNATELY, WE DON'T EVEN ACKNOWLEDGE ITS ALARM ANYMORE. I CRUISED BY THERE JUST TO MAKE SURE IT WAS O.K.

THE STREETS ARE DEAD SO I'LL TALK ABOUT MY "OFF" DAYS IF THERE IS SUCH A THING. YESTERDAY, WHILE ON MY WAY TO SCHOOL, A B/F (30'S) FLAGGED ME DOWN. SHE WAS LOOKING FOR DIRECTIONS TO THE NEAREST HARDWARE STORE. AS

IT TURNED OUT, I HAD MET HER ONCE BEFORE (LIKE OVER A YEAR AGO). WHEN WE MET, I WAS SITTING IN A FAST FOOD RESTAURANT PARKING LOT AND SHE WAS GOING THROUGH THE DRIVE THRU. SHE KEPT STARING SO I MADE SOME SMART REMARK. AFTER THAT, WE CONVERSED FOR A WHILE. SHE USED TO GO TO BED TOO EARLY SO I STOPPED CALLING HER. SHE SAID SHE DIDN'T RECOGNIZE ME AT FIRST BECAUSE I DIDN'T HAVE A MUSTACHE ANYMORE. BACK THEN SHE WAS A MORTGAGE LENDER. NOWADAYS, SHE'S A CONGRESSIONAL AIDE. (THAT EXPLAINS LOOKING FOR THE HARDWARE STORE. PROBABLY LOOKING FOR MATERIAL TO PUT UP SOME CANDIDATE SIGNS.) SHE LEANED OVER THE TOP OF HER CAR AND WROTE HER NEW NUMBERS DOWN I COULD TELL SHE WAS PURPOSELY POKING OUT HER BACKSIDE AS SHE WROTE. SILLY HER, SHE MUST HAVE THOUGHT I WAS LOOKING.

A COUPLE OF DAYS AGO I GOT A CALL FROM THIS FEMALE DJ (B/F, 30'S) IN TOWN THAT I KNOW. I MET HER WHEN HER RADIO STATION WAS HOSTING A CONCERT AT A NIGHTCLUB AROUND HERE. THAT WAS SEVERAL MONTHS AGO. I GUESS SHE'S STILL A DJ. SHE CALLED ME FROM A RADIO STATION AND LEFT A MESSAGE. I CALLED HER TO SEE WHAT SHE WANTED. I CALLED YESTERDAY AND THEY SAID SHE'D BE IN AT 4 A.M. THIS TIME I GOT NO ANSWER.

0411 -I WENT TO GET SOME GAS AND TRIED THE DJ AGAIN. I'M ASSUMING SHE'S GOT A FRIEND WHO'S GOT A FRIEND THAT GOT IN SOME TROUBLE WITH THE LAW AND NEEDS ADVICE.

0427 - (S) TRAFFIC STOP
I STOPPED A H/M (40'S) BECAUSE HIS LICENSE WAS SUSPENDED. THE SUSPENSION WAS FOR FAILING TO MAINTAIN INSURANCE COVERAGE. HE SAID HE COULD SHOW ME THAT PAPER THAT PROVED HE PAID HIS INSURANCE A YEAR IN ADVANCE. HE ALSO SAID HE UTILIZED THE SAME COMPANY FOR THREE YEARS. HE SAID HE HAD CHANGED AGENTS, BUT NOT COMPANIES. HE SAID HE STUDIED INSURANCE AND KNOWS THAT THEY ARE SUPPOSED TO INFORM YOU WHEN THEY CANCEL YOU. I TOLD HIM, "IT MAY BE THEIR ERROR, THEREFORE I'M NOT TAKING YOUR TAG. I AM, HOWEVER, GIVING YOU THIS TICKET AND TAKING YOUR LICENSE. IF IT

TURNS OUT THEY WERE WRONG, YOU WON'T HAVE TO PAY. GOOD LUCK SIR. I HOPE IT TURNS OUT IN YOUR FAVOR."

0443 - ON THE WAY TO GET SOME BREAKFAST, I CALLED THE DJ ONCE AGAIN. I WISH AT LEAST A MACHINE WOULD PICK UP. THERE WOULD BE DOCUMENTATION AND THE BALL WOULD BE IN HER COURT. AS IT STANDS NOW, THE BURDEN OF PROOF THAT I EVER RETURNED HER CALL LIES WITH ME...

AS I PULLED UP AT THE RESTAURANT, I GOT A HOLD OF HER. SHE SAID SHE WAS GOING THROUGH HER BOOK AND CAME ACROSS MY CARD. SHE WANTED TO KNOW WHICH NUMBERS ACTUALLY WORKED. SHE SAID, "I BET YOU THOUGHT IT WAS SOMETHING SERIOUS, HUH?" SHE SAID, "MAYBE WE CAN GO FOR COFFEE, OR SOMETHING." I DON'T DRINK COFFEE, BUT I SAID, "SURE." SHE SAID SHE WAS ABOUT 45 SECONDS AWAY FROM SHOW TIME AND WANTED TO KNOW IF SHE COULD CALL ME BACK AT 7:30 A.M. I TOLD HER I'D BE SLEEPING THEN BECAUSE I WORKED 6 P.M. TO 6 A.M. SHE SAID, "HOW ABOUT LATER IN THE AFTERNOON?" AGAIN I SAID, "SURE."

0540 - (D) DOMESTIC DISTURBANCE

WHILE I WAS EATING BREAKFAST I WAS DISPATCHED TO A DOMESTIC DISTURBANCE. THE PARTIES INVOLVED WERE A B/M (40'S) AND A W/F (40'S). SHE WAS INTOXICATED AND HANGING OUT IN HER VEHICLE WHICH WAS PARKED IN THE DRIVEWAY. THE B/M WAS STANDING AT THE DOOR. THE W/F WAS UPSET BECAUSE HE WAS DENYING HER ENTRY. I SPOKE TO HIM AND FOUND OUT THEY HAD LIVED THERE TOGETHER. EARLIER, SHE AGREED TO MOVE OUT. SHE ACTUALLY REMOVED ALL HER BELONGINGS FROM THE HOME AND THEY WERE STUFFED IN HER CAR. APPARENTLY SHE HAD PLANNED TO MOVE IN WITH SOME OTHER GUY, BUT IT DIDN'T WORK OUT. SHE THOUGHT SHE COULD JUST EASE ON BACK TO THIS GUY. SHE THOUGHT WRONG. HAD SHE NOT VOLUNTARILY MOVED OUT, WE WOULD HAVE TOLD THE MAN SHE HAD A RIGHT TO THE HOME. (THEY WERE FORMER BOYFRIEND AND GIRLFRIEND.) THIS WAS THE SECOND TIME WE WERE CALLED OUT TO THAT RESIDENCE. I WASN'T ONE OF THE RESPONDERS ON THAT INITIAL CALL. THE OFFICERS THOUGHT THEY RESOLVED THE MATTER. THE WOMAN AGREED TO JUST SLEEP IN HER VEHICLE UNTIL

MORNING WHEN SHE COULD LOOK FOR SOMEWHERE TO GO. (THERE HAD BEEN NO PHYSICAL CONTACT.) I TOLD HER, "I THOUGHT YOU AGREED TO STAY OUT HERE AND LEAVE YOUR EX-BOYFRIEND ALONE." SHE SAID, "I KNOW. BUT I LOVE HIM AND I GAVE HIM EVERYTHING." I TOLD HER HE DIDN'T SEEM TO FEEL THE SAME ABOUT HER. I ALSO SAID SHE VOLUNTARILY LEFT AND HE WAS NOT OBLIGATED TO LET HER RETURN. SHE SAID SHE UNDERSTOOD, BUT IT HURT. SHE THEN SAID SHE COULD GET A KEY FROM THE LANDLORD AROUND THE CORNER BECAUSE TECHNICALLY SHE WAS STILL ON THE LEASE. I TOLD HER IF SHE HAD A KEY AND WAS ON THE LEASE, THAT WOULD BE A DIFFERENT STORY. SHE THEN PROCEEDED TO WALK DOWN THE STREET TO THE LANDLORD'S. SHE FLAGGED ME DOWN AS I DROVE OFF. SHE SAID, "HERE'S THE PHONE NUMBER TO MY OFFICE WHERE I'LL BE LATER. WILL YOU CALL ME LATER?" I SAID, "TO DISCUSS WHAT?" SHE SAID, "THIS ISN'T BEING RECORDED IS IT?" I SAID, "NO, IT'S NOT BEING RECORDED. CALL YOU TO DISCUSS WHAT?" SHE SAID, "TO DISCUSS US." (AND WOMEN CALL MEN DOGS?)

BEFORE GOING TO THE ABOVE CALL, I TOLD THE COOK AT THE RESTAURANT THAT I HAD TO GO TO A DOMESTIC DISTURBACE. I TOLD HIM SOME OTHER OFFICERS HAD GONE OUT THERE EARLIER, BUT I DIDN'T BECAUSE I WAS ON A TRAFFIC STOP. HE SAID, "YOU ALL SHOULD HAVE ARRESTED SOMEONE THE FIRST TIME, WASTING OUR TAX DOLLARS GOING BACK AND FORTH OUT THERE!" WE BOTH LAUGHED.

10/20

1800-BRIEFING

1821 -I LEFT BRIEFING AND HEADED TO DINNER.
   BEING THAT IT'S PAYDAY FRIDAY, I FIGURED I'D CALL MY CREDIT UNION TO SEE HOW MUCH MONEY WAS NOT DEPOSITED INTO MY ACCOUNT.

1837 - A W/M (40'S) PULLED UP BESIDE ME IN TRAFFIC AND ASKED, "IS THERE ANY WAY YOU CAN GET INTO A LOCKED CAR?" I TOLD HIM, "NO, WE DON'T CARRY SLIM JIMS." I THEN GAVE HIM THE NAME OF A LOCKSMITH. HE SAID, "THANKS, I HAVE A CALL INTO ONE."

1840 - (D) 9-1-1 HANG-UP
   I RESPONDED TO A PAY PHONE INSIDE OF A MALL WHERE A 9-1-1 CALL HAD BEEN PLACED. THERE WAS NO ONE AROUND THE PHONE.

1851 - SECOND ATTEMPT AT DINNER.I WAS GOING TO EAT AT MY FRIEND'S (B/M, 31) PLACE OF EMPLOYMENT. JUST AS I PULLED UP, HE PAGED ME 9-1-1 FROM HOME. I THEN REALIZED HE WASN'T AT WORK (I'M SMART LIKE THAT). HE HAD SOME DISTURBING NEWS. HE WAS FIRST ON THE SCENE AT A "LIKELY" SUICIDE SITE. A MAN HAD LAIN DOWN ACROSS SOME RAILROAD TRACKS BEHIND MY FRIEND'S PLACE OF RESIDENCE. THE TRAIN SOUNDED ITS HORN AND LOCKED UP ITS BREAKS, BUT WAS UNABLE TO AVOID CRUSHING THE MAN. MY FRIEND NOTIFIED THE LOCAL AUTHORITIES AS HE ATTEMPTED TO LOCATE THE MAN'S MISSING BODY PARTS. NEEDLESS TO SAY, MY FRIEND DIDN'T JOIN ME FOR DINNER THAT NIGHT.
   I DECIDED TO GO ELSEWHERE TO EAT. AS I PULLED UP TO THE HOTEL WHERE I WAS GOING TO BE DINING, FIRE/RESCUE WAS ENTERING THE PROPERTY. I FOUND OUT FROM SECURITY THAT A YOUNG, W/F HAD FALLEN AND BROKEN HER LEG. HE CLAIMS SHE WAS DOING SOME FANCY CROSSOVER MOVES ON HER ROLLER BALDES IN FRONT OF THE HOTEL AND "LOST IT." THE POOR GIRL WAS ON DAY ONE OF A SIX-DAY VACTION.

ON A LIGHTER NOTE I HAD LEMON PEPPER CATFISH, RICE, BABY RED POTATIOS, AND NEW ENGLAND CLAM CHOWDER. THE CHOWDER, I MIGHT ADD, WAS DELICIOUS. ORDINARILY, I DON'T LIKE CLAM CHOWDER.

1944 - (BU) NON-EMERGENCY BACK-UP
I RESPONDED TO BACK-UP AN OFF-DUTY OFFICER WHO WAS WORKING AT A SHOPPING MALL. HE WAS OUT WITH TWO YOUNG, W/MS IN THE PARKING GARAGE. THEY HAD A BOTTLE OF VODKA IN THE CAR THAT THEY HAD BEEN DRINKING. THEY ALSO HAD A SMALL AMOUNT OF MARIJUANA. THE OFFICER CHARGED THEM AFTER GIVING THEM A GOOD LECTURE. (THE TWO MALES WERE FROM TAMPA.)

2010 - MY FRIEND (F, 23, BRAZ) CALLED ME. SHE TOLD ME, "I LIKE READING THE SITE AND I SENT YOU AN E-MAIL SAYING SO. WHY DIDN'T YOU RESPOND TO IT? YOU BETTER SEND ME AN E-MAIL ON MY BIRTHDAY." SHE TOLD ME HER FRIEND HAD LEFT HER HUSBAND AND TOOK THE KIDS BECAUSE SHE DIDN'T WANT TO BE MARRIED TO HIM ANYMORE. THE HUSBAND TOLD HER THAT HE CALLED THE POLICE AND SHE WAS GOING TO BE ARRESTED IF SHE DOESN'T COME BACK TO HIM. FOR FEAR OF BEING ARRESTED, SHE HASN'T GONE TO WORK FOR THREE DAYS. MY FRIEND WANTED TO KNOW IF THAT WAS RIGHT. I TOLD HER SHE HAD THE RIGHT TO LEAVE HIM, BUT DID NOT HAVE THE RIGHT TO KEEP HIS CHILDREN FROM HIM. AFTER WE TALKED ABOUT THAT A BIT, SHE SAID, "I LOVE READING THOSE STORIES. OH, IT'S THURSDAY. YOU HAVE SOME NEW ONES!" I SAID, "NO, IT'S FRIDAY. YOU'RE LATE." SHE SAID SHE DIDN'T HAVE TIME TO CHECK IT YESTERDAY BECAUSE OF WORK. BUT SHE'D READ THEM AFTER WE GOT OFF THE PHONE.

2033 - AFTERWARDS, I SPOKE WITH ANOTHER FRIEND (F, 26, BRAZ). SHE WAS TAKING A BATH AND ASKED IF I CARED TO JOIN HER. I DECLINED. (I'M MORE OF A SHOWER KIND OF GUY.)

2050 - (D) DISTURBANCE

A THIRD PARTY CALLED IN ADVISING A MALE AND FEMALE WERE FIGHTING. HE ONLY HEARD THE DISTURBANCE AND DIDN'T KNOW EXACTLY WHICH APARTMENT IT WAS COMING FROM. ANOTHER UNIT GOT THERE BEFORE ME AND SAID I COULD CANCEL MY RESPONSE.

2129 - (D) VEHICLE BURGLARY

A TOURIST FROM ENGLAND SAID SOMEONE STOLE THEIR DAUGHTER'S GAMEBOY AND CAMERA FROM THE BACK SEAT WHILE THEY WERE DINING AT A RESTAURANT THAT SPECIALIZES IN B-B-Q RIBS. AFTER TAKING THE REPORT, I ASKED THEM IF THEY LIKED THE RESTAURANT. THEY SAID IT WAS O.K. I ASKED IF THEY HAD THE RIBS. THE WOMAN RUBBED HER STOMACH AND SAID, "YES, NOW I'M GOING TO HAVE A BIT OF WHISKEY." I SAID, "AH, NOW THE FUN BEGINS." THEY LAUGHED AND THANKED ME AND WERE ON THEIR WAY.

2230 - (S) TRAFFIC STOP

I STOPPED A YOUNG, B/M AND A YOUNG, B/F IN A RED CHEVROLET CAPRICE. THE TAG HAD BEEN EXPIRED FOR TWO MONTH. I THOUGHT ABOUT GIVING HIM A WARNING, BUT IT WAS TWO MONTHS. I DECIDED TO WRITE HIM A TICKET. AFTER EXPLAINING THE PAYMENT PROCESS TO HIM, HE ASKED ME HOW TO GET TO THE HOTEL WHERE HE AND HIS GIRLFRIEND WERE GOING TO STAY. AFTER I TOLD HIM, HE SAID, "THE EXPIRATION SLIPPED HIS MIND BECAUSE THE TAG WAS SEIZED AND HE JUST GOT IT BACK. IT WAS SEIZED FOR FAILING TO MAINTAIN INSURANCE COVERAGE.

2320 -I WENT TO EAT AGAIN. I HAD A CHICKEN BREAST AND MORE OF THE RICE AND CLAM CHOWDER.

0000 -I DID A CHECK OF SEVERAL HOTEL PARKING LOTS.

0005 - (D) SUSPICIOUS INCIDENT
A RESTAURANT CALLED REQUESTING WE PROVIDE SOME TRAFFIC CONTROL. A TOUR BUS BROKE DOWN WITH ITS REAR HALF WAY IN THE INTERSECTION. A TOW TRUCK PULLED IT OUT, BACKING UP TRAFFIC IN BOTH DIRECTIONS.

0010 - MY FRIEND (F, 26, BRAZ) CALLED TO SAY SHE WAS OFF TO BED AND WOULD CALL ME TOMORROW.

0034 -I WENT TO A RESTAURANT PARKING LOT TO WORK ON MY PAPERWORK. 0057 -I DID ANOTHER HOTEL CHECK.

0110 -I WENT TO THE STATION TO TURN IN MY PAPERWORK AND GET SOME FREE OFFICE COOLER WATER. HEY I DON'T WANT TO HEAR IT. I PAID FOR THE INTIAL PLASTIC BOTTLE. I CAN KEEP REFILLING IT AND ACTING LIKE its AQUAFINA IF I WANT.

0130-(D) ALARM
I RESPONDED TO AN ALARM IN A RESIDENTIAL NEIGHBORHOOD. THE NEIGHBOR FROM ACROSS THE STREET WAS STANDING OUTSIDE. HE WAS WEARING ONE OF THOSE GERMAN OUTFITS WITH THE SHORTS AND SUSPENDERS. HE SAID HE'D SEEN NOTHING UNUSUAL AT THE RESIDENCE THAT I WAS RESPONDING TO. I CHECKED IT AND IT WAS SECURED. I ASKED THE GUY ACROSS THE STREET TO LOOK OUT FOR HIS NEIGHBORS AND HE SAID, "I ALWAYS DO. THANKS OFFICER."

0155-I PULLED INTO A SHOPPING PLAZA TO WORK ON ADDITIONAL PAPERWORK.

0229 - (BU) DISTURBANCE
I RESPONDED TO A HOTEL WHERE A HEATED VERBAL ALTERCATION BETWEEN A CAB DRIVER AND A PASSENGER WAS ALLEGEDLY OCCURRING. I GOT THERE AND FOUND NOTHING GOING ON. FURTHER, THE PERSON WHO CALLED IT IN DIDN'T WANT TO MEET. I CLEARED THE CALL AND LEFT.

0245 - I WENT TO A CONVENIENCE STORE TO WORK ON PAPERWORK AGAIN.

0305 - (BU) DISTURBANCE

THIS WAS A DISPUTE BETWEEN TWO CONVENIENCE STORE CLERKS. IT WAS THE B/M'S (40'S) FIRST DAY ON THE JOB. HE WAS UPSET WITH AN ASIAN FEMALE (40'S). HE SAID HE HELPED ALL THE CUSTOMERS WHILE THE FEMALE AND ANOTHER GUY TALKED ON THE PHONE WITH EACH OTHER. WHEN HE RAN OUT OF MONEY, HE DIDN'T HAVE THE SAFE COMBINATION TO GET MORE. HE TOLD HER THAT WAS FINE. HE'D DO SOMETHING ELSE AND SHE COULD WORK THE REGISTER. SHE GOT UPSET AND BEGAN USING RACIAL SLURS. HE SAID INSTEAD OF "JACKING HER UP", HE OPTED TO CALL US.

0533 -I WENT TO A DONUT SHOP FOR BREAKFAST. HOLD IT! I DIDN'T HAVE A DONUT. I HAD A CINNAMON APPLE PECAN MUFFIN. SEE YA TOMORROW.

10/21

1800-BRIEFING

1814 - MY SERGEANT WAS DUE IN LATE. BRIEFING WAS HELD BY THAT SUPERVISOR FROM THE OTHER SQUAD THAT I KIND OF GOT INTO IT WITH. IT WENT WELL. I'M NOT HOLDING ANY GRUDGES, AND I DON'T THINK HE IS EITHER. PROFESSIONALS MUST REMAIN PROFESSIONAL.

OUR SERGEANTS DECIDED TO SETTLE THE MATTER AS FOLLOWS: MY PARTNER AND I ARE TO SLACK OFF OF THE AGGRESSIVE PATROL FOR THE FIRST FEW HOURS OF OUR SHIFT. THAT MEANT NOT SO MANY TRAFFIC STOPS AND TRIPS TO JAIL UNTIL LATER. THIS WAS SUPPOSED TO ALLOW THE EARLIER SHIFT TO CATCH UP ON THEIR PAPERWORK AND GET SOMETHING TO EAT. WHAT CAN I SAY? I'M A TEAM PLAYER.

1816-I ATE BEFORE COMING IN. MY FRIEND (F, 26, BRAZ) COOKED FOR ME. I TOLD HER IT WAS GREAT. AND IT WAS GOOD AS FAR AS LIVER AND ONIONS GO.

1821-I SAT IN THE LOT OF A JUVENILE DETENTION FACILITY IN MY AREA AND CAUGHT UP ON SOME PAPERWORK.

2138-I GOT HUNGRY AGAIN AND DECIDED TO GO EAT AT MY FRIEND'S (B/M, 31) HOTEL. THE ONE WHO DIDN'T GO TO WORK YESTERDAY BECAUSE OF THE SUICIDE. I WENT TO SEE HOW HE WAS DOING.

1943-I FIGURED I BETTER STOP AND GET SOME GAS FIRST. I WOULDN'T WANT TO GET INVOLVED IN A HIGH SPEED CHASE WITH ONLY A QUARTER OF A TANK FULL.

MY FRIEND WAS DOING FINE EMOTIONALLY. HE WAS JUST DISPLEASED WITH THE COVERAGE THE SUICIDE VICTIM RECEIVED. A GUY SPENDS THIRTY-ONE YEARS ON THIS EARTH TRYING TO FIND HIS WAY. FOR WHATEVER REASON, HE DECIDES THAT HE CAN NO LONGER BARE HIS EXISTENCE AND LIES DOWN ON SOME TRAIN TRACKS. COVERAGE OF HIS LIFE AND DEATH IS REDUCED TO A MERE FIVE LINES IN THE

NEWSPAPER'S LOCAL SECTION. LIFE GOES ON, YOU SAY? BOY DOES IT EVER.

2200 - I STOPPED BY A DRUG STORE TO USE THE RESTROOM, BUY SOME JUICE AND A SMALL LIGHT SO I CAN SEE MY LAPTOP AT NIGHT.

2215-ON PATROL

2230 -I DID A CHECK OF A FEW HOTELS.

2243 - (D) 9-1-1 HANG-UP
   THE DISPATCHER ADVISED A 9-1-1 HANG-UP CALL THAT WAS RECEIVED FROM AN AREA HOTEL. UPON MY ARRIVAL, HOTEL PERSONNEL ADVISED THAT ALL WAS WELL.

2300 - I CHECKED A FEW MORE HOTEL PARKING LOTS.

2315 -I SPOKE TO A FEMALE FRIEND OF MINE. YOU KNOW WHAT? IT DAWNED ON ME THAT I DIDN'T KNOW WHAT FRIEND NUMBER SHE WAS. IN FACT, I COULDN'T REMEMBER WHICH NUMBER HALF OF THEM WERE. THAT'S WHY I JUST STARTED SAYING MY FRIEND AND PROVIDING A BRIEF DESCRIPTION OF THEM.
   THE ONE I WAS TALKING TO WAS A 23 YO FEMALE FROM BRAZIL. (THE WOMAN I USED TO CALL FG3 (F, 23, PR, USED TO CALL ME 24/7) SAID, "I'M NOT CALLING YOU ANYMORE. YOU KNOW WHERE I LIVE IF YOU WANT TO GET A HOLD OF ME." ANOTHER FRIEND (F, 26, BRAZ) ALSO CALLED. SHE TOLD ME ABOUT HER BIRTHDAY CELEBRATION FOR HER SON THAT HER EX-HUSBAND ATTENDED. IT WAS HELD AT THE HOUSE OF SOME PEOPLE THAT HER EX GOES TO CHURCH WITH. SHE SAID SHE FELT EXTREMELY UNCOMFORTABLE BECAUSE ALL THE PEOPLE KEPT REFERRING TO HER AS HIS WIFE, WHICH SHE NO LONGER WAS. WHEN SHE FINALLY MADE UP AN EXCUSE TO LEAVE AFTER BEING THERE FOR FIVE HOURS, SOMEONE SUGGESTED THEY PRAY FOR HER BEFOR LEAVING. SO THEY DID. THEY GATHERED TOGETHER, FORMED A CIRCLE, AND HELD HANDS. SHE SAID SHE KNEW THEY WERE PRAYING FOR THEM AS A COUPLE. THE FEW PEOPLE THAT KNEW THEY WERE NO LONGER TOGETHER TRIED TO CONVINCE HER TO

GET BACK WITH HIM. THEY TOLD HER, "WE CAN REALLY SEE A CHANGE IN HIM."

2330 - A K-9 OFFICER IN MY AREA REQUESTED SOME ASSISTANCE. A WALK-UP ADVISED HIM OF A MAN WHO WAS RUNNING DOWN THE MIDDLE OF THE STREET IN TRAFFIC. WE MADE CONTACT WITH THE H/M (30'S). HE WAS SHAKING AND OUT OF BREATH. HE SEEMED TO BE UNDER THE INFLUENCE OF A CONTROLLED SUBSTANCE. HE HAD APPARENTLY JUST BEEN RELEASED FROM THE HOSPITAL UP THE ROAD, SO THERE WAS NO SENSE IN TAKING HIM BACK THERE. THE PAPERWORK HE HAD ON HIM STATED THAT HE HAD BEEN TREATED FOR SEIZURES AND RELEASED. THE H/M WAS MEXICAN AND PRIMARILY SPOKE SPANISH, BUT HE SPOKE ENGLISH PRETTY GOOD. WE HAD A DIFFICULT TIME TRYING TO ASCERTAIN WHERE HE LIVED. HE KEPT SAYING HE LIVED IN HOLLYWOOD, FLORIDA, BUT HAD BEEN IN CENTRAL FLORIDA FOR TEN MONTHS. WHEN I ASKED WHERE HE HAD BEEN STAYING ALL THAT TIME, HE CAME UP WITH A COUPLE OF ANSWERS. FIRST, HE SAID HE WAS HOMELESS. THEN, HE SAID HE LIVES IN A ROOM BEHIND HIS EMPLOYER'S HOUSE. HE SAID HE WORKED AS A LAWNCARE ASSISTANT. THE MORE TIME WE SPENT TALKING TO THE H/M, THE MORE RATIONAL HE BECAME. HE DID, HOWEVER, KEEP SAYING THAT SOME PEOPLE WHERE THREATENING HIM AND THEY WANTED TO KILL HIM. HE WAS UNABLE TO ADVISE HIS ADDRESS. WE ASKED FOR LANDMARKS AROUND HIS NEIGHBORHOOD IN AN EFFORT TO NARROW DOWN THE POSSIBILITIES. HE SAID THERE WAS AN "EL POYO" (CHICKEN) IN THE AREA, BUT THAT DIDN'T HELP MUCH. AFTER PRODDING HIM FOR ABOUT AN HOUR, HE NAMED A BAR THAT WAS IN THE AREA. BEING THAT THERE WAS NO BED SPACE IN ANY OF THE HOMELESS SHELTERS, I FOUND OUT THE ADDRESS OF THE BAR THROUGH THE DISPATCHER AND TOOK HIM TO THAT AREA. EARLIER, THE H/M ASKED THAT I JUST TAKE HIM TO JAIL. THE POOR GUY JUST WANTED SOMEWHERE WARM TO STAY WHERE THREE MEALS ARE GUARANTEED. I TOLD HIM, "THE JAIL IS OVERCROWDED. THEY SET MOST CRIMINALS FREE. THEY CERTAINLY AREN'T GOING TO TAKE YOU. YOU HAVEN'T COMMITTED A CRIME." I TRANSPORTED HIM TO

THE LOCATON WHERE HE SAID HE STAYED. AFTER I LET HIM OUT THE CAR AND BEGAN TO DRIVE OFF, HE CHASED ME DOWN WITH HIS ARMS FLAYLING. I SAID, "WHAT IS IT?" HE POINTED ACROSS THE STREET AND SAID, "THOSE ARE THE MEN WHO WANT TO KILL ME!" I SAID, WHERE?" HE POINTED INTO THE DARKNESS AND SAID, "DONT YOU SEE THE TWO MEN OVER THERE? ONE IS WEARING A RED SHIRT." THERE WAS NO ONE FOR MILES, BUT THIS GUY WAS STARTING TO CREEP ME OUT. I'M NOT A DOCTOR, BUT I REALIZED HE WAS SUFFERING FROM SOME FORM OF PARANOIA. I TOLD HIM TO WALK THE OTHER WAY AND I'D STAY AROUND FOR A WHILE. JUST AS SOON AS HE TURNED THE CORNER, I TOOK OFF, THAT INVISIBLE MAN WITH THE RED SHIRT ON WASN'T GOING TO GET ME!

I WENT TO THE HOTEL WHERE MY FRIEND (B/M, 31) WORKS AS A SECURITY OFFICER. THEY HAD A BIG EVENT THERE AND I WENT TO PATROL THE PARKING LOT. HIS SECURITY VAN HAD LIKE TWO FLAT TIRES AND THE OTHER TWO WERE MISSING AIR. THE LOT WAS FAIRLY QUIET. I FOUND MY FRIEND DRIVING AROUND ON A GOLF CART THAT HE BORROWED FROM ANOTHER HOTEL. (NOW THAT'S DEDICATION. HE COULD HAVE JUST FORGETTEN ABOUT PATROLLING OUTSIDE UNTIL HIS VAN WAS REPAIRED.)

0222 - (BU) TRESPASSER

THERE WAS A TRESPASSER AT AN AREA HOTEL. JUST AS I ARRIVED, ANOTHER GUY ON MY SQUAD CANCELLED ME. HE WAS GOING TO BACK THE INITIAL RESPONDING OFFICER

I WENT TO THE STATION FOR WATER AND TO USE THE RESTROOM. I ALSO CHECKED MY MESSAGES. MY DAUGHTER'S MOM HAD CALLED. I'M NOT CALLING HER BACK BECAUSE SHE RECENTLY GOT ON MY NERVES. THE NEXT TIME I CALL FOR MY DAUGHTER, I'M SURE SHE'LL GET ON THE PHONE AND SAY WHATEVER IT WAS SHE HAD TO SAY.

0319 - (D) DOMESTIC BATTERY

I WAS DISPATCHED TO A DOMESTIC BATTERY WITH BOTH PARTIES PRESENT. THE COMPLAINANT WAS THE WIFE, WHO SAID HER HUSBAND HIT HER. THE DISPATCHER ADVISED THE HUSBAND WAS POSSIBLY DRUNK. UPON ARRIVAL, I FOUND THAT THE HUSBAND (W/M 50) WAS NOT POSSIBLY DRUNK.

HE WAS DRUNK. AND SO WAS HIS WIFE (W/F, 40'S). SHE WAS CRYING HYSTERICALLY. THE HUSBAND WALKED UP TO ME AND SAID, "YOU MAY AS WELL TAKE ME TO JAIL." I ASKED THE LADY, "DID HE HIT YOU?" SHE SAID, "HIT ME? HE DRUG ME BY MY HAIR ACROSS THE FRONT LAWN AND KICKED ME." I THEN ASKED HIM IF HE HIT HER. HE SAID, "YOU CAN SAY THAT." I IMMEDIATELY TOLD HIM HE WAS UNDER ARREST AND HOOKED HIM UP. HE STARTED SAYING TO HIS WIFE, "DON'T DO THIS!" I SAID, "WHAT DO YOU MEAN? A MINUTE AGO YOU WERE SAYING TAKE YOU TO JAIL." I HAD HER FILL OUT A STATEMENT AS TO WHAT HAD HAPPENED. SHE WAS BARELY LITERATE IN HER DRUNKEN STATE. SHE WAS UNABLE TO WRITE IT, BUT MANAGED TO TELL ME THAT HER HUSBAND GOT JEALOUS ABOUT A COMMENT SHE MADE ABOUT GETTING HOME TO SEE HER FATHER. THAT WAS WHEN HER HUSBAND LOST IT. HIS PERCEPTION OF THE COMMENT WAS THAT IT WAS A PERVERSE ONE. (HOW THAT COULD BE PERCEIVED AS PERVERS, I DON'T KNOW.) ANYWAY, WHEN THEY GOT HOME, HE YANKED HER OUT THE CAR BY HER HAIR AND PROCEEDED TO KICK HER ABOUT HER BODY. AS SHE WROTE OUT THE STATEMENT, SHE PULLED LOCK AFTER LOCK FROM HER HEAD, WHICH HER HUSBAND HAD DETACHED FROM HER SCALP. SHE ALSO HAD CUTS ON HER HAND THAT WERE PROBABLY DEFENSIVE WOUNDS AND A BRUISED HIP. I CALLED RESCUE OUT TO TAKE A LOOK AT HER. I ASKED HER IF SHE WAS GOING TO PROSECCUTE HIM FOR THIS. SHE WAS STILL CRYING FRANTICALLY AND SAID, "I'M NOT SURE. THIS IS ONLY THE SECOND TIME IN FIVE YEARS SINCE WE'VE BEEN BACK TOGETHER THAT HE'S DONE THIS." (THE TWO WERE PREVIOUSLY MARRIED FOR NINE YEARS, BUT DIVORCED AS A RESULT OF DOMESTIC BATTERY. IMAGINE THAT. THEY WERE ON THEIR SECOND MARRIAGE TO ONE ANOTHER.) THE COUPLE HAD TWO KIDS; FOURTEEN AND NINE. THEY WERE ASLEEP INSIDE THE HOUSE. BOTH THE MAN AND WOMAN KEPT SAYING THEY DIDN'T WANT THEM TO HEAR WHAT WAS GOING ON. I TOLD THE HUSBAND HE SHOULD HAVE THOUGHT ABOUT THAT WHEN HE SNATCHED HIS WIFE OUT THE CAR. THE HUSBAND THEN SAID, "I WAS LYING EARLIER. MY WIFE WAS THE AGGRESSOR." HE SHOWED ME A BITE MARK ON HIS SHOULDER. I TOLD HIM, "I'M SURE SHE DID BITE YOU AFTER YOU YANKED HER BY THE HEAD." HE SAID HE ONLY DID THAT TO KEEP HER IN THE CAR. SHE WAS

TRYING TO JUMP OUT WHILE IT WAS MOVING.   ON THE WAY
TO JAIL, HE STARTED SAYING HE WAS CLAUSTROPHOBIC AND I
MIGHT HAVE TO STOP FOR HIM TO PUKE. HALF WAY THERE, HE
ASKED IF I COULD SLOW DOWN DUE TO HIS SUDDEN ILLNESS.
I TOLD HIM I WAS TRYING TO HURRY AND GET HIM OUT THE
BACKSEAT. WHEN WE PULLED UP TO THE JAIL, HE GOT A
SUDDEN ATTACK AND SAID, "PULL OVER PLEASE." AFTER I DID,
HE STUCK HIS HEAD OUT THE DOOR AS IF HE WAS ABOUT TO
PASS OUT AND SAID, "HOW MUCH FURTHER?" I SAID, "JUST
AROUND THE CORNER AND INTO THE GARAGE." HE SAID,
"JUST HURRY!"   I GOT HIM INSIDE AND TURNED HIM OVER
TO THE CORRECTIONAL OFFICERS. HE LOOKED INTO THE
HOLDING CELL, WHICH WAS HALF PACKED WITH WHAT WOULD
APPEAR THE BE LESS THAN MODEL CITIZENS, AND SAID TO
ME, "I DONT HAVE TO STAY OVERNIGHT IN THERE, DO I?" I
SAID, "YOU SURE DO." HE SAID, "YOU MIGHT AS WELL GET ME
A LAWYER NOW, BECAUSE I DONT DESERVE THAT. WE HAVE
TO NEGOTIATE." I TOLD HIM HE NEEDED TO NEGOTIATE WITH
THE BOOKING OFFICERS. FORESEEING WHAT WAS TO COME.
I SAID TO THE BOOKING OFFICER, "HE WANTS A LAWYER AND
HE WANTS TO NEGOTIATE ON WHETHER OR NOT HE GOES IN
THE CELL. HE WAS IMMEDIATELY BUM RUSHED BY ABOUT FIVE
CORRECTIONAL OFFICERS WHO PHYSICALLY PLACED HIM IN
THE CELL. HE WAS BIG AND BAD WHILE HE WAS DRAGGING
HIS WIFE ACROSS THE FRONT YARD. NOW, HE'S A LITTLE
CLAUSTROPHOBIC WIMP.

0500 -I LEFT THE JAIL AND HEADED TO THE STATION TO
TURN IN PAPERWORK.

0530 -I WROTE OUT THE ABOVE NOVELA, THEN WENT TO
GRAB A QUICK BREAKFAST BEFORE HEADING HOME. I
CAN'T WAIT TIL TOMORROW TO TALK TO YOU AGAIN. OH
YEAH, I SURE YOU WERE WONDERING, SO HERE IT IS: I
HAD TWO STRIPS OF BACON, TWO PANCAKES, AND AN
OMELETTE WITH EVERYTHING.

0636 - TO THE HOUSE

10/22

2000 – BRIEFING. AFTER BRIEFING, I TALKED TO A SQUAD MEMBER ABOUT HIS LONG TERM GOALS. HE'S CONSIDERING THE CALIFORNIA HIGHWAY PATROL. HE USED TO LIVE ON THE WEST COAST AND WAS VERY FOND OF IT.

2105 - (S) SUSPICIOUS VEHICLE
   I CHECKED OUT A CAR IN A NIGHTCLUB PARKING LOT WITH A PUNCHED IGNITION THAT HAD BEEN THERE FOR ABOUT TWO WEEKS. I CHECKED IT BEFORE AND IT HAD NOT BEEN REPORTED AS STOLEN. I RAN IT THROUGH THE SYSTEM AGAIN. HAD STILL NOT BEEN REPORTED AS STOLEN.

2108 - (BU) DISTURBANCE
   THIS WAS AN EMERGENCY CALL IN REFERENCE TO A MALE V. FEMALE FIGHT IN A HOTEL PARKING LOT. UPON MY ARRIVAL, BOTH PARTIES HAD ALREADY GONE. SECURITY HAD CALLED THE DISTURBANCE IN AND ALSO ADVISED THEY HAD LEFT THE PROPERTY.

2127 - I STOPPED BY MY FRIEND'S (B/M, 31) HOTEL AND SPOKE WITH HIM FOR A WHILE. IN THE BACK OFFICE, THEY HAD A DONUT BOX WITH TWO DONUTS LEFT IN IT; ONE POWDERED, AND ONE SUGAR. PRIOR TO SCARFING DOWN THE SUGAR DONUT, I TOLD MY FRIEND, "I CAN'T WALK OUT WITH THIS." HE SAID HE SHOULD HAVE TAKEN A PICTURE AND POSTED IT ON THE SITE.
   AFTERWARDS, HE TOLD ME THAT A CO-WORKER OF HIS HAD A CRUSH ON ME AND HAS BEEN BUGGING HIM ABOUT ME DAILY. TO GET HER TO LEAVE HIM ALONE, HE SAID HE'D MAKE SURE HE INTRODUCED HER TO ME. WHEN HE DID, SHE (F, 30'S, PR) WAS EXTREMELY SHY, BLUSHING ALL OVER THE PLACE. I HANDED HER MY NOTEPAD AND TOLD HER TO WRITE DOWN HER NUMBER. SHE SAID, "OHH NO, I CAN'T DO THAT. I HAVE A BOYFRIEND." INSTEAD, SHE WROTE DOWN HER ADDRESS AND SAID, "YOU CAN COME OVER WHENEVER YOU WANT." (YOU DO THE MATH.)

0105 - (S) TRAFFIC STOP

I STOPPED A GREEN FORD EXPLORER OCCUPIED BY THREE H/MS AND THREE H/FS. THE OWNER'S DRIVER'S LICENCE WAS SUSPENDED THREE TIMES. TWICE FOR FAILING TO MAINTAIN INSURANCE COVERAGE AND ONCE FOR FAILING TO PAY CHILD SUPPORT. (THEY DO THAT HERE.) AFTER ASKING THE DRIVER HIS NAME, I HOOKED HIM UP. HE WANTED TO KNOW IF I COULD EXTEND HIM A PROFESSIONAL COURTESY BECAUSE HE WAS A BONDSMAN. I TOLD HIM, "NO. I HEAR A LOT OF SAD STORIES AND I REMAIN CONSISTENT." THEY WERE ON THE WAY BACK TO MIAMI. THE ARRESTED H/M HAD BROUGHT HIS GIRLFRIEND UP FOR VACTION. SHE WAS IN THE FRONT, PASSENGER SEAT CRYING HYSTERICALLY. THE H/M ASKED IF I COULD TAKE THE CUFFS OFF HIM SO HE COULD CALM HER DOWN. HE SAID, "I'M NOT GOING ANYWHERE." I TOOK THEM OFF FOR A WHILE AND ALLOWED HIM TO MAKE ARRANGEMENTS. ON THE WAY TO THE JAIL, HE SAID HIS ONLY CONCERN WAS THAT HE PUT SOME OF THOSE PEOPLE THERE. I TOLD HIM I WOULD ADDRESS THAT WITH THE CORRECTIONAL OFFICERS. ONCE AT THE JAIL, HE THANKED ME FOR TREATING HIM LIKE A GENTLEMAN AND UNCUFFING HIM WHILE HE DEALT WITH HIS FIANCE. I LATER TOLD THE C. O. THAT HE WAS A BAIL BONDSMAN AND HE SAID HE'D TAKE CARE OF HIM. I ASSUMED THAT MEANT THEY'D SEGREGATE HIM FROM THE OTHER INMATES.

0218 - AFTER LEAVING THE JAIL, I WENT TO GET SOME GAS.

0245 - (S) SUSPICIOUS VEHICLE

I WENT TO CHECK THE VEHICLE WITH THE PUNCHED IGNITION AGAIN. IT STILL HAD NOT BEEN REPORTED AS STOLEN. I WAS NOT AUTHORIZED TO TOW IT AS AN ABANDONED VEHICLE BECAUSE IT WAS ON PRIVATE PROPERTY.

0251 - (S) TRAFFIC STOP

I STOPPED A BRONZE COLORED CHEVY IMPALA. THE OWNER'S LICENSE WAS SUSPENDED THREE TIMES. I DISCOVERED THAT THE DRIVER WAS NOT THE OWNER. THE DRIVER (YOUNG, B/M), HOWEVER, GOT OUT OF THE CAR AND IMMEDIATELY SAID HIS LICENSE WAS SUSPENDED. I HOOKED HIM UP. HE ASKED WHY HE WAS GETTING

ARRESTED WHEN HE STEPPED TO ME LIKE A MAN AND TOLD ME THE TRUTH. I TOLD HIM BECAUSE HE WAS DRIVING WITH A SUSPENDED LICENSE. I CHECKED HIM OUT. HE HAD NINE SUSPENSIONS; ONE FOR CHILD SUPPORT DELINQUENCY, TWO FOR FAILING TO APPEAR IN COURT, AND SIX FOR FAILING TO PAY TRAFFIC FINES. HE SAID THE ONLY REASON HE WAS DRIVING WAS BECAUSE THE GUY WHOSE CAR IT WAS HAD BEEN DRINKING. HE SAID, "I WAS JUST TRYIN' TO SAVE A LIFE. OUT OF THE KINDNESS OF YOUR HEART, YOU SHOULD UNDERSTAND, AND LET ME GO." HE LATER SAID, "I WAS SUPPOSED TO GO PICK UP MY LICENSE TOMORROW. THE PEOPLE SENT ME A NOTICE TELLING ME TO." ALL THE WAY TO JAIL, HE KEPT GIVING ME REASONS WHY HE WAS DRIVING. I TOLD HIM, "WHEN THEY SUSPENDED YOUR LICENSE, THEY DIDN'T SAY DON'T DRIVE UNLESS... THEY SAID DON'T DRIVE!" HE SHUT UP AFTER THAT. EXCEPT FOR LATER, WHEN HE ASKED, "CAN YOU PUT IN MY REPORT THAT I WAS HONEST WITH YOU AND TOLD YOU STRAIGHT UP THAT MY LICENSE WAS SUSPENDED?" I TOLD HIM THAT I HAD INCLUDED THAT ALREADY. (I HAD COMPLETED THE CHARGING PAPERWORK WHILE AT THE SCENE OF THE ARREST.)

0355 -I LEFT THE JAIL AND HEADED BACK TO MY AREA.

0400 -I CHECKED SOME HOTEL PARKING LOTS IN MY AREA. (I KNOW, I DO A LOT OF THAT. I HAVE A LOT OF HOTELS IN MY AREA.)

0440 -I TURNED IN MY PAPERWORK AND CHATTED WITH MY SERGEANT FOR A WHILE.

0500 -I STARTED TO SLOWLY MOVE IN A HOMEWARD DIRECTION. I'LL TALK TO YOU IN A COUPLE OF DAYS. I HAVE TWO DAYS OFF. TRANSLATION: TWO DAYS IN WHICH TO WORK OFF-DUTY JOBS.
   POORMEPOORMEPOORMEPOORMEPOORMEPO
ORMEPOORMEPOORME...

10/25

1800-BRIEFING

1820-I WENT TO DINNER. I HAD CHICKEN TERRYAKI, MASHED POTATOES, AND PEAS WITH CARROTS.

1909-I WENT OUT ON PATROL.

2026 - IT WAS RAINY OUT, SO I JUST PARKED AND WATCHED THE TRAFFIC.

2100-I STARTED PATROLLING AGAIN.

2114-I CHECKED ON SOME OF MY HOTELS.

2121-I WAS APPROACHED BY A W/M (40'S). HE WAS WAITING FOR A CAB AND WANTED TO KNOW WHERE A NEARBY CLUB OR BAR WAS THAT HAD NICE LADIES. I TOLD HIM ABOUT A RESTAURANT/BAR DOWN THE STREET AND THE HOTEL/NIGHTCLUB WHERE MY FRIEND (B/M, 31) WORKS. I TOLD HIM THE LADIES THERE WERE VERY FRIENDLY. (THAT'S WHAT I HEARD.)

2143-(D) STOLEN CAR
   I MET WITH A YOUNG, AMERICAN INDIAN IN THE PARKING LOT OF A LOCAL THEME PARK. SHE SAID HER GREEN MITSUBISHI GALANT HAD BEEN STOLEN. AS I MENTIONED BEFORE, AT THESE PARKS, THEY'RE USUALLY JUST MISPLACED. SECURITY HAD DRIVEN HER ALL AROUND THE LOT TO BE SURE. SHE WAS DISPLEASED WITH THEM BECAUSE THEY DIDN'T TAKE HER WORD WHEN SHE SAID, "I VISIT HERE FREQUENTLY AND I KNOW WHERE I PARKED." SECURITY GOT UPSET WHEN SHE ASKED, "CAN YOU CALL THE POLICE NOW?" SHE ASKED ME WHAT THE PROCEDURE WAS AS FAR AS REPORTING STOLEN CARS. I TOLD HER I DIDN'T KNOW THEIR PROCEDURE. WHEN I FIRST MET WITH SECURITY, HE SEEMED TO GET UPSET WITH ME WHEN I TOLD HIM I WAS GOING TO PERSONALLY CHECK THE LOT PRIOR TO TAKING THE REPORT. HE TOLD ME THE SECURITY OFFICERS HAD SCOURED THE LOT ALREADY. I STILL CHECKED IT FOR MY OWN PEACE OF MIND. WHILE TAKING

THE REPORT, THE VICTIM HAD A PROBLEM WITH THE RELEASE OF LIABILITY PORTION. SHE DIDN'T LIKE THE IDEA OF HER VEHICLE BEING DAMAGED WHILE WE WERE APPREHENDING THE SUSPECT. SHE AGREED TO SIGN AFTER BOTH HER MOTHER AND I TOLD HER THE ONLY ALTERNATIVE WOULD BE NOT GETTING HER CAR BACK AT ALL..

AFTER FINISHING UP WITH THE VICTIM, MY FRIEND (F, 26 Y/O, BRAZ) CALLED. SHE TOLD ME SHE RECENTLY PICKED HER FIVE Y/O SON UP FROM HIS DAD'S HOUSE. HE ALWAYS GETS UPSET WITH HER AND SAYS, "I WANT TO STAY WITH MY DAD. I LIKE HIM MORE THAN I LIKE YOU." LATER ON, AFTER THEY HAD COME FROM CHURCH, HE APOLOGIZED TO HER AND SAID, "BIBLE MAN SAYS GIVE YOUR ANGER TO JESUS AND HE'LL GIVE YOU YOUR HAPPINESS BACK. SO, I'M NOT MAD AT YOU ANYMORE." SHE SAID SHE USED THE BIBLE MAN THING ON HIM LATER ON WHEN HE WAS BEING BAD. IT WORKED. HE STRAIGHTENED UP. I SAID TO HER, "HE'S GONNA BE LIKE: MAN, WHY DID I HAVE TO TELL HER ABOUT BIBLE MAN? I SHOULD NEVER HAVE DONE THAT!"

2230 - (BU) - MAN DOWN
THIS WAS IN REFERENCE TO A W/M IN A CAR WHO WAS SLUMPED OVER THE STEERING WHEEL. THE CALLER SAID THEY DIDN'T KNOW WHETHER OR NOT HE WAS BREATHING. AS IT TURNED OUT, HE WAS INTOXICATED. THE INITIAL RESPONDING OFFICER ARRESTED HIM FOR DRIVING UNDER THE INFLUENCE AND MULTIPLE TRAFFIC INFRACTIONS.

2250 - I WENT TO GET GAS AND USE THE RESTROOM AT THE GAS STATION/CONVENIENCE STORE WHERE THE ELDERLY W/M WORKS. WHEN I ASKED HIM HOW HE WAS DOING HE SAID, "AS WELL AS CAN BE EXPECTED."

I CALLED HOME TO CHECK MY MESSAGES. MY SON'S MOM HAD CALLED AND SAID MY SON HADN'T BEEN FEELING WELL LATELY. ALSO, MY FRIEND (F, 24, PR) HAD CALLED. SHE SAID, "I KNOW I SAID I WASN'T GOING TO CALL YOU ANYMORE, BUT I COULDN'T HELP IT."

0005 - (BU) POSSESSION OF DRUGS

SEVERAL OTHER OFFICERS AND I RESPONDED TO AN OFFICER BEHIND A RESTAURANT/BAR. HE HAD ARRESTED A YOUNG, H/M WHO WAS IN POSSESSION OF A LARGE AMOUNT OF PRESCRIPTION PILLS. WITH HIM IN THE CAR WAS TWO MORE H/MS AND TWO H/FS. THE CAR WAS A BROWN HONDA ACCORD. AFTER DOCUMENTING THEIR PERSONAL INFORMATION, THOSE FOUR WERE RELEASED. ONE OF THE H/FS SAID THAT ONE OF THE OFFICERS WAS EXTREMELY RUDE TO HER. SHE ASKED ME WHAT HIS NAME WAS. I TOLD HER TO GO AND ASK HIM WHAT HIS NAME WAS. SHE ASKED IF I HAD SOMETHING FOR HER TO WRITE IT DOWN WITH. I HANDED HER A PEN AND A SHEET OF PAPER FROM MY NOTEBOOK.

0109-I WENT TO EAT AGAIN. I HAD FRIED CHICKEN, PIZZA, AND PASTA SALAD. I TOOK A BAG OF PRETZELS TO GO SO I WOULDN'T HAVE TO STOP FOR BREAKFAST.

0130-I DID A CHECK OF A FEW LOCAL HOTELS.

0223 -I RAN EVERY TAG I CAME ACROSS. FORTUNATELY, EVERYONE WAS "GOOD-TOGO." I TOOK A CARWASH BREAK.

0208 -I SAT IN THE LOT OF A DRUG STORE THAT HAD BEEN ROBBED IN THE RECENT PAST AND DID MY PAPERWORK.

0300 -I WENT TO THE STATION TO DROP OFF MY PAPERWORK.

03 15 - I BROKE OPEN MY BAG OF PRETZELS AND HIT THE STREETS.

0330 - MY SERGEANT CALLED MY PARTNER AND ME TO MEET WITH HIM IN A RESTAURANT PARKING LOT. HE SAID HE NEEDED SOMEONE TO TALK TO SO HE WOULD STAY AWAKE. WE STOOD AROUND AND TALKED FOR A WHILE ABOUT EVERYTHING FROM OFFICERS WHO HAD GOTTEN FIRED TO SPEAKING

ENGAGEMENTS AT ELEMENTARY SCHOOLS.

0441-I WENT BACK OUT ON PATROL. IT WAS STILL DEAD OUT.

0545 - I HEADED HOME. HAVE A GOOD MORNING.

10/26

2050 -I GOT OUT OF CLASS AND WENT TO EAT. I HAD BBQ PORK CHOPS, RICE, AND CARROTS.

2118-I WENT OUT ON PATROL.

2133 - (D) DOMESTIC BATTERY
  I WAS DISPATCHED TO AN AREA APARTMENT COMPLEX. A H/M (30'S) HAD BATTERED HIS GIRLFRIEND (H/F, 40'S) AND HER FRIEND (H/F, 40'S). HE WAS UPSET WITH THEM BECAUSE THEY CAME AND GOT HIM FROM A BAR. HE VIEWED THAT AS BEING DISRESPECTFUL. HE CHOKED HIS GIRLFRIEND AND THREW HER DOWN ON THE PARKING LOT PAVEMENT. HE GRABBED THE FRIEND BY HER SHOULDERS AND SHOOK HER WHEN SHE TRIED TO BREAK UP THE ALTERCATION. THE GIRLFRIEND STARTED TO CRY UNCONTROLLABLY. NOT BECAUSE OF HER INJURIES, BUT BECAUSE I WAS TAKING HER PRECIOUS BOYFRIEND TO JAIL. SHE BEGGED AND PLEADED WITH ME NOT TO DO SO. TOLD HER IT WAS NOT HER DECISION TO MAKE. I TOLD HER I WAS OBLIGATED BY LAW TO ARREST HIM. SHE SAID, "PLEASE SIR. I PAY PART OF YOUR SALARY. YOU CAN LET HIM GO AND I WON'T SAY ANYTHING." SHE CONTINUED TO PLEAD WITH ME TO RELEASE HIM. FINALLY, I TOLD HER, "MAM, YOU DO OBVIOUSLY NOT COMPREHEND WHAT I'M TELLING YOU, SO I'M NO LONGER DISCUSSING IT. SHE THEN APOLOGIZED TO HER BOYFRIEND IN MY BACKSEAT AND WALKED AWAY AS HE CONTINUED TO SHOUT, "YOU SEE WHAT YOU DID!" (SHE WON'T PROSECUTE. HE'LL BE OUT IN A FEW DAYS AND THEY'LL BE BACK TOGETHER. THE CYCLE WILL CONTINUE.)

0015 - (S) WARRANT SERVICE
  I SERVED A WARRANT ON ONE OF THE INMATES BEFORE LEAVING THE JAIL. POLICE OFFICERS FROM OTHER AGENCIES IN THE AREA ARE NOT AUTHORIZED TO SERVE WARRANTS. THEY BRING THE PEOPLE IN AND JAIL PERSONNEL HAVE OFFICERS SERVE THEM ON BEHALF OF THE SHERIFF, WHENEVER WE'RE AROUND.

2254 - A SQUAD PARTNER OF MINE WAS DISPATCHED TO AN UNSTABLE MAN WITH A HANDGUN INTENDING TO INFLICT HARM ON HIMSELF. CONTACT WAS NEVER MADE.HE WAS GONE WHEN THE OFFICER ARRIVED.

0200 -I STOPPED CRUISING FOR A WHILE AND TOOK A GAS AND SNACK BREAK. I MUNCHED ON SOME PRETZELS. I SAID PRETZELS, NOT BEN AND JERRY'S HOOCHIE COOCHIE OR SOME OTHER CREATIVELY TITLED FLAVOR. EVERYBODY HAPPY? THE ROLD GOLD PEOPLE AREN'T TRYING TO GET ANYONE OUT OF JAIL, ARE THEY?

0230 - (BU) TRAFFIC STOP
  I ASSISTED ANOTHER OFFICER WHO WAS DEALING WITH ONE/HALF OF A DISTURBANCE. (MEANING, 1/2 THE PARTIES INVOLVED WAS NOT PRESENT.)

0240 - (S) TRAFFIC STOP
  I STOPPED A W/M (30'S) WHO WAS DRIVING A 4WD BLACK JEEP. I WAS PARKED AT AN OFF-RAMP AND HE BLEW BY ME AS IF I WAS STANDING STILL. (I WAS STANDING STILL, BUT THAT'S NOT THE POINT.)   I ASKED HIM WHAT HIS RUSH WAS. HE SAID, "I DON'T KNOW. WAS I SPEEDING?" I SAID, "YOU TELL ME." HE SAID, "PROBABLY." I SAID, "YOU NEED TO SLOW DOWN, MAN." I THEN HANDED HIM HIS LICENSE AND REGISTRATION BACK AND WALKED OFF.

0305 - (S) SUSPICIOUS VEHICLE
  IN AN ATTEMPT TO STAY AWAKE, I CHECKED OUT A HONDA CIVIC THAT I NOTICED PARKED IN A HOTEL LOT. THE TAG ATTACHED WAS NOT ASSIGNED TO IT. I CHECKED TO SEE IF IT WAS STOLEN. IT WAS NOT.

0331 - I STOPPED BY THE 24-HOUR DRUG STORE WHERE MY FRIEND (F, 31 Y/O, HAITI) WORKS TO TALK TO HER FOR A WHILE. SHE'S A PHARMACY TECH, OR SOMETHING. I KNOW SHE'S IN SCHOOL TO BECOME A PHARMACIST. SHE SAID SHE JUST BROKE UP WITH HER ITALIAN BOYFRIEND BECAUSE SHE NO LONGER WANTED THE RESPONSIBILITY. WE TALKED ABOUT HER

SICKLE CELL ANEMIA. SHE SAID SHE'D RATHER LIVE
LIFE LIKE SHE WANTED AND DIE WHENEVER, THAN TO
LIVE BY A DOCTOR'S STRICT REGIMEN. (A DOCTOR TOLD
HER WHAT SHE NEEDED TO EAT AND HOW FREQUENTLY
SHE NEEDED TO EAT IT. SHE DOESN'T LIKE TO EAT AT
ALL.)

0500 -I REMEMBERED I HADN'T TURNED IN MY
PAPERWORK. WE USUALLY GET IT TO THE SERGEANT
BY 0430. I CALLED HIM AND HE SAID TO MEET HIM IN THE
PARKING LOT OF THE STATION.

0538 - AFTER GETTING HIM MY PAPERWORK, WE
CHATTED A BIT. I THEN ROLLED OUT TO THE HOUSE. I'LL
TALK TO YOU IN ABOUT FOUR DAYS.

10/30

1800-BRIEFING
  AFTER BRIEFING, MY ZONE PARTNER AND I HAD OUR PHOTOGRAPHS TAKEN FOR OFFICER OF THE MONTH. THE PHOTOGRAPHER WAS THE OFFICER I HAD THE DISPUTE WITH THAT TIME. HE SAID, "YOU SEE, ALL THAT BITCHIN' I DID DIDN'T MATTER ONE BIT YOU GUYS' HARD WORK PAID OFF. CONGRATULATIONS. IF YOU CAN'T HAVE FUN OUT HERE, YOU MAY AS WELL GO HOME." I SAID, "I HEAR YA," AND SMILED.

1841 -I HEADED TO DINNER, BUT BROKE FOR A CALL...

1848 - (D) MISSING PERSON
  TWO TEN Y/O, W/FS WERE MISSING FROM THE CONVENTION CENTER. THE MOTHER OF ONE OF THEM WAS RESPONSIBLE FOR THE TWO. SHE HAD BEEN IN MEETINGS ALL DAY AND HER CO-WORKER WAS RUNNING THEIR EXHIBIT BOOTH. THE GIRLS HAD BEEN RUNNING AROUND THE CONVENTION CENTER, BUT THEY CHECKED IN AT THE BOOTH EVERY TEN MINUTES. WHEN THE BOOTH CLOSED DOWN AT THE END OF THE DAY, THE GIRLS WERE NOWHERE TO BE FOUND. THE MOTHER AND THE CO-WORKER WERE BOTH WITH SECURITY CRYING AND NERVOUS. EVENTUALLY, ANOTHER CO-WORKER WALKED INTO THE SECURITY OFFICE WITH THE GIRLS. THEY HAD COME BACK TO THE BOOTH AT 6 P.M., BUT IT WAS CLOSED DOWN. SHORTLY THEREAFTER, THEY MADE CONTACT WITH THE CO-WORKER WHO BROUGHT THEM TO THE OFFICE. EVERYONE WAS HAPPY IN THE END AND THEY ALL HAD A BIG HUG. THE MOTHER AND THE CO-WORKER CONTINUED TO CRY ONLY THIS TIME, THEY WERE HAPPY TEARS. (AWWWHHH)

1906- I GAVE DINNER ANOTHER SHOT. I HAD SALSBURY STEAK, MASHED POTATOES, MACARONI AND CHEESE, AND MIXED VEGATABLES WHILE I STUDIED. (I KNOW, TWO STARCHES. I SHOULD BE HANGED.)

1949 - I WENT TO MY FRIEND'S (B/M, 31) HOTEL TO CHECK IT AND HIM OUT.

2035 - (D) SUSPICIOUS INCIDENT

A W/F CONVENIENCE STORE CLERK CALLED AND SAID AN UNKNOWN PERSON WAS DRIVING BY PERIODICALLY AND LOOKING INTO THE STORE. THAT FRIGHTENED HER. ANOTHER OFFICER PICKED UP AND CLEARED THE CALL FOR ME. MY GUESS IS THAT HE TOLD HER HE'D CRUISE BY PERIODICALLY TO CHECK ON HER AND TO CALL AGAIN IF ANYTHING HAPPENED.

2100 - MY FRIEND (F, 26, BRAZ) CALLED ME AND SAID SHE AND SOME FRIENDS WERE HAVING A COOK OUT AT HER HOUSE. I TOLD HER I'D SWING BY FOR DINNER IF I GOT THE CHANCE. (TRANSLATION: I'D GO BY AND TRY TO ACT HUNGRY.)

2338 - I WENT TO GET A CARWASH.

0005 - (S) TRAFFIC STOP
  I STOPPED TWO YOUNG, H/FS IN A BLUE VOLVO 740. THE TEMPORARY TAG ON THE VEHICLE WAS UNREADABLE. UPON CLOSER EXAMINATION, I SAW THAT WHITEOUT HAD BEEN USED TO CHANGE THE EXPIRATION DATE. THEY BLAMED IT ON THE DEALER, AS THEY HAD RECENTLY PURHCASED THE CAR. THEY SAID THE DEALER KEEPS SAYING THE NEW TAG IS NOT IN YET. I GAVE HER THE BENEFIT OF THE DOUBT AND TOLD HER TO TELL THE DEALER YOU WANT EITHER THE ACTUAL TAG OR A NEW TEMPORARY TAG. I TOLD THEM TO GET IT TAKEN CARE OF BECAUSE THE DRIVER COULD BE GOING TO JAIL.

0128-(S) TRAFFIC STOP
  AS I WAS PULLING OUT OF A CLOSED ESTABLISHMENT, A YOUNG, W/M IN A WHITE MITSUBISHI ECLIPSE BLEW BY ME. HE JUMPED ON HIS BREAKS, BUT IT WAS TOO LATE. I ASKED HIM WHAT HIS HURRY WAS. HE SAID, "SORRY 'BOUT THAT OFFICER. I SLOWED DOWN WHEN I REALIZED IT. I'M JUST TRYIN' TO GET BACK TO WORK. I WORK AT THAT PIZZA PLACE OVER THERE AND I'VE BEEN DRIVING ALL NIGHT." I CHECKED HIS LICENSE AND IT WAS VALID. I TOLD HIM, "SLOW DOWN!" HE SAID, "SORRY 'BOUT THAT OFFICER."

0141-I STOPPED AT A 24 HOUR DRUG STORE IN MY AREA AND PULLED UP BESIDE AN INJURED BIRD.

EITHER IT FLEW INTO THE BUILDING OR SOMEONE HIT IT. IT WASN'T BLEEDING, BUT ITS CHEST WAS RISING AND FALLING AS IT LAY STILL ON ITS SIDE. I WAS TOO CHICKEN TO PICK IT UP WITH MY HANDS, SO I USED A TAG THAT I HAD IN MY TRUNK. I MOVED IT TO A SPOT BELOW A TREE NEAR SOME SHRUBBERY. A B/F (40) CLERK WHO WAS ON A SMOKE BREAK SAW ME AND ASKED, "IS EVERYTHING ALRIGHT OVER THERE? THERE AREN'T NO DEAD BODIES AROUND THERE, ARE THERE? "I SAID, "NO, JUST AN INJURED BIRD." SHE SAID, "OH, THE RATS WILL GET IT. WE HAD ONE IN THE STORE THAT WAS SO BIG, I ALMOST CLOCKED OUT." THEN SHE STARTED TALKING ABOUT HER SMOKING. SHE SAID SHE WAS QUITTING. SHE SAID, "THE ONLY PROBLEM IS THAT I FEEL THE WEIGHT COMING ON. LORD KNOWS I DON'T NEED NO MORE ON MY BACKSIDE AND HIPS." I TOLD HER, "WEIGHT IN THOSE AREAS CAN'T BE A BAD THING." SHE SAID HER FATHER, WHO ALSO SMOKES, WAS IN THE HOSPITAL. FOR SOME UNKNOWN REASON, HE HAD BEEN LOSING BLOOD. SHE SAID IT COULD BE RELATED TO SMOKING. SHE PROMISED HIM SHE'D QUIT. I HAD GONE TO THE STORE BECAUSE I NEEDED TO BUY THIS POOR LITTLE KITTEN SOME FOOD. IT HAD BEEN HANGING OUT AROUND MY FRONT DOORSTEP. I'VE BEEN GIVING IT MILK, SO IT MEOWS WHENEVER I COME OUT THE HOUSE. THE POOR THING'S SO SKINNY, I DECIDED TO START GIVING IT FOOD. THE B/F KEPT COMING UP WITH STUFF TO TALK ABOUT. I MANAGED TO SLIP OUT AS SOON AS SHE GOT TIED UP WITH SOME OTHER CUSTOMERS.

0212-(D) ALARM
I WAS DISPATCHED TO AN ALARM AT A CLOSED DINNER THEATRE. I MET WITH THE MANAGER (ITALIAN MALE, 40'S). WHEN HE FIRST SHOWED UP, I ASKED HIM IF HE WAS THE OWNER. HE SAID, "NO, I'M JUST THE MANAGER, BUT I'M TRYING TO OWN IT." I LEFT AFTER WE CHECKED THE BUILDING.

0233 - (D) SUSPICIOUS PERSON
A 64 Y/O, WHITE TRANSIENT (HOMELESS) WAS FOUND WANDERING AROUND THE PROPERTY OF AN AREA HOTEL. MY

GUESS WAS THAT HE WAS LOOKING FOR A WARM PLACE TO SLEEP. (IT WAS PRETTY CHILLY OUT.) SECURITY WANTED HIM TRESPASSED FROM THE PREMISES. HE GAVE US ALL A LAUGH WITH THE NONSENSE HE WAS TALKING. OUR INTELLIGENCE REPORTS HAVE A SECTION FOR NICKNAMES. HE SAID HIS WAS "THE TENNESSEE STUD." HE SAID THE YOUNG LADIES COULDN'T RESIST HIS SEX APPEAL. WHEN I ASKED HIM WHERE HE LIVED, HE SAID, "ON CARDBOARD. IT'S CHEAPER THAT WAY."

0301-I DID A CHECK OF SEVERAL OTHER HOTELS IN THE AREA.

0315 -I CALLED TO CHECK MY MESSAGES. A FRIEND (F, 24, PR) HAD LEFT THREE MESSAGES. MY SON'S MOM WANTED ME TO CALL MY SON AND STRESS THE IMPORTANCE OF KEEPING HIS ASTHMA MEDICATION ON HIM AT ALL TIMES. HE KEEPS FORGETTING IT AT HOME AND IN HIS UNCLE'S TRUCK AND EVERYWHERE ELSE. (SHE THROUGHT I'D BE THE PERFECT PERSON TO DO THAT. NOT BECAUSE I'M HIS FATHER, BUT BECAUSE I HAVE ASTHMA.)

0345 - I SAT IN THE PARKING LOT OF A RESTAURANT AND FINALIZED MY "STATS" (STATISTICS) ON MY COMPUTER. WE HAVE TO TURN THEM IN AT THE END OF EACH MONTH. CONTRARY TO POPULAR BELIEF, WE HAVE NO QUOTA FOR TICKETS OR ANYTHING ELSE. ON THE OTHER HAND, IF YOU TURN IN A SHEET WITH VERY LOW STATS, IT'S GOING TO LOOK LIKE YOU DID NOTHING ALL MONTH.
  SPEAKING OF DOING NOTHING, IF YOU DON'T SEE AN ENTRY FOR SEVERAL HOURS, OR IF THERE ARE ONLY A FEW ENTRIES FOR AN ENTIRE SHIFT, IT DOESN'T MEAN I'M NOT WORKING. IT DOES MEAN THAT I WASN'T DISPATCHED MANY CALLS, BUT IN THE MEANTIME, I'M PATROLLING AROUND. I'M RUNNING TAGS, CHECKING NEIGHBORHOODS AND BUSINESSES, AND SIMPLY BEING VISIBLE. YOU BELIEVE ME, DON'T YOU?

0359 -I WENT TO THE STATION TO TURN IN MY

PAPERWORK.

0410-(D) MAN DOWN

SOMEONE SAID A PERSON WAS ON THE GROUND IN A DITCH OFF THE INTERSTATE BESIDE A CHEVY BLAZER WITH THE PASSENGER DOOR OPEN. I ARRIVED AND FOUND THE BLAZER, BUT NO ONE WAS AROUND. THE HELICOPTER FLEW OVER AND DIDN'T LOCATE ANYONE IN THE AREA EITHER. MY SERGEANT ALSO RESPONDED TO THE SCENE. THE VEHICLE SEEMED TO HAVE BEEN DISABLED AND POSSIBLY BURGLARIZED. THE PASSENGER WINDOW SEEMED TO HAVE BEEN SMASHED OUT AND THE STEREO WAS POSSIBLY MISSING. (IT MAY HAVE NEVER HAD ONE.) MY SERGEANT SAID TO HOLD OFF ON TAKING ACTION UNTIL THE OWNER CALLED A CRIME IN. I WENT AHEAD AND RAN THE TAG TO FIND OUT THE OWNER'S ADDRESS. IF IT WAS LOCAL I WOULD HAVE GONE BY THEIR HOUSE TO FIND OUT WHAT THE DEAL WAS. AS IT TURNED OUT, I DIDN'T RECOGNIZE THE ADDRESS.

0450 - I TALKED TO MY SERGEANT AND ANOTHER SQUAD MEMBER IN THE STATION PARKING LOT FOR A WHILE.

I GOT SOME GAS FROM A STATION IN THE HEART OF MY WORK AREA. I STUDIED A BIT FOR SCHOOL WHERE I HAD TO BE IN ABOUT SEVEN HOURS.

A B/M (40'S) WALKED UP TO ME AND SAID, "THE HARDEST THING TO DO IS GET A CAB IN THE CITY." I ASKED IF HE CALLED ONE AND HE SAID HE HAD, TWICE. HE SAID HE CALLED ONE FROM HIS HOUSE, BUT THEY REFUSED TO RESPOND THERE. (HE LIVES IN A NEIGHBORHOOD THAT IS KNOWN FOR DRUG ACTIVITY.) HE THEN CAUGHT A BUS TO THE GAS STATION WHERE WE WERE. I WENT TO USE THE RESTROOM. WHEN I RETURNED, THE B/M WAS RIDING OFF IN A CAB.

0600 - I HEADED HOME. I'LL TALK TO YOU AGAIN LATER TONIGHT.

10/31

2000 - BRIEFING

2016 - (D) SUSPICIOUS VEHICLE
  I WAS DISPATCHED TO AN AREA NEIGHBORHOOD. A RESIDENT CALLED IN A COMPLANT OF A KNOWN SEVENTEEN Y/O WHO WAS DRIVING HIS WHITE CHEVY LUMINA THROUGH THE AREA AT HIGH RATES OF SPEED. HE WAS ALSO THROWING EGGS AT TRICK-OR-TREATERS. UPON ARRIVING TO THE NEIGHBORHOOD, THE CHEVY WAS NOWHERE TO BE FOUND, NEITHER WERE ANY TRICK-OR-TREATERS. HE PROBABLY LEFT AFTER HE RAN OUT OF KIDS.

2100-I HAD A HAMBURGER, HOT DOG, FRENCH FRIES, TATOR TOTS, CORN ON THE COB, AND BAKED BEANS.
  IT'S HALLOWEEN AND THERE ARE A LOT OF FOLKS ON THE STREETS. IN ADDITION, SOME POLITICIANS ARE IN TOWN, SO TWO OF MY SQUAD MEMBERS WERE DESIGNATED TO WORK SOME KIND OF DIGNITARY DETAIL. MY AREA PARTNER IS OUT SICK AND CALLED IN TONIGHT. THAT LEAVES ONLY ANOTHER SQUAD MEMBER AND ME TO WORK OUR DIVISION. MY SERGEANT SAID, DON'T BE DICKIN' AROUND OUT THERE TAKIN' PEOPLE TO JAIL AND STUFF BECAUSE WE'RE SHORT-HANDED. THAT IS, UNLESS IT'S UNAVOIDABLE, AND THEY NEED TO GO." I JUST LAUGHED OUT LOUD, BUT OTHERWISE KEPT MY COMMENTS TO MYSELF.

2125-I CALLED MY FRIEND (F, 26, BRAZ) AND GOT HER MACHINE. SHE CALLED ME BACK SHORTLY THEREAFTER. I TOLD HER WHAT I LEARNED IN PORTUGUESE EARLIER THAT DAY. WE ALSO TALKED ABOUT MY WORKING MIDNIGHTS. SHE SAID I SHOULD CHANGE MY SCHEDULE SO SHE CAN SEE ME WHEN SHE NEEDS TO.

2132 -I SAT IN THE PARKING LOT OF A GAS STATON IN THE HEART OF MY AREA. BESIDES PROVIDING A VISUAL PRESENCE, I COULDN'T DO POLICE WORK, SO I

WAS FORCED TO STUDY.

2233 - (D) ALARM
I WAS DISPATCHED TO AN ALARM AT A BUSINESS IN A STRIP MALL. ANOTHER UNIT WHO WAS CLOSER PICKED UP THE CALL.

2306 - (BU) TRAFFIC STOP
I WENT TO BACK-UP MY SERGEANT WHO HAD STOPPED A RED FORD PICK-UP TRUCK WITH THREE MALES; ONE YOUNG, W/M AND TWO YOUNG, H/MS. TWO WERE WEARING HALLOWEEN MASKS; "BOB HOPE" AND "ALIEN." HE STOPPED THEM BECAUSE AN ARMED ROBBERY HAD JUST OCCURRED IN A NEIGHBORING JURISDICTION INVOLVINIG A MAN WEARING A MASK. THESE WEREN'T ROBBING ANYONE, BUT THEY WERE UP TO NO GOOD. THEY HAD SEVERAL ROLLS OF TOILET PAPER AND CARTONS OF EGGS. THEY SAID THEY WERE THROWING THE EGGS AT SIGNS, NOT PEOPLE. I WAS JUST GOING TO GET THEIR PERSONAL INFORMATION AND SCOLD THEM A BIT AND VERBALLY BANISH THEM FROM THE AREA. HOWEVER, MY SERGEANT INSISTED I TAKE THEM TO JAIL FOR UNLAWFUL ASSEMBLY. THAT'S A SECOND DEGREE MISDEMEANOR WHICH INVOLVES THREE OR MORE PERSONS WHO MEET TOGETHER TO COMMIT AN UNLAWFUL ACT. ONE OF THE GUYS ASKED, "YOU'RE NOT GOING TO CALL MY JOB ARE YOU?" I ASKED HIM, "IS THIS SOMETHING YOU WOULDN'T WANT YOUR EMPLOYER TO KNOW ABOUT?" HE SAID, "NO." I TOLD HIM, "WELL, YOU PROBABLY SHOULDN'T BE DOING IT THEN." HE SAID, "YES SIR, IT WAS STUPID. THEN I SAID, "TO ANSWER YOUR QUESTION, NO, I'M NOT GOING TO CALL YOUR JOB."

0127 -I TRIED TO MAKE IT TO THE CHOW HALL BEFORE THEY CLOSED AT 2:00 A.M. I MADE IT AND HAD A BURGER AND TWO HOT DOGS AGAIN.

0200 -I PULLED INTO A GAS STATION TO WORK ON SOME PAPERWORK.

0205 - CHANGE OF PLANS. MY SERGEANT CALLED ME TO AN ARSON SCENE INVOLVING A GROUP OF TEENAGERS.

HE WANTED ME TO BRING HIM A PAIR OF HANDCUFFS.

0217 - (D) DISTURBANCE
I WAS DISPATCHED TO A LOUD PARTY IN AN APARTMENT COMPLEX. I RESPONDED TO THE AREA AND FOUND THE SOURCE OF THE LOUD MUSIC WAS A HALLOWEEN PARTY. THE RESIDENT WAS A YOUNG, W/M. I TOLD HIM IF I HAD TO COME BACK AGAIN SOMEONE WOULD GO TO JAIL. THE W/M WAS VERY COOPERATIVE. HE APOLOGIZED AND SAID, IT WON'T HAPPEN AGAIN.

0306 -I WENT TO GET A CARWASH AND SOME GAS.

0315-I WENT TO THE GAS STATION ACROSS THE STREET FROM WHERE MY FRIEND (F, 32, HAITI) WORKS, SO I DROPPED IN TO SEE HOW SHE WAS. I TALKED TO HER UNTIL SHE GOT A CUSTOMER. SHE WORKS IN THE DRUG STORE'S PHOTO LAB AND IN ANOTHER DRUG STORE AS A PHARMACY TECH. SHE'S GOING TO SCHOOL TO BE A PHARMACIST. SHE WANTED ME TO WISH HER LUCK FOR HER HEARING LATER THAT DAY. SHE GOT A TICKET FOR GOING 65 MPH IN 35MPH ZONE. I TOLD HER, "GO AND FIGHT IT IF YOU THINK YOU WERE IN THE RIGHT AND WEREN'T GOING THAT FAST. BESIDES, THE OFFICER PROBABLY WON'T SHOW UP TO COURT ANYWAY."

0335- (S) TRAFFIC STOP
I STOPPED A WHITE CHEVY BECAUSE THE OWNER'S LICENSE WAS SUSPENDED. THE YOUNG, H/M DRIVER CLAIMED HE PAID HIS TICKETS AND DIDN'T KNOW HIS LICENSE WAS SUSPENDED. I GAVE HIM THE BENEFIT OF THE DOUBT. I TOOK HIS LICENSE AND WROTE HIM A TICKET. I TOLD HIM IF HE HAD IN FACT PAID THE TICKET, HE WOULDN'T HAVE TO PAY AGAIN. I TOLD HIM IF HE GOT STOPPED AGAIN, HE'D PROBABLY BE ARRESTED. JUDGING FROM THE WAY HE SAID, "THANK YOU SIR", I COULD TELL HE KNEW ABOUT THE SUSPENSION. THAT'S O.K.; HE SEEMED LIKE A NICE KID. HE PROBABLY JUST HAD SOME BAD BREAKS AND COULDN'T AFFORD TO BAIL HIMSELF OUT OF IT.

0356-I WENT BACK TO THAT GAS STATION IN THE HEART

OF MY AREA TO TRY AND COMPLETE MY PAPERWORK.

0421 - A YOUNG, W/M WALKED UP TO ME. HE WAS LOOKING FOR FRIENDS IN A NEARBY HOTEL, BUT DIDN'T KNOW WHAT NAME THEY CHECKED IN UNDER. HE NEEDED TO CALL THEM TO FIND OUT WHERE THEY WERE IN THE HOTEL. THE PHONES IN THE AREA WOULDN'T LET HIM CALL HIS FRIEND'S LONG DISTANCE CELL PHONE NUMBER. HE WANTED TO KNOW IF I KNEW WHERE ANOTHER PHONE WAS. I SAID I DIDN'T, BUT IF HE HAD A CREDIT CARD, HE COULD CHARGE THE CALL. HE WAS PLEASED WITH THAT SUGGESTION AND SAID, "OH YEAH, I DO. THANKS."

0500 - I DID A CHECK OF A FEW HOTELS.

0510 - I WENT TO THE STATION TO TURN IN MY PAPERWORK.

0536 - I EASED TO THE HOUSE. HAVE A GREAT DAY.
   *OFF-DUTY EMPLOYMENT UPDATE:
   WHILE WORKING OFF-DUTY, I HEARD A BURGLARY IN PROGRESS CALL GO OUT. AN EIGHTY-ONE YEAR OLD, BLIND MALE CALLED IN ADVISING HIS RESIDENTIAL ALARM WAS GOING OFF. HE SAID IT WOULD ONLY GO OFF IF THE DOOR WAS OPENED. HE AND HIS WIFE WERE HOME ALONE. WHEN ASKED IF THERE WERE ANY WEAPONS IN THE HOUSE, HE SAID HE HAD A .38 COLT. I WASN'T A RESPONDING UNIT, SO I DON'T KNOW WHAT THE OUTCOME OF THE CALL WAS. THAT'S O.K., IT'S PROBABLY BETTER LEFT TO YOUR IMAGINATION. WELL I NEED TO RUN BUT I WILL TELL YOU ABOUT MY NEXT CALL. IT WAS DISPATCHED AS A 911 HANGUP FROM A LIQUOR STORE. IS IT A ROBBERY IN PROGRESS? I GUESS YOU WILL HAVE TO WAIT FOR VOL.II OF SILENT PARTNER LAW ENFORCEMENT ADVENTURES.
   REMEMBER, CHECK ROADDEPUTY.COM FOR UPDATES AND ALWAYS SUPPORT LOCAL LAW ENFORCEMENT.
   SEE YA ON THE ROAD!!!!

www.ingramcontent.com/pod-product-compliance
Lightning Source LLC
Chambersburg PA
CBHW030320290526
45785CB00001B/451